£1-00

SUNDAY BEST 2

Edited by Donald Trelford

SUNDAY BEST 2

London
The Observer/Victor Gollancz Ltd
1982

© The Observer Limited 1982

British Library Cataloguing in Publication Data
Sunday best 2.
   1. Anthologies
   I. Trelford, Donald
   082   PN6014

   ISBN 0-575-03190-5

Published by Victor Gollancz Ltd
14 Henrietta Street
London WC2E 8QJ

Photoset in Great Britain by
Rowland Phototypesetting, Bury St Edmunds, Suffolk
and printed by St Edmundsbury Press,
Bury St Edmunds, Suffolk

9. A Backward Glance 178

10. Hail and Farewell 203

Editor's Introduction
Donald Trelford

Nobody is too important to write for the newspapers, said George Orwell, who did a fair bit of it himself, often in *The Observer*. This year's collection of *Sunday Best* contains a fair number by outside writers, usually novelists or academics of whom Orwell might have approved. But there was also the Falklands, an old-fashioned war that called for old-fashioned reporting, the Pope's historic visit and an apparently endless stream of Royal events. The tragedy of the Lebanon is foreshadowed in Gavin Young's report from the West Bank, while John le Carré captures what Conrad called 'the moral, the emotional atmosphere of the place and the time'. Five of the staff writers represented here won Press awards during the year.

The selection of articles is unashamedly personal; I have cut and revised them where this seemed to be needed. As before, the guiding principles of selection were that the article should be a good read in itself, that its appeal should have lasted, and that the combination of articles should hold together as a book. It was not intended, and could not be, a 'representative' selection of *The Observer*; but I hope that something of the newspaper's characteristic flavour, style and values comes through. These qualities are perhaps most in evidence in the recollections of *The Observer*'s own Suez crisis and in the obituary of the paper's most distinguished reporter, Patrick O'Donovan.

Thanks are due to my wife, Kate, to my secretary, Barbara Rieck, and to Geoffrey Care and his staff in *The Observer* library, for help in preparing the material for publication.

1.
An Old-Fashioned War

A Majority for Blood
Simon Hoggart

In its fury yesterday, the House of Commons turned on a discredited, tinpot Goverment which, in order to divert attention from its crippling domestic problems, had got itself engaged in a dreadful foreign imbroglio.

MPs also had some harsh words for the Argentine junta. But there was no doubt where they expected to see the first blood spilled – on the Conservative front bench. At this darkest hour of his career the Defence Secretary, Mr John Nott, behaved as we have come to expect all the great politicians to behave – he made an ass of himself.

The House was packed for the first Saturday sitting since Suez in 1956. Outside the public gallery there were long queues, longer than had been seen in London since, well, since the first night of 'Evita'.

Inside the mood was bellicose. This was particularly true on the Labour benches. One half expected to see Mr Michael Foot handing out white feathers, or old naval hands like Mr Callaghan crying 'Eat death, Johnny Gaucho!'

Mrs Thatcher began. Friday, she said, had been a day of 'rumour and counter rumour.' This was not strictly true, since anyone who read the papers or listened to the radio knew exactly what was happening. The Prime Minister continued: 'Yesterday morning we sent a telegram . . .' The Labour side erupted in ersatz mirth for the first time. Hadn't they all read last week that British Telecom had stopped telegrams?

She continued to jeers and booing. The Government had not wanted to escalate the dispute, fear of precipitating the events they had wanted to prevent, and so forth. Then she made her big mistake. She introduced a party point.

Exactly the same thing had happened to the Southern Thule in 1976, and the then Government hadn't even told the House until 1978. Labour backbenchers, many of whom until that moment had thought that the Southern Thule was a new disco step, bayed back in disbelief. Mr Ted Rowlands, the Minister then responsible, stood up and pointed out that unlike the Falklands, Southern Thule was 'totally uninhabited with the exception of penguins and a vast amount of bird droppings.'

Mrs Thatcher continued with the logistical problems which would have been involved in doing something about the problem. She sat down to cries of 'resign', which brought a comforting note of sameness and continuity in these disturbing times.

Mr Foot rose. He was later praised by warlike Conservative back-benchers for having 'spoken for England' – the first time this has happened to the white-haired old pacifist. He called for a counter-invasion. 'The Government must prove itself by deeds, because they will not, I believe, do it by words.' He sat down to the biggest cheers he has heard from the Labour Party since he announced in Brighton last year, 'I am an inveterate peacemonger.'

Mr Edward du Cann began by praising the Government. This is usually the sign that he is going to make a scornful attack on it, and so it proved to be. It was 'astounding' that we were so woefully ill-prepared, 'extraordinary' that forces were not already deployed, 'fatuous' that anyone should have thought it could be solved diplomatically.

'We have nothing to lose except our honour. . . . I am quite certain that it is safe in the hands of the Prime Minister,' he finished. That, from the Chairman of the 1922 Committee, was like a jewelled dagger in Mrs Thatcher's back.

Enoch Powell began by making a short speech about Northern Ireland – which was unusual for him. He generally makes a much longer speech about Northern Ireland, but clearly even he felt the circumstances were special. He appeared to be looking forward, perhaps with relish, to a court martial of the hapless Royal Marines on the islands. He described the 'infamy' to this country. MPs' vocabulary at least was escalating. A huge task force from 'Roget's Thesaurus' had been assembled and was even now being deployed.

Sir Nigel Fisher wanted the most extreme measure of all. Argentina should be banned from the World Cup in Spain. Labour MPs took a moment off from laughing at Mr Nott to laugh at that.

David Owen told the House for roughly the four hundred and sixty-seventh time that a similar situation had blown up when he was Foreign Secretary and that he had solved it. The Government said it had no idea what the Argentines would do – yet their intentions had appeared in the *Guardian* (and *The Observer* for that matter) as long ago as February. This seems a shade harsh on Lord Carrington; after all, few people read the foreign pages of the quality papers, and certainly not the Foreign Office.

Dr Owen suggested a blockade of the islands. This was what the House wanted to hear. Was it the former Foreign Secretary's leadership bid? Probably not, because when he sat down Roy Jenkins said, loudly, 'Well done, David.'

By this time it was clear that MPs had three enemies in their sights: in descending order, Mr Nott, the Foreign Office, and the Argentines. Everybody spoke for England, except the SNP leader Donald Stewart, who spoke for Scotland. This turned out to be exactly the same. The entire Dreadnought class of Tory MPs – Mr Julian Amery, Sir Bernard Braine and other names familiar from previous wars, were mobilised and put to sea.

It appeared that Mr Nott had left the front bench and had disappeared. At 12.40 Mr Barry Sherman (Lab, Huddersfield) demanded to know where he was. We expected to hear the sharp crack of a pearl-handled revolver any minute as Mr Nott did the decent thing, and shot an underling. But 20 minutes later he was back.

Mr John Silkin, winding up for the Opposition, wanted the answers to three key questions, otherwise Mr Nott, Lord Carrington and the Prime Minister herself would have to go. 'It was a collective decision of the three most guilty people in this Government. It is these three who are on trial today,' he declared.

Finally Mr Nott rose confidently to speak. His confidence did not last long. He quibbled desperately about exactly what had happened in 1977 when Labour had faced a similar crisis.

Dr Owen scored another hit on the stern by pointing out that if a Defence Secretary didn't understand about negotiating from strength, he had no right to be a Defence Secretary. When Mr Nott announced to jeers that 'no other country could have reacted so fast. We were not unprepared at all,' you could see the smoke pouring from his engine room, hear the band playing 'Nearer My God, to Thee.'

By this time the Tories were in open despair, burying their heads in their hands, rolling their eyes to heaven, shaking their heads in pity, and all the other over-theatrical gestures favoured on such occasions.

Nothing could save Mr Nott from sinking with all hands except a sudden, thick fog. Miraculously this came with the end of the debate at

2 p.m. prompt. Whether he can now get back to port remains to be seen. *(4.4.82)*

The Nuremberg Factor
James Neilson

If ever there had been a society heading for a monumental breakdown, that society was Argentina before 2 April.

Ever since the end of 1980, Argentines had been aware that their country was approaching a spectacular upheaval. For months before the invasion of the Falklands, the atmosphere crackled with frustration and resentment. The yearning for some kind of violent catharsis was palpable. Civilian politicians talked of the coming 'social explosion' with unconcealed relish. Economists wondered what national bankruptcy would be like. And insiders warned that strange right-wing military groups, which regarded President Leopoldo Galtieri as a dangerous moderate, were preparing to discard him for someone far tougher and more nationalist.

Argentina, in other words, had been in a state of collective hysteria for some time, and was evidently a threat not only to itself but also to its neighbours, of which, thanks to the Falklands, Great Britain was one.

Argentine chauvinists had never made any secret of their belief that the Falklands should be appropriated by force, and since Galtieri took power last December they had been openly discussing the pros and cons of an invasion. More sensible Argentines thought that, desirable as this might seem, the costs would be far too high. But Galtieri's regime was in such a desperate situation in the weeks before 2 April that these costs seemed insignificant when set beside the possibility of escaping from its predicament.

But what, one might well ask, was so dreadful about the prospects confronting Galtieri and his henchmen? Surely they could have merely called elections and let the civilians rule for a while? Unfortunately, things were not that simple. The Argentine generals cannot afford to give up power because they would then find themselves obliged to answer for the many crimes they committed while holding it. For Galtieri and his friends, democracy is more frightening than almost anything else in the world, war included.

After the military coup in 1976 that installed them in government, the Argentine armed forces threw themselves into a ruthless campaign against anything they thought tainted with Marxism. During this campaign, torture was used as a matter of course. Thousands of people, among them at least a hundred infants, 'disappeared.' Although it is taken for granted that most of the kidnapped people were murdered, often in a sadistic manner, the military have refused to acknowledge their responsibility.

In addition to this, a number of senior officers are said to have acquired large fortunes during the six years of military rule, thanks to a variety of imaginative schemes. If a constitutional government took office, there would be nothing to stop the courts carrying out a full investigation into all these crimes and punishing anyone found guilty. Argentine dissidents call this the 'Nuremberg factor,' and it is by far the most important obstacle in the way of democratic government.

The invasion of the Falklands, then, was obviously a desperate stratagem to get the regime out of a nasty situation at home by plunging headlong into a popular adventure abroad. Had its calculations been right, it might just have got away with it – there is hardly an Argentine alive who is not passionately convinced that the islands belong to Argentina – but even then it would have been a close-run thing. There is a substantial difference between the politicians' jingoistic public utterances and their private comments about the military, whom they despise as corrupt, cruel and incompetent.

The regime's calculations, however, went disastrously wrong. Great Britain did not content itself with token protests, few foreign countries approved of Argentina's action, and British troops, it turned out, weren't the degenerate long-haired drug-addicts of the Argentine military imagination. Neither the Argentine rulers nor the Argentine public had bargained with much opposition, and when it came, they indignantly accused Margaret Thatcher of 'over-reacting'; they also, of course, began bickering among themselves.

The misjudgment of Argentina's rulers has been a tribute to their astonishing capacity for self-deceit. The Argentine public wants to believe what it is being told, but it is so used to official mendacity that it cannot do so, and finds the frequent outbursts of military braggadocio disturbing rather than inspiring. At the start of April, Argentines pleasurably surrendered to a lighthearted euphoria, such as we are told seized much of Europe in August 1914. By the time April ended, Argentina was again sunk in its now habitual anguish.

The nature of the individuals ruling Argentina has been a matter of common knowledge for years, but few governments – Jimmy Carter's was an honourable exception – cared to accept the implications. They told themselves that murderous and assertive as Argentina's generals might be, they threatened only their fellow Argentines. But three years ago Argentina almost went to war with Chile over three tiny islands generally recognised as Chilean. Then it intervened in Bolivia, helping to destroy a democratic experiment and trying to instal a replica of itself.

Some right-wing Argentines, moreover, nurse extravagant ambitions for their country. Just after the Falklands had been invaded, a mass-circulation magazine close to the military, *Gente*, published a map suggesting that Argentina had 'lost' territories in Chile, Bolivia, Peru, Brazil, Paraguay and Uruguay. The Paraguayans took this seriously enough to make an official protest. The others were incredulously silent.

The Argentine obsession with the Falklands owes more to Argentina's unhappy experience this century than to British skulduggery 150 years ago. Had Argentina developed into a prosperous democracy respected by all, and not into a poverty-stricken dictatorship noted for its eccentricities, the Falklands would not have mattered very much. Indeed, if Argentina had become a kind of Spanish-speaking Australia, it is entirely possible that Great Britain would by now have asked it to take the islands off its hands.

But Argentina is anything but a satisfied power. It is a stridently unsatisfied one, a seething mess of neuroses, of resentments, of hates, of fantasies, of aggressive xenophobia, a gnawing sense of failure and an assertive, bristling pride. It is not, therefore, very strange that British possession of the archipelago should have swollen into an affront of monstrous proportions in so many Argentine minds. *(2.5.82)*

James Neilson is ex-Editor of the Buenos Aires Herald; he was forced to flee the country after death threats.

The Clever Pigs of Animal Farm
Conor Cruise O'Brien

People often don't object to terrorism as much as they say they do. Take Mrs Thatcher, for example. If you were to accuse Mrs Thatcher of being an habitual accomplice and armourer of terrorists, she would be sincerely indignant. For her, terrorists are scruffy characters with left-wing opinions. They go around dressed like Mr Michael Foot on his way to the Cenotaph.

She would never dream of providing people like that with guns. No one with any moral sense could do such a thing. It would be *wrong*, and that's that.

There are conditions, however, in which that is no longer quite that. If murderers and torturers are in control of a territory and a treasury, if they are carefully and expensively dressed, and clearly opposed to Communism, then terrorist is not the appropriate word to apply to these people. What's the word that American woman at the United Nations uses? Authoritarian! That will do nicely.

To sell guns to terrorists is immoral. To provide authoritarian governments with weaponry is morally neutral. When the 'terrorist' sign is extinguished, and the 'authoritarian' sign is switched on, you know that you have moved from the domain of moral judgment into that of pragmatism.

It is true that you may have to move back again, and in a hurry too. Thus, if the authoritarian government which you have armed to the teeth suddenly turns these arms against you, then the light of moral judgment flashes on again, and in that light the criminal nature of these people is clearly to be seen.

Not by everybody, though, and that's the awkward part. The leading ally – if that's the correct expression right now – remains firmly in the domain of pragmatism. That American woman keeps her conspicuous cool, and from her lips is still to be heard that blessed word 'authoritarian.' Hard to get these people to see that such terminology is no longer appropriate.

I have had a good many occasions to observe democratic statesmen in contact with the different categories of murderers and torturers who hold power over most of the earth. I imagine the interior monologue of the average democratic statesman on making such a contact, to run more or less as follows:

'This fellow is a bit of a stinker, of course. To get where he is and stay there he must have had to do some pretty stinky things. His is a pretty stinky country, after all. Still, the point is that he did get where he is; the stink is no affair of mine. If they ever do get rid of him they'll only put in some other stinker, who may not suit our book as well as this fellow. In any case, the important thing is that he's in charge over there, just as we're in charge over here. So let's chat this fellow up and see what we can get out of him.'

Even that monologue, morally unpretentious though it is, doesn't quite tell it all. There is a freemasonry among governments, which transcends ideology, regimes, and methods. Those who have made it in one set of circumstances have an instinctive respect for those who have made it in another set of circumstances, whatever the methods required by the other set of circumstances may be.

General Galtieri, if fate had formed him in Finchley, would have been a democrat. Margaret Thatcher, born in Buenos Aires, would have become, well, authoritarian. Hard to credit, I know, but that's how it is.

The world's rulers – not just the Communist ones, but the lot of them – are Orwellian pigs. They resent one another and scheme against one another, but they know they have one precious thing in common. They are smarter than other animals and that is why they are where they are. This forms a bond.

From every great international gathering rises the rich aroma of a global sty.

You can get a fine whiff of the same from Henry Kissinger's marvellous memoirs. Henry really is the smartest thing on four trotters. His memoirs are bursting with cleverness, and joy in cleverness, and joy in power. More unexpectedly, there is also a current of magnanimity. Henry is a schemer for sure, and wallows in it, but he is no resenter. He appreciates the rival pigs, and enjoys communicating with them. He outsmarts them, of course, and tells us all about that, but he is too smart himself to outsmart them too much. He savours the general communion of the clever and the powerful: the porcine ecumenism.

All this makes for delightful, as well as instructive, reading. The only bad bits in these memoirs are the bits when Henry moralises. To be a successful hypocrite, you have to be free from intellectual vanity: an ailment to which Henry is unfortunately a martyr. The competent hypocrite has to be prepared to sound as if he genuinely does not know the score. Henry would die rather than sound like that, so all his pious passages are coldly perfunctory. Reading each one of them, I found myself saying: 'Come off it Henry, do! Give us another good grunt.' And, of course, he always does.

While reading Henry's memoirs, I was also reading Jacobo Timerman's. The two books have something in common: they are both by very clever men, both Jewish; both books are well written, and both about power. There the resemblances end. Henry's is an upstairs book: Timerman's a downstairs one. Henry's is about the exercise and enjoyment of power; Timerman's is about what power feels like when it is inflicted on you. Henry's is about life at the top table, among his own kind, Timerman has been down on the floor at the mercy of the dogs – dogs corresponding to those whom Orwell's Napoleon trained.

All animals have their pride, of course, and dogs are no exception. Timerman's Argentine torturers worked 'in basements or abandoned kitchens,' but liked to give themselves airs:

'The torturers, nevertheless, try to create a more sophisticated image of the torture sites, as if thereby endowing their activity with a more elevated status. Their military leaders encourage this fantasy; and the notion of important sites, exclusive methods, original techniques, novel equipment, allows them to present a touch of distinction and legitimacy to the world.'

Dogs pretending to be pigs, in fact.

Mr Timerman's book is authentic and moving, as well as subtle, but had no appreciable effect on Western support for anti-Communist terrorist regimes. General Galtieri may perhaps prove more persuasive in that matter. It should now be apparent that authoritarian regimes cannot be relied upon to confine their aggression to their own people. Rulers who are restrained by no law within their own territories are not likely to respect international law either. The argument that arming such rulers is immoral has not impressed Western (or other) governments. But General Galtieri has shown that arming such rulers can also be unsafe. It can hurt the country that does the arming, and it can also endanger international peace.

Henry would understand that. Pity, in a way, that Henry is no longer around, politically speaking. Since pigs – in an Orwellian sense – there must always be, it is probably safer to have very bright pigs indeed in places of power, rather than ones who are no brighter than you have to be, in order to qualify as a pig at all. Most of those who are entrusted with the management of the present crisis seem to fall into that latter category. (25.4.82)

A World Beyond the Islands
Editorial

Since the beginning of the crisis in the Falklands, the world has taken on a strange shape for Britain. Islands 8,000 miles away, which two and a half months ago few of us could accurately position on a map, have swollen to occupy almost the whole space of our political world. Other events and dramas that will have more effect on our future have shrunk almost to invisibility. The war between Iraq and Iran, the cautious edging closer of America and Russia on strategic weapons talks, even our tortured dealings with our Common Market partners over farm prices and the budget, have seemed irrelevant to the unexpected national saga of the South Atlantic. The Falklands loom as immense as a new-found continent, and we can see little beyond them.

There is nothing odd about this. We are in the middle of the sort of crisis that consumes the energy of a country's leaders and the attention of its people. The simple patriotic emotion of loyalty towards one's own troops has been powerfully developed by the belief, skilfully implanted by the Prime Minister, that our well-being as a people depends on how we acquit ourselves in the conflict. The opinion polls suggest most Britons agree. National feeling has acquired what it always seeks but does not always find: a purpose that seems to justify and ennoble it.

Those who have had doubts about sending the British task force to retake the islands have had as much difficulty constructing their case as a climber trying to ascend a polished rock wall. It has been difficult to establish a foothold against the military logic of events, against Argentina's refusal to withdraw its troops on reasonable terms, and against the feeling that a wrong had been done by the Argentine invasion and that Britain should use the power it possesses to put it right. But the moment has arrived when the Government and the country should lift their eyes from the obsessing islands and consider the world beyond.

The Government and the British armed forces have proved to themselves, to us and to the world that they have determination and bravery. But now that it is plain that the Argentine garrison on the Falklands is waiting only for defeat, Britain needs to show other qualities as well, qualities that are not less those of a decent nation proud of its history.

Some have said that for the British Government to show magnanimity is to be condescending to the Argentines, to suggest that they are not quite grown-up. Magnanimity is a vague word but its opposite is clear enough: it is small-mindedness. Mrs Thatcher sometimes equates magnanimity with treachery. She should regard the aim of letting Galtieri off his hook as pragmatic statesmanship, the exercise of skilled experience that knows the importance of ending a war well.

We do not know what the military situation on the islands is at this moment. Some among Argentine's leaders and fighting soldiers may, faced with inescapable defeat, believe their national honour calls for regiments of martyrs. They may think this could save the leaders' skins and the nation's soul. In that case there is no hope of negotiating an end to the fighting. But even after the collapse of the latest United Nations cease-fire attempt the task force, which has proved beyond doubt its ability to beat the Argentines, must be ready to seize the first chance to negotiate surrender.

For our main preoccupations now must be: How do we prevent the consequences of this war, which we did not expect or want, exploding in the faces of our allies and ourselves? How can we reach a settlement that does not leave us at perpetual daggers drawn with Argentina, and the Falklands as the Israel of the South Atlantic?

Many ill-tempered remarks have been made about American hesitations to support us. The United States ambassador to the United Nations, who is known to value highly US relations with South America, has for some people become the wicked witch of the crisis, trying to put a wavering President under her Latino spell. But America's future relations with Latin America are of direct concern to a British Goverment, particularly this British Government with its world-view so close to Washington's. We will do ourselves and our allies great damage if we finish the battle in a way that endangers still further America's chances of re-thinking and reconstructing its relations with its neighbours.

We need also to finish the war in a way that gives the Falklands a future that is not perpetually under threat from a raging Argentina. We must finish it in a way that we can afford and that British voters, when present feelings are forgotten, will believe they can afford. The British Government should not be expected yet to provide definite plans for the islands' future. But it should be expected to conduct the war's last days in a way that does not make the future more difficult than necessary.

Both Government and country must realise that the Falklands are not our only world. There is a real world, too, where it is in our interest to show the magnanimity and imagination of the victor. *(6.6.82)*

The Quiet Liberation of Port Stanley
Patrick Bishop

The scale of destruction grew more spectacular the closer we got to the town. The last few miles were lined with abandoned Argentine gun emplacements, still smoking from the British artillery bombardment, and scattered around them lay the pathetic squalor of the defenders: piles of comic books, ration tins and underclothes.

We arrived on a concrete road. In the distance Port Stanley looked like a southcoast retirement haven until you noticed the damage. Every house we passed had suffered in the shelling of the past days, and a few fires were burning feebly in the wreckage.

The only sign of the welcome was a little Union Jack hanging in the broken front window of a pink clapboard bungalow. There was a huge hole in the roof where a British shell had landed. The streets were deserted, apart from a pair of Argentine conscripts digging a grave.

We stopped at the first big empty building we came to. The Marines' faces were dark with dirt and tiredness and they gratefully abandoned their back packs and waited to be told what to do next. An officer came out of the building. No one was to be allowed into town because hundreds of armed Argentines were still roaming the streets.

The troops went inside to make cups of tea but a British shell had landed on the town filtration plant and the water was off. The electricity had been hit too, and there was no light.

They settled down in darkening rooms and began to reckon up who had died and who had been injured. It was not the triumphal entry into the capital we had been hoping for, but by then we were getting used to changes in the script.

In the end, the fall of Stanley was conducted more like the conclusion of a terrorist siege than a military surrender. For 10 days previously, Spanish-speaking Marine Captain Rod Bell had been in touch with the Argentine garrison on the islands' radio network during its medical programme. Supervised by the commanding officer of 22 SAS (who had ended the Iranian Embassy siege in London), he had worked at establishing a relationship of trust with the beleaguered Argentines, inquiring constantly after the well-being of the 600 civilians left in Stanley in the hope that the Argentines would be persuaded that the British wanted to end hostilities bloodlessly and humanely if possible.

When the British call came through at the appointed time of 2.30 GMT on Monday, the Argentine forces were already streaming off Sapper Hill, the last remaining high ground, and General Mario

Menendez, the military Governor of the island, came to the radio for the first time.

He agreed to Rose and Bell flying into town at 7 p.m. for talks. They lasted until 9 p.m. when Menendez agreed to include the West Falklands in the deal and to a cease-fire zone around the islands. At a minute to midnight he and the British Land Forces Commander, Major General Jeremy Moore, signed the surrender.

It should have been a moment for jubilation, but the people of Stanley reacted to the news with the same enigmatic reserve that nearly everyone on the island has displayed throughout the war. The troops were given hot drinks and home-made cakes, but there was no champagne, and there were no bouquets under the tank treads.

To an outsider, the Falklanders have often seemed curiously unmoved by the loss of life and property that their crisis has produced. At times it was hard to believe that they had any connection with the war. They behaved, it sometimes appeared, like peasantry caught in an eighteenth-century European dynastic clash – getting on with their farming as best they could while the rival armies swirled around them. They certainly appear to have little idea of how hard the fight has been.

It was supposed to have been a neat little war with not many dead, but it turned out messy and vicious, and far from the foregone conclusion everyone seemed to be talking about at home. It was an old-fashioned war. Despite the helicopters and the snowcats, most of the troops marched towards the front, and the regimental aidposts were full of people hobbling around with trench foot.

The battlegrounds, when they got to them, were sheer and rocky; perfect defensive positions that a more determined enemy could have held for weeks. The pace of the campaign was set by the Argentine Air Force. Until its fighters had been thinned out by the Harriers and ground defences after the initial few days of the landing, the task force was stuck on the beach head.

Less than a week before the fall of Stanley, the combat air patrol was incapable of protecting the landing ship *Sir Galahad*, which sat for six hours in broad daylight loaded with Welsh Guards before she was finally hit by the Argentine Skyhawks.

The day before the Argentine collapse I cowered in a stone 'sangar' outside 3 Commando Brigade Headquarters beside Major General Moore and his deputy, Colonel Tom Seccombe, while enemy fighter bombers swooped in unmolested to strafe our position. Had they been successful they would have destroyed most of the senior brigade personnel and the bulk of 3 Commando Brigade's communications.

Even the night before the end, a conclusion looked far away. The Argentine guns were giving the British troops the worst malleting of the campaign. Marines from 42 Commando were dug in right below the Argentine artillery observers on Mt William, and when I got there at dusk shells were falling every 30 seconds.

Every now and then the descending whistle ended in silence; another one had failed to explode because the soggy peat soil was too soft to detonate it. After a few minutes I decided to move somewhere safer and walked down the road towards Fitzroy. The Argentine guns started sending up paralume shells that lit up the sky and mountains like a stage set by some over-the-top designer.

The Marines had set up their regimental aid post in an abandoned lorry container parked by the side of the road and Surgeon Lieutenants Ross Aldley and Martin Ward were waiting for the first casualties of the night's fighting. At about midnight four Scimitars and Scorpions rumbled past laden with Scots Guards on their way to a diversionary attack. A little later the offensive began.

The side of Mount William began to flicker with tracer fire and the crashing of guns and mortars got more intense, but in the dark it was impossible to tell who was winning and who was losing. We tried sleeping. After a few hours we heard the tanks coming back. The story came out while the doctors patched up the wounded. The Guards' attack had started well. The Argentines hadn't spotted them until they were right upon the enemy positions, but in the fire fight that followed two Guardsmen had been killed and several were wounded before the Argentines ran away.

The survivors collected the casualties and headed back to the road, but on the way blundered into a minefield. There were 10 casualties in all. One man had been carrying his wounded 'oppo' on his back when he stepped on to a mine and both his feet were shattered.

They sat in silence while the doctors stripped off the blood-sodden boots and cleaned out the worst of the shrapnel. They were not even front-line troops, but a collection of rear echelon storemen and clerks rounded up for the night and put under an SAS major.

One of the patrol asked for a cigarette. 'You've got a heart of gold, mate, you should have been a bloody social worker.' He was silent for a while then he started getting angry. 'Two dead,' he said, 'two fucking dead, all for some pimple on the arse end of the world.' *(20.6.82)*

No Tears for Galtieri
Editorial

An episode that began three months ago as farce, with the landing of Argentine scrap dealers among the penguins of South Georgia, has ended in a mixture of triumph and tragedy, with the British recapture of Port Stanley and the sacking of General Galtieri after the loss of a thousand lives.

No tears will be shed for Galtieri, a brutal and stupid man who brought shame, death and despair to his long-suffering people. His removal makes it at least conceivable that working relations between Britain and Argentina can be restored once the wounds have begun to heal. Without such a relationship, the long-term future of the disputed islands must remain bleak and uncertain.

The conduct of the Falklands campaign itself redounds greatly to the credit of the war Cabinet, especially Mrs Thatcher's decisive leadership, and to the courage and professional efficiency of our fighting forces. Now that the campaign is won, however, public attention will shift away from the heroism and horrors of war towards the origins of the crisis and to what kind of future the Falklanders can now expect.

An inquest is necessary for three main reasons. First, it is owed to those who died or otherwise suffered in the crisis, including Lord Carrington and those who resigned with him. Secondly, the operations of the task force have raised serious questions about our defence policy, equipment and capabilities that need to be resolved. And, crucially, an inquiry may put the whole episode into a fuller historical perspective and thereby, one suspects, remove or modify some prevailing myths which may have sustained the public in war but lie across the path to a sensible and satisfactory peace.

The sending of the task force clearly involved considerable risks. Equally clearly, Mrs Thatcher enjoyed considerable luck. The force was originally sent as a back-up to diplomacy, but the decision to begin repossession by force was dictated as much by the approach of winter weather as by the state of negotiations with Argentina and successive mediators. It was one of Galtieri's many miscalculations that he failed to recognise the diplomatic advantage he enjoyed while the United Nations was active and the British fleet was bobbing about in the South Atlantic. He was actually being offered nearly everything he wanted, and he let Mrs Thatcher off an uncomfortable hook by foolishly turning it down.

Mrs Thatcher has so far publicly ruled out any further talks about the future of the islands, at least for the time being. She believes that British public opinion, after the war losses, would not now understand any deal involving an Argentine share in sovereignty over the islands, and that it would be unthinkable now to ask the islanders themselves to accept such a change.

Looking further ahead, however, it is already clear that it will not be easy to get the co-operation of other countries – of the United States, Latin America or Europe – in establishing an international security umbrella over the islands unless there is Argentine participation in a political settlement. And the lack of a political settlement with Argentina will deter foreign economic investment in the islands.

Without a political settlement, without international security guarantees, without foreign economic aid, the financial burden of maintaining a Fortress Falklands policy could become formidable. Estimates of the cost, including a force adequate to deter further Argentine hostilities, vary from £600 to £800 million a year.

To this large sum must be added the broader political and economic effects of a continued state of tension in the South Atlantic. It would damage our relations with other Latin American States and reduce our outlets for trade in those countries. It would also mean either a reduction in our contributions to NATO or a substantial increase in our defence budget, which is already too high for a country with three million unemployed.

Mrs Thatcher may be right in her view that public opinion in Britain would not understand or tolerate any immediate move towards the Argentinians. But the British public can see clearly enough that the islands are a long way from home and barely viable, and that we cannot afford to fight a war for them indefinitely. Our people have learned to accept the long retreat from empire.

In time they would accept a deal that offered security to the islanders in the context of a long-term political settlement that included Argentina, the United Nations or the Organisation of American States. The islanders – and the world at large – would be more likely to accept such a deal, however, if a democratic regime began to emerge in Buenos Aires. In this respect, the destruction of Galtieri could yet prove to be the best service Britain has given to the Argentine people. *(20.6.82)*

Adiós Ushuaia
Ian Mather

It ended as it had begun: at an airport, being bundled in and out of cars, surrounded by armed police and soldiers, with passports changing hands. There was the same sense of confusion, even the same prickle of anxiety. 'Excuse me,' the naval officer had said at Rio Grande, where the three of us sat waiting in the bar for our plane to Buenos Aires. 'Will you please come with me in a bus?'

Now, 77 days later, we sat locked in the VIP lounge 'for our own protection' at Ezeiza Airport with our Iberia tickets in our hands, three suspected spies going home on bail.

But even at this late stage, it crossed my mind that some disaffected military group waving machine pistols might seek to reverse the judge's order. . . . At one particularly low point a few weeks earlier the three of us had even considered refusing bail should it mean staying in Argentina: we knew all about the right-wing 'death squads'.

But it was all right. We were on our way. As we flew north, the other two – *Observer* photographer Tony Prime and Simon Winchester of the *Sunday Times* – slept the sleep of those who know that, in the words of Argentine justice, they are 'no longer a danger to society.' I couldn't sleep, just as I hadn't been able to during the early days of our capture. It was hard to stop the mind racing. I remembered anticipating this moment in my prison diary. It was a Sunday morning notable for the beauty of the dawn, with the sun fingering the mountain-tops across the Bay of Ushuaia, and for the depths of my gloom, as I paced the narrow corridor between the cells:

'You can be alone when you want to, even in prison; your mind learns to cut out other people. You spend so much time thinking about your own case. Is this healthy, or not? I have no idea what I shall be like when I'm released, if and when I ever am. Will I collapse? Shall I be normal?'

Still normal, perhaps, but certainly not the same. Just as events outside had changed utterly – the war for the Falklands ended, Galtieri toppled – so our lives inside had changed us. I had made firm friends with an embezzler, a child molester and an Argentine commissar of police. I had read Harold Robbins for the first time and Sophocles for the second. I had learned Spanish with a Tierra del Fuego accent (rrrolling my Rs as in Rrio Grrrande). I had discovered surprising things about myself and about the immense kindness of other people.

And I had learned to value, as I never imagined I would, the simple privilege of freedom.

Re-reading my diary now for the first time, I see the word cropping up again and again, sometimes in Spanish: *libertad!* . . .'Everyone shares in the joy when a prisoner is released. All crowd round and offer their congratulations, without jealousy. We all share in the process of liberation.' Freedom, like imprisonment, is a great equaliser.

We kept our diaries (Simon and I, that is: Tony's journal was his sketchbook) religiously. Mine is a spiral-bound school exercise book purchased for me in Ushuaia by a friendly Swiss diplomat. The cover is an incongruous photograph of skindiving equipment, goggles, flippers, etc. On the fly leaf I have written my prison motto, in Spanish: '*Paciencia, tranquilidad, valor, humor.*' Courage, humour – they were hard virtues to cling to during the early days of our arrest.

Things had happened so quickly. One minute, it seemed, we were being embraced by President Galtieri's press secretary, as he gave us *carte blanche* in Buenos Aires to travel anywhere in Argentina. The next we were being hustled from police stations to airports, from barracks to jail, our press credentials politely put aside.

I had been arrested before in other parts of the world in the course of journalistic duty. I knew the first few days were the worst and the most dangerous. There was a chilling moment at Ushuaia jail early on when we were taken away singly, stripped, searched and made to lie naked on a prison cot. A small man in a white coat came into the cell. Earlier, I had caught a glimpse of some kind of electrical equipment on a trolley. Was the man in the white coat, who now began to examine me, checking my ability to stand up to torture? Were we to join the *desaparecidos*? He seemed nice enough and wished me luck as he left. Later we were to learn that he was a police doctor who had merely been ensuring that we had not been hurt in any way by our naval captors.

We had more visitors. Marine Captain Grieco, whom we were to get to know well, introduced himself and asked if we were suffering 'anxiety.' Yes, we said. 'Is it supportable?' (It was Capt. Grieco, with contacts at naval HQ in Ushuaia, who was to tell us later, before the sinking of the *Sheffield*, that the Argentines were holding back from using their Exocets – 'a terrible weapon.') Then came the judge, in gold-rimmed spectacles and speaking reasonable English. Have faith in Argentine justice, he urged. 'Remove from your minds any thought of "Midnight Express".' And to our immense relief he said we could all move into the same cell.

Diary. Friday, 16 April: 'The BBC reported that there was concern about the whereabouts of three British journalists. . . . A few World Service bulletins later we heard that the Editor of *The Observer*,

Donald Trelford, had issued a statement saying that everything possible would be done to secure our release. Good old Donald! Good old
BBC!'

That diary entry is an understatement. The news that our arrest was
known in London was hugely cheering. Until then, all our attempts to
get messages out had been ignored. Now, we thought, it would just be
a matter of time. That night, as we took our 'exercise' pacing up and
down the corridor outside our cell, three apples were rolled across the
floor to us by an unseen hand. Later, when we were allowed to mix with
the other prisoners, we learnt that our benefactor was Humbert, a
Chilean businessman in prison for stealing whisky.

Tuesday, 20 April: 'I was taken to court just before 11 a.m. in a
car with three large men. They smiled and were friendly. They
drove slowly so that Argentine TV could film us arriving at the court-
house. One of the guards wiped the window so I could be filmed inside
the car. I did not like to look out of the window and see the outside
world . . .

'It is perhaps better not to think too much about this morning's
hearing, or to contemplate the future too much. I have come through
this so far in reasonable psychological shape. . . . There is a glacier
right opposite the prison, and the air is so clear you feel you can touch it
through our murky double-glazing. The water in the shower – a
perforated disinfectant can – is so cold it might have come straight from
the glacier. It seemed to freeze on my head. But I have decided to
shower every day, to keep up standards.'

That entry in the diary concludes claustrophobically: 'I am nervous
about seeing a door closing on me. When anyone appears to be about
to close our cell door from the outside I leap up and shout "Don't close
the door!" Shall I be as nervous about closed doors when I get back
home?' As I write this, I see I have left the door open.

Friday, 23 April: 'At around 6 p.m. we were summoned to the court
to hear the judgment. It was left to Isabel Hilton (of the *Sunday Times*)
to read the verdict. Gradually, as she translated, it emerged that not
only were we being accused of taking illegal photos, but also of having
the intention to spy for the British Government and working as a team.
It was all ghastly and I held my head in my hands. I felt so sorry for
Isabel. At our council of war afterwards with Isabel and the lawyers
and Hugh O'Shaughnessy (of *The Observer*) Hugh went round muttering, 'Shit and botheration.'

As our imprisonment lengthened, the days shortened. It got light
later and later, dusk ate into the afternoon. The first snow of winter
transformed the landscape and hurt my eyes when I stood on the chair
in our cell to peer outside (I learnt to blink rapidly before submitting

them to the full glare of snow-reflected light). I stood by the window partly to avoid the cigarette smoke: everyone in the jail smoked except Simon and me.

At first I found it hard to look out of the window. It reminded me too much of freedom. Then I discovered the pleasure of pretending to climb one of the surrounding mountains in my mind's eye, cheating a little now and then by donning seven-league boots to jump across an inconvenient ravine.

Sunday, 23 May: 'An interesting feature of prison life is the amount of pretending that is normal among the prisoners. One prisoner, Ullman, an armed robber, is always pretending to be a sports commentator or an opera singer. Rocky, our devoted friend, in jail for hitting an officer while doing his National Service, takes his imaginary dog for a walk along the passage.'

Simon and I also went for long walks along this passage, which was 30 paces long, pretending that we were rambling in the country. The shower at the end was a waterfall. The other cells, where gourds of *maté*, the local version of tea, were usually being brewed, were cafés conveniently situated along our route.

The most common form of fantasising among the prisoners concerned sex. There seemed to be no homosexuality; but a large, clandestine sex manual was passed around constantly and our fellow inmates would helpfully point to the illustrations and say 'fucky, fucky' with relish. One evening I described how, on an assignment in Afghanistan, I had seen a peasant having intercourse with a donkey while the creature placidly carried on eating grass. Not to be outdone, one of the prisoners described a similar adventure with a pig. He had tucked the animal's hindquarters down the front of his wellington boots.

The two women in the jail were fortunately out of earshot in the female wing – not that they would have been shocked, anyway.

One of them, a 22-year-old 'dancer' from the 'Igloo' nightclub called Maria, had taken out another girl's eye with a broken bottle. The other, Rosa, was an infanticide (a common crime in these parts, apparently).

I dreamed a lot, but not often about sex (did they put bromide in our bean stews and tripe?). To start with, my dreams were about food, always laid out before a foggy yellow backdrop. Then they were regularly about home, about my wife and children, always strictly naturalistic. Simon and Tony had the same experience. Perhaps, in our nightmare situation, dreams were the reality – a reversal of the normal sleep/waking pattern.

There were other distractions besides sleeping. We told each other our life stories: I, raised in the shadow of Preston's Great Avenham Street Mount Zion Strict and Particular Baptist Tabernacle; Tony, an East End likely lad; Simon, a Dorset-educated public schoolboy. We laughed hysterically reading 'Scoop' aloud to each other, we acted our parts in Shaw and Sophocles – books kindly sent in by a teacher in Ushuaia who doubled up as the court interpreter. An Englishwoman married to an Argentine sent us a computer chess set. I became convinced the machine was cheating.

At other times it was impossible to keep the realisation of our predicament at bay. Simon and I would have long, obsessive talks about what lay ahead for us, analysing minutely whether a British victory in the Falklands would help to free us – or be the signal for our fellow prisoners or our guards or even an impromptu 'death squad' to wreak vengeance. (Comisario Barosso told us not to worry. If a death squad came – and he made machine-gun noises.)

At first Simon and Tony insisted on answering 'Present' in English at our daily roll-call instead of '*Presente*' in Spanish, as I did. One of our regular arguments concerned this question of whether defiance or compliance was the best policy. I believed it would be safer, especially in the event of all-out war (one of our fears was that the RAF would bomb Ushuaia airport, yards from the jail), for us to keep a low profile, not draw attention to our Englishness. This upset Simon a good deal at the time, who felt that it was important not to lose our identity in prison.

I suppose, looking back at these diaries, I was the pessimist among the three of us. Tony, beavering away at his sketching, performing miracles with the electrical wiring and plumbing in our cell, was the convinced optimist. When I argued with the other two about the need to preserve our few extra rations in case of worse times to come, Simon rewarded my (to my mind sensible) homily by calling me Job's Comforter. Simon and Tony were each convinced it was the other's fault that we had been arrested. I assume, when I was out of earshot, they agreed that I was the one to blame.

Monday, 14 June: 'Comisario Barosso did not yet know the Argentines had surrendered. "That's terrible," he said when we told him, once again quoting the BBC World Service to tell our captors what they had been prevented from knowing.

'"On Saturday the Argentine boxing champion lost. Yesterday our football team lost in the World Cup. And today the Argentine Army loses!"'

The surrender was too much for Marine Captain Grieco. Unlike the Army, he said, the Marines had fought to the last. 'One thousand Gurkha dead in front of their position!'

Friday, 18 June: 'Katie's birthday. Imagine New College cloisters in June. I love having a daughter at my old college.'

Sunday, 20 June: 'Father's Day in Argentina, too. Telegrams from the family. On TV the bellicose slogans have vanished. Watched West Germany beat Chile in the World Cup. . . .'

Monday, 21 June: 'Willy (our Argentine lawyer) and Isabel arrived. Lots of hugs and kisses. The judge seems to have made a complete *volte face*. All we are waiting for now is the arrival of the bail money. . . . Given two whiskies by the Comisario, which went to my head.'

I always wanted this saga to end happily, with handshakes and fond farewells from all the prisoners and prison staff. Eventually, it did – thanks to an enormous amount of effort by an enormous number of people. I shall treasure one letter in particular from a hardened Fleet Street man who, surprisingly, said he was praying for us – 'At least it can't do any harm.'

Officially, my home address is now the Canal Beagle Hotel, Ushuaia. I am at home in London on bail for two months. Will it really be Adiós Ushuaia? (*4.7.82*)

The Chocolate Soldier
Patrick Bishop

He was in Port Stanley buying chocolate in the supermarket when I saw him again, a shy Para lieutenant who was 22 years old and looked 17. The last time we had met had been on *Canberra*, four weeks and a small war before. 'They tell me you're a hero now,' I said; he looked both pleased and embarrassed.

Three Para were pinned down by Argentine machine gunners on Mount Longdon and the lieutenant had led an attack to knock out the position. Now there was talk of a medal.

The lieutenant made a slightly surprising hero. On the way down he had been regarded as the baby of the unit and the butt of some mild joking. His transformation, though, was just another example of the dramatic difference between the way things appeared on the journey down and how they turned out to be in fact.

A fortnight before the landing, none of us really believed that it would happen. The night before we set sail, the journalists held a sweepstake on the date that *Canberra* would turn round. My bet was within seven days. The longest was 27 May.

I was issued with dog-tags bearing my name and religion, and a phial of morphine. I started to take first aid classes seriously and to listen intently at lectures on how to dig a shell-scrape.

Gradually the need to maintain one's independence from the military felt less and less pressing. I began pounding round the deck behind the 'Toms' as they stomped along chanting 'If You've Got a Low IQ, You Can Be a Para Too,' breaking in my new boots.

I stopped talking about 'equipment.' It seemed much easier to refer to everything, as the military did, as 'kit.' (Though this could be taken to extremes: I heard an officer refer to his girlfriend as a 'good bit of kit.')

The night before the landing I went to a Mass of general absolution in the ship's cinema, where Father Noel Mullen absolved all present of their sins. Sitting beside me was a radio reporter who had not appeared in church before and who had expressed fiercely modern opinions on every subject throughout the voyage. Things were getting serious.

Despite the mental bracing that had gone on throughout the voyage, nothing could have prepared us for the experience of being on a ship on Friday 21 May in San Carlos Water. On *Canberra* it started with a scene of bizarre innocence with the ladies of the P&O crew (girls from the Purser's office and medical staff) strolling around the Promenade Deck to get their first sight of the Falklands, rather like inquisitive nineteenth-century memsahibs docking at Bombay.

An hour later they were lying flat on the decks while the Argentine air force tried to sink the ship. The civilian crew behaved with incredible *sangfroid*, especially as they had been told repeatedly that the ship would not be going anywhere near the fighting, calmly taking cover as attack after attack went in. Their coolness was in contrast to the marine major who dived into a strongroom slamming the door behind him every time the planes arrived. We all remembered with horrible clarity the statistics for survival in the icy waters of the South Atlantic – about five minutes if you were lucky.

Sitting out the attacks below decks was much worse than watching what was going on above, as it was impossible to tell whether the shudders and thuds were the sound of the ship being hit or the noise of friendly fire. By contrast, watching the Argentine planes coming in was exhilarating. All hopes that I could report these events dispassionately vanished when I found myself cursing as an Argentine pilot desperately twisted his Skyhawk to safety out of the track of a pursuing Sea-Cat missile.

At last 42 Royal Marine Commando, the unit I was attached to, were ready to go ashore. 'You lucky bastards,' said a kitchen porter as we filed out of the galley door and into the landing craft. He was right. Being ashore was always better than being afloat. With shellfire you quickly learned to distinguish between friendly outgoing ('bang . . . whizz') and incoming ('wheee . . . bang!').

The paralume (parachute illumination) shells were in some ways the most upsetting. They lit up the already dramatic scenery like a Hammer horror film set.

During the few hours I was under shellfire I experienced brief, intense moments of fear; but you knew that if you were dug in only a direct hit was likely to kill you, although this was rumoured to have happened to one unlucky man who had his head knocked off by a shell.

For the marines and paras, waiting for the action appeared more nerve-wracking than the fighting itself. I spent the night that 42 Commando were due to go up Mount Kent, which was thought to be held by a company of Argentine troops, with the officers in their billet in the San Carlos social club.

They prepared for battle with the deliberation of matadors, dressing with slow ritual. First their Arctic underwear, then camouflage trousers, quilted Mao suits and windproof smocks. With the final application of black camouflage cream, the transformation from avuncular jovial types into fighters was complete. They wrote last letters to their wives and families then struggled into their kit. Some of them were carrying so much that they had to put it on sitting down before being hauled upright. Another image came to mind: medieval knights before a joust.

'Hey, I've always really fancied those binoculars of yours,' said an officer who was staying behind. 'Can I have them if you don't come back?' It was an old joke in keeping with the black humour all the Services used.

In the end, the marine attack didn't go in that night because the weather was too bad for the helicopters to land. Four-Two were lucky to get any helicopters at all. At that stage of the war they were in such short supply that servicing was practically non-existent. Some units had only one day's supply of rations. Snow Cats were setting off towards the front with only half a tank of fuel, in the hope that they could be topped up en route.

Returning from days spent on the hills, I marvelled that the Booties (marines) were not only staying cheerful in such conditions but actually seemed to be enjoying it. Their bivouacs grew more and more grandiose. They started off as a shallow pit, built up with rocks round the sides and covered with a waterproof poncho. Then the men started adding peat cladding for camouflage and extending walls like suburban DIY enthusiasts.

They showed the same ingenuity with the rations. A favourite meal was combat porridge, a calorie-packed mixture of instant oats, chocolate powder and pulverised biscuits all mixed with hot water, that was guaranteed to kick-start any Bootie or Tom into a new day regardless of how bitter the night before had been.

By the time we got to Stanley, everyone was too weary for celebrations and the fantasies of drink and rapine talked about along the way went unrealised. It was all talk anyway. Everyone discovered, with increasing concern, that one of the first casualties of the war was the libido.

Standing on Stanley airfield waiting for a Hercules home, an SAS captain remarked that if we had been fighting a better Army it would have been a different story. We won, he said, because the Argentines were 'military pygmies.'

Apart from their Air Force, and their gunners at Goose Green, the Argentine troops did show a remarkable disinclination to fight. They knew a landing was imminent in the Port San Carlos area because several hours before the troops went ashore a high-flying plane spotted the Task Force fleet creeping along Falkland Sound: the pilot signalled back to the land forces a message that was intercepted by British signals intelligence. No move was made to move troops by helicopter to the area. If even half an Argentine regiment had been shifted to Port San Carlos, it is unlikely that the Marines and Paras would ever have got ashore.

Their equipment could not be faulted. At Goose Green I saw stacks of wicked-looking Browning heavy machine guns that hadn't been taken from their cases. The most sought-after items of loot were £25,000 night sights found in many Argentine positions. On top of Mount Harriet I saw a brand new radar system that had never been set up.

Nor, contrary to the propaganda, were they ill-fed or badly clothed. To the great annoyance of the British troops, Argentine ration packs came complete with tins of beef, powdered fruit juice, letters and envelopes, cakes of soap and razors and a miniature bottle of whisky. They slept on foam mattresses.

What was lacking was will. The NCOs were incapable of keeping their men in position when the shooting got serious. After the raid on Pebble Island, where the troops had melted away once their officer had been shot by the SAS, British officers were told to 'shoot the guy who's waving his arms about.'

Intelligence reports suggest that the Argentine garrison gave up hope immediately after Goose Green. A signal from General Menendez, the Argentine forces commander at Port Stanley, to General Galtieri was intercepted by British signals intelligence on the evening of the Goose Green surrender: Menendez reported that defeat was inevitable.

The Marines and Paratroopers, on the other hand, were models of discipline and resolution. No British generation of men has had less to do with the military than mine, and to my surprise the experience of living alongside them for 10 weeks turned out to be an enlightening and enjoyable one.

Most of the 15 journalists on *Canberra* began the voyage feeling mild dread at the prospect of the enforced company of so many soldiers. We ended up 'troopie groupies' of varying degrees of intensity, loyal to our units, and fluent in military slang.

At best, I patronisingly thought, the military would be amiable but bone-headed. Many of them emerged as intelligent and tolerant. Among the Marines and Paras there was less of the canyon-like class divide that separated Guards officers from their men, and they often spoke with the same accents.

On the whole they behaved well and despite the opportunities there were no orgies of killing, though I heard of one or two disturbing incidents. In one, a gunner told me that artillery fire had been called down on Argentines who had been driven off a hilltop near Stanley. A witness later described a pathetic band of soldiers scrambling over the rocks in the moonlight while artillery observers coolly directed shells onto them.

There was some ghoulishness. A young Argentine soldier who was shot through the mouth during the battle for Mount Harriet, and buried where he fell, was disinterred by a 'Bootie' who wanted to photograph him for his album.

The soldiers showed each other remarkable loyalty and kindness.

Many of my memories of the war are already receding; the cold, the wet and the fear seem distant now. It is the smells that are easiest to recall: the hot, eye-watering blast of aviation spirit exhaust that hit you every time you got on and off a helicopter, the powdery tang of artillery smoke, and the acrid smell of a hexamine stove fuel block.

Some memories are too strong to fade. I remember the awful stillness of a dead Argentine I nearly trod on while wandering around the back of a house in Stanley, and the sight of a row of survivors from the *Ardent*, their expressionless faces smeared a ghastly white by Flamazime anti-burn cream, lying on the floor of the Ajax Bay field dressing station. They lay silently, not moaning.

As wars go, it was not a bad one. It was short and decisive and, given the huge potential for destruction on either side, surprisingly cheap in lives. During the slack middle period in the war, we listened on our short wave radio to World Service reports of the Israeli attack in the Lebanon and at first envied the astonishing speed of their advance. We changed our minds when we heard the casualty figures. Perhaps, we reflected, if wars have to be fought at all, it would be best if they were all like this one. *(11.7.82)*

2.
The Way We Are

Not the Dinner Party
Edward Mace

Gradually, people in London have stopped giving dinner parties. At least, if these grisly rites persist, they've stopped inviting me. I gave them up long ago.

Dinner parties were the social horror story of the Sixties and Seventies. Asked weeks beforehand, when you would agree to anything, you struggled home from work, longing to put your feet up, for sausages and Match of the Day. Instead, you were forced to take another bath, change into your best suit – even, bizarre though it sounds now, into a dinner jacket – and set off out again.

Always the debate: how to get to Blackheath, Hampstead, Islington, or, as the Sixties progressed into the Seventies, further and further down the Fulham Road? To risk taking the car, hoping to dodge the breathalyser on the way back? It was either that or hanging on the telephone for half an hour hoping that Radio Cabs would answer in the end, and, if they did, that there would be a cab within a radius of five miles not already grabbed by somebody on their way to a dinner party.

Then the dinners themselves. Eight of us round a table for four. The heat of the candles. Complicated dishes that the hostess had burst herself over – running like a hare in her lunch hour to Berwick Street Market for the eggplant; doubling back to Paxton's cheese shop in Jermyn Street, fit to drop.

Wine that the host had fatally economised on, sometimes buying too little of what would have been all right if there had been enough, or, more likely, buying too much of what definitely wasn't all right so that the misery would be protracted through half the night and some of the next day.

The talk and the tension. Girls in long dresses quoting from the women's pages of *The Guardian*; chaps who cared about the Third World and chaps on the make who didn't. The obsession with giving up smoking; stories of holidays in the Seychelles, just discovered.

After dinner you usually perched in agony on a low Victorian maternity chair or something of the sort, picked up in a junk shop in Suffolk.

And if getting there had been a problem, getting home was a nightmare. This was the era of mushrooming mini-cab firms. Everybody had sheaves of little cards that had been pushed through their letter boxes, offering prompt late-night service. The trouble was the firms never stayed in business long enough.

Only the rich escaped this gruesome scene, with their professional cooks and butlers. Unperturbed by pretension, they ignored fashion and continued to ask you at the last minute, telling you to come as you were, straight from work. Thank God for the casual hospitality of the super-rich.

Now it's over at last. We're dining on the made-up dishes from Marks and Spencer now. And the cookery books have been relegated to where they do most good, the bedside table.

It was the custom in the Sixties and Seventies to decry the cocktail party which had been much in vogue in the Fifties. Only at a dinner party, trendsetters said, could you hope to meet people *properly*. Can you think of anyone worth knowing you would ever have got to know properly at a dinner party? *(23.5.82)*

Sex on the Dole
Carole Brightside

I got pregnant when I was 15. I didn't want to get pregnant, but I wanted a baby. That's about all I did want. I thought if I had a baby to look after it would make everything seem real and then I wouldn't have to pretend about everything all the time.

I've lived in the same house all my life. We've got two rooms at the top. All we've got in the kitchen is an old gas stove that dad got off a tip, a tap and a yellow sink that's got so many cracks that it will fall to bits any day now. When we want to pee or do the other thing, we have to go downstairs and use the bog. Mrs Thing says she's doing us a favour. When I want to pee in the night nothing would get me downstairs, so I use a tin that I keep under the bed. When I've finished I pour it down the sink and turn on the tap. I never thought there was anything wrong in it.

I love my baby; it's a feeling, not talking. She takes up all my life and when I take her out I'm watching her all the time. It's like looking up at the sun, it's so bright you can't see anything else and it makes your eyes water. All the thoughts in my head go into her. She's real to me like nothing else is. She's beautiful and no-one is going to take her away from me, ever. I can manage.

She's got big brown eyes, like me, and when she gets hold of my hand she holds me so tight, it's because she loves me.

I don't think much about her father. I never told him I was pregnant. I knew what I was doing when it happened. I let him have me because all I could think about was having a baby. Having him wasn't much of a thrill really, not like he told me it was for him. He doesn't know where I live or anything like that. If I meet him, I'll just walk straight past him without saying anything.

I didn't mind telling Mum. She said: 'Well you've told me straight out, I'll say that for you. What your Dad'll say I don't know.' I've never been frightened of Dad. He said they'd had so many ups and downs that another down wouldn't kill us. Sometimes Mum acted as if she'd like to turn me out of the house, but she never would. It was as if she didn't know what to think. I mean it was stupid her thinking I'd have a career or anything. No one's got a job round our way.

All the lot I went round with know about contraception, so I don't know what they are going on about in the newspapers. Some of the girls want to have a baby, like me, but then they get frightened so they have to have an abortion. I'd never let that happen to me; fancy killing a little baby. A lot of the boys tell them they've got something on when they haven't, so some get caught that way. I've never taken the Pill.

Some of the girls won't use any sort of contraception, just for the thrill. It's like when we were kids running across the road in front of the cars; it's like breaking a school rule, like jumping down the corridors and screaming about something rude.

It's doing what they say is wrong, because we want to; we want to go against them. We know we can't be like them, so not being like them is being against them. We're doing something just as good, being us, then we don't mind about not being like them. They can't talk to us properly because they don't know what it's like having a tin under the bed. I'm not going to tell them – they'd make me feel silly and ashamed and I'm not going to be ashamed, it's not my fault. So we pretend all the time and have a good laugh.

I never have to pretend with my baby, because she's clean and beautiful and I made her, she's mine and I love her. I'm not going to pretend I didn't get pregnant on purpose, because I did. I talk to her all the time. I know she can't understand but it doesn't matter. She will one day. I can say just what I like, things I could never tell anyone else. My Mum did this to me, I know that now.

Some kids I know talked to their dolls but I never had any. I had an old bit of my Mum's old coat. I'd take that out with me and pretend it was a doll. See what I mean about pretending all the time? Pretend this, pretend that, pretend the other, so that no-one knows what the real me is like. Sometimes I don't even know myself. That's why I don't pretend to my baby, not yet anyway. We laugh a lot.

I'm on social security of course, but having my baby doesn't make any difference. I'd still be on it. It's not my fault, I didn't make the world. Having my baby means everything to me – it makes things make sense. *(16.8.81)*

Must Boys be Boys?
Nigel Hawkes

It's an article of faith, I suppose, that children are cajoled into adopting their sex roles by their parents. Girls are taught to be girls and boys – barring accidents – taught to be boys.

Without such misplaced guidance, the feminist argument goes, we would have a society with a much fairer distribution of opportunity. Girls would rush off in hordes to Imperial College and become engineers and start designing bridges and . . . well, you know the rest.

But is it true? Becoming a parent makes one wonder. How on earth have I managed to condition my younger son so successfully that virtually the first word he ever spoke was 'car'? How did he manage to work out that cars are things boys are meant to be interested in before he even knew up from down?

Equally, why is his sister so spontaneously interested in clothes and jewellery? The truth seems to be that even before social pressures can have had much influence, little girls are very girlish, and little boys very masculine. Every parent knows this: it's only the textbooks that deny it.

The child psychologists have an answer, of course, though I don't promise it's very convincing. According to them, parents condition their children *without even realising they are doing it.* This is an explanation possessing the great advantage that it is impossible to disprove; if I claim to treat my children exactly alike, I am deluding myself. Subtle cues, invisible even to the parents themselves, are supposed to be enough to create those very considerable differences between girls and boys. If only potty training were as easy.

Mothers who do admit to treating their children differently 'tended to interpret such differences as natural reactions to innate differences between boys and girls,' say the psychologists Sears, Maccoby and Lewin in their 'Patterns of Child Rearing.' Poor, misguided mothers! When they thought they were responding to differences, they were in fact creating them.

To take a specific example: psychologists would interpret my son's interest in cars as a classic result of the process they call 'canalisation' – the directing of a child's interest on to toys or objects thought to be appropriate to his or her gender. Boys are given cars to play with, girls get dolls. Appropriate forms of play with these toys elicit approving noises from parents, reinforcing the sexual differentiation.

This may look tidy on paper, but it doesn't really meet the case. Boys get dolls, too, or at least teddy bears and some of them, astonishingly, still treasure them when middle-aged. And girls get cars, and show a modest interest in them. There simply isn't that much difference, these days, in the toys boys and girls get given; but there is an unmistakable difference in how they respond to them.

To be fair to the psychologist who devised the term canalisation, Ruth Hartley, I should say that it is only one of four processes by which she believed gender is established. The other three are manipulation, verbal appellation, and activity exposure.

Manipulation is the tendency of mothers – and, presumably, fathers – to treat the genders differently, making more of a fuss of a girl's hair, dressing her more carefully, and so on. Verbal appellation is simply saing things like 'You're a naughty boy' or 'What a pretty girl.' Activity exposure is the observation by children of the traditional activities of men and women, though this does seem to beg the question a bit. Why should a boy who sees so much of his mother's activities choose instead to identify with his father's, which he only sees at weekends?

Without denying for a moment that all these four processes go on, they do seem to me rather thin as an explanation of gender differences. One doubts they would be effective at all if they were not working a clay predisposed to fit the mould.

Present attitudes seem to me to be little better than the mirror-image of the absurd views held in the nineteenth century. Anatomists then went to enormous lengths to prove what society wanted to believe: that women were fitted by nature to lead less adventurous lives than men.

In the 1870s the French anatomist Paul Broca measured skulls and proved that men's brains are on average 14 per cent larger than women's, accounting for what were then believed to be the innate differences in intelligence. It is now known that brain size tends to be related to body size – which is why men's tend to be bigger – but to have no relation to intelligence.

But because the Victorians were blinded by prejudice, that is no reason for us to be. Today any attempt to demonstrate or explain differences between the sexes is certain to fall foul of feminist wrath. The situation is even worse in the US, where psychologists who dared to undertake work which might subvert the feminist ideology have been bombarded with offensive mail and phone calls.

As a result, those willing to argue a biological basis for the undeniable differences between boys and girls have been reluctant to come out of the woodwork. Far safer is the attitude taken by biologist Richard Lewontin of Harvard, who says that speculation about which sex is more analytical, or better at maths, is just 'the garbage-can of bar-room speculation presented as science.'

So, dipping for a moment into the garbage-can, what differences are generally accepted? Eleanor Maccoby (she of Sears, Maccoby and Lewin, and a Nurture rather than Nature believer) accepts only four traits as well established: the greater verbal ability of girls, and the greater visual-spatial ability, skill at mathematics and aggression of boys. (This excludes, obviously, anatomical differences and those based on size.)

Others are prepared to go a little further. The development of male characteristics is controlled by the hormone testosterone, and there is a theory that exposure to such hormones in the womb does something to the fine structure of the brain, wiring it up differently for boys than for girls. Supporting evidence comes mostly from animal studies.

Among canaries, for example, it is only the male birds that sing, a behaviour apparently controlled by a cluster of brain nuclei which grow and shrink with the coming and passing of the mating season. Female birds possess these nuclei, but in smaller numbers. But when they are treated with testosterone, their singing nuclei develop and they even burst into song, just like the males.

Songbirds are rather remote from human beings and it would be nice to have some evidence from closer home. The best that has been done so far, however, is some studies on children who have been exposed to male hormones in the womb, either as a result of adrenal gland malfunctions in their mothers, or because synthetic hormones had been prescribed to prevent miscarriage.

These studies do suggest that girls exposed to these extra doses of hormone before birth show more 'tomboyish' behaviour, tend not to play with dolls so much, and show more aggression than their sisters who did not suffer such exposures. The results are not completely convincing: the sample is small and the effects observed depend on subjective judgment. But they do suggest that hormones provide the predisposition on which the effects of environment can work.

Most people might feel that the differences do not matter anyway, since the point is not to provide a rationale for sexism but to try to eliminate it. Even if the differences are primarily biological, they provide no justification for denying either men or women opportunities to do what they want.

But they may help explain things which otherwise remain rather bewildering. The Israeli Kibbutz movement is one of the largest experiments in sexual equality yet attempted, and for a while seemed to be getting results. Women went into many unfamiliar occupations. But as time passed, there was a backsliding towards more traditional roles, a change more marked in the second generation than the first. If sexual conditioning were wholly the result of social pressure, exactly the opposite outcome would have been predicted.

If injustice exists – as it does – it is likely to be easier to counter when armed with the truth, whatever that may turn out to be. Besides, I can see no reason why people should feel guilty when they raise daughters who turn out to be girls. *(27.9.81)*

An Only Childhood
Ian McEwan

At a dinner recently, I heard someone described as 'a typical third child.' The company murmured in recognition and assent and, without pause, moved on to another subject – as it happened, TINA, whom we might reasonably have described as the 'typical product of a single parent family.'

Even more potent in the currency of family types is the only child. What do the words suggest? Immediately we see before us a doleful eight-year-old, nose pressed against a window pane watching a sunlit procession of merry children, siblings all, chanting and cartwheeling past his house; behind him, in the gloom of the sitting room, slightly out of focus, slumped like the figures in Sickert's 'Ennui,' are his parents, their taut expressions telling of wounded, possessive love; on the mantelpiece a clock beats like a snare drum, measuring out the infinite solitude of childhood. Indeed, one friend (from a large family, of course) confessed that she had grown up believing the term to be *lonely* child.

Recently I carried out a little survey among friends. I asked them which words best described the adults they knew to have been only children. Some key words from my respondents were *selfish, self-absorbed, spoiled, over-ambitious, demanding* and even *emotionally dishonest*.

On behalf of only children everywhere, I would like to submit my own list: *sensitive and secure* (a rare combination, that), *a great capacity for love* (giving as well as accepting it), *a deep sense of responsibility* (almost to a fault), *a rich imagination* (only an only child could compile such a list) and, most important, a lack of fear of, even a taste for, *solitude*. I know of people who grew up in large families who cannot keep their own company for more than an hour or two, after which they begin to wonder if they exist – surely a serious inadequacy in a civilised adult.

We all carry around with us, like a visiting card, a little autobiography – part history, part fiction, part mythology – which occasionally a new friend or acquaintance will ask us to produce. Mine goes: I have a half-brother and a half-sister who are both more than 10 years older than me, and because they both married fairly young and because the family was often abroad, they were not around much while I was growing up.

And so, continues my visiting card, I consider myself, psychological-

ly, an only child. As far as I can remember, no one has ever asked me
what this 'psychology' is and, until now, I have never asked myself.

My childhood was dominated by the presence of other children, real
and imaginary. After I was born, my mother was not able to have any
more children, and when I was seven my parents decided to adopt a
little boy to keep me company. The elaborate arrangements were
finally completed and Bernard (are you out there?) was all set to join
us at Christmas.

The preparations that year were particularly intense. The house
filled with the sweet, warm smells of my mother's mince pies. I helped
my father tie bunches of balloons into every corner of the living room
and 'our' bedroom. I learned that Bernard had fair hair, and began to
address him in my mind. Presents were bought for us both that either
matched or duplicated each other. I doubt if ever a more loving,
expectant household stood ready to greet an adopted child.

Then, quite suddenly, the bureaucracy at Dr Barnardo's decided
that, since the family, like all Army families, would have to move every
few years, this would be too insecure and unstable an environment for
a growing boy. Last-minute interventions by the local mayor were of
no use. I woke on Christmas morning to a double pile of presents. For
me Bernard was real enough – there were his things – and I adopted
him as an invisible playmate. My parents, especially my mother, were
deeply stung by the insinuation that they were unable to provide a
decent home, and the attempt to adopt was never repeated.

As well as imaginary friends, I devised elaborate mental games,
though I would not have called them games at the time; they were
compelling necessities and to have failed to engage in them would have
invoked punishment, usually disguised as misfortune. When I was
eight I read a story which featured a courtroom scene. The defendant,
who happened to be innocent, explained his behaviour and motives to
a deeply sceptical judge. For two or three years after that I did not let a
day pass without imagining for a while that my present actions were
under scrutiny by a court of law.

I saw my present self from the future and made it into a past. If I was
walking along a street I would hear the judge say, 'And what did you do
when you reached the corner?' 'I turned left m'lud.' 'And *why*
exactly?' 'Well you see, I wanted . . .' This became for me a means of
self-observation and exploration. As my replies became more elaborate, the judge, barely convinced, would probe further. In this daydream I could easily walk half a mile past my destination and then the
judge would demand to know all about that.

If this was a protean super-ego, I took it on board without discom-
fort. In the hours I played alone I deveveloped powerful relationships

with inanimate objects. Once, a kite I had built refused to fly. I took it to my bedroom, laid it on the bed and, addressing it in my mind, tried to persuade it of the great pleasures of flight. I gave it one last chance. However, out in the garden it refused to go and I beat it to shreds with a broom, then forgave it and buried it.

The only child can get an awful lot of reading done. I sometimes think I did most of my serious reading between the ages of seven and 11. Certainly I have never been able to achieve the same absorption and excitement in books as I had then. We were living in Tripoli, Libya, by this time and my mother worked in the YMCA bookshop. Three or four times a week she brought home a new hard-back book for me, and took away the one I had just finished to slip it back on the shelves.

I read without direction – pleasure was all that mattered. Biggles, Gimlet, Billy Bunter, Jennings, and probably every word that Enid Blyton had written to date. I wonder now if my pleasure in books would have been quite so intense if I had been presented with books I *ought* to read. When the public libraries began the move against Enid Blyton, I was pleased to think that I had grown up on the subversive work of a banned author.

But for all this interior life, I was not lonely. My friendships had all the intensity of love affairs. When I was seven and we were still living in England, my cousin Paula came to stay with us because her mother was ill. We became close friends and even shared a desk at school, facing out together the derision of a class in which the boys and girls kept, or were kept, determinedly apart. Because our house was not very large, Paula and I had to share a huge double-bed. Night-times became a delirium of whispering and giggling under the blankets.

One night, not long before she was due to return home, I woke to find that Paula had rolled against me and was sleeping with her head on my arm. So great was my pride and protective tenderness that I lay without moving till dawn, my arm racked by pins and needles and, later, total numbness.

Perhaps there is a tendency among only children to idealise situations, to incorporate them into fantasy. Had Paula been my sister, I would have longed for a single bed.

What is distinctive about the only child's lot is his or her relationship with its parents. The only child stands at the apex of a tight little triangle, the focus of love, expectation, indifference, even cruelty – whatever is on offer, the only child gets it all. Probably, in most cases, it is love, and then the question is whether the child is sustained or stifled by being the sole recipient of parental love.

During my childhood I was unquestionably sustained. Our triangle,

at least the sides of it that I could see, was constructed of uncompli-
cated affection. Complication set in later with boarding school and
adolescence. Then the usual problems of growing up in and away from
the family circle were intensified, perhaps by the smallness of that
circle.

I remember playing with my parents much as I played with other
children. We played separately rather than all three together. Out-
doors was my father's domain, indoors my mother's. And yet, characteristically, for one of the happiest moments of my childhood I was
alone. During a school holiday when I was 10, my mother dropped me
off at the beach on her way to work. It was eight o'clock in the morning
as I walked along the bluff that overlooked the long curve of beach and
calm water.

The early morning sunlight made everything familiar look newly
made, and I remember stopping, quite overcome by joy and a feeling
of oneness with the world. In retrospect it seems to have been a
moment of an intensity described by William James in his 'Varieties of
Religious Experience.' What was crucial at the time was that the beach
was entirely deserted, and as I descended the bluff I pretended that I
was the first ever to set foot there.

When I was 11 I went to boarding school. My secure domestic
triangle and the freedom of the Mediterranean were replaced by a
bewildering lack of privacy, by a non-stop jostling, pummelling and
shouting, by obscene words and rites which one dared not ignore, by a
terrifying bully of a games master, and by mediocre food.

I ticked off the days of that interminable first term like a convict in a
cell, and when I returned home I was unable and unwilling to describe
my new life to my anxious parents. I could pass no judgement on it – for
me it simply existed. One week I was an only child, the next I had 60
brothers.

A year or two later, when this estrangement was compounded by the
beginnings of adolescence, I felt baffled by the changes within me, and
guilty too. It was then that Bernard, my lost adopted brother, might
have been of use. I might have discovered from him just what was
particular to me in my situation, and what was shared by all growing
boys. There was no question of comparing notes at school. There one
either boasted about one's parents or said nothing at all.

We were boys, almost men, and our emotional training was such
that we did not admit confusion or pain even to ourselves, let alone to
one another.

What was once security for the only child can become, for the only
adolescent, an over-focused isolation. Adolescents naturally and
urgently need to reach out for standards other than their parents' to

judge themselves and the world by; the only adolescent reaches out and experiences more often than not a sense of guilt at his or her betrayal of a unique family relationship.

I mark the end of my childhood by the end of that first holiday home from school. The three of us had picked up on our lives together easily enough, but when it came for me to return to England I knew this time exactly what I was returning to, and I felt keenly for what I was leaving. As we drove out across the semi-desert to the airstrip, we were all three intent on being brave. There was cheery talk about the next holiday, and there were long silences.

In the aeroplane two elderly ladies kindly moved to let me have the window seat so that I could wave to my parents. Of course, I could see them more clearly than they could see me. They were barely 40 feet away from the tip of the wing, standing arm in arm just where the tarmac met the sand. They were waving and smiling pluckily. I saw my mother surreptitiously dab at her eyes. I had a distinct intimation then that a period of my life, a time of unambiguous, only child affinities, was over and I began to cry, misting up the porthole.

When I wiped it clear my parents mistook the movement of my hand and waved again. The plane began to move and they slipped out of sight. I turned towards the cabin and felt dreadfully confirmed in my intimation of loss when I saw that the two old ladies at my side were watching me and crying too. *(31.1.82)*

Rise of the Rastaman
Shiva Naipaul

On sunny Saturday afternoons on the Portobello Road, the blacks with the tangled braids of hair – called dreadlocks – look alluring and picturesque. They blend into the lively scene which still evokes memories of the Sixties; they are an accepted part of the masquerade. Venture, however, a street or two to the north, to All Saints Road, and the innocuous quality disappears. One strays from a realm in which the masquerade of racial assertion, of ostentatious Blackness, is suddenly stripped of its eccentric and theatrical charm, assuming an altogether harsher aspect. Being black on All Saints Road is no joke.

Whether by night or by day, it takes courage to enter one well-known public house in the area. Near the entrance cluster knots of dreadlocked blacks. If you look a promising prospect, you will, in all probability, be surrounded. The litany of illicit commerce will be hummed into your ears.

Fending off the hawkers and the pimps, summoning resolution, you force a passage into the pub. Within, the odour of ganja (marijuana) is unmistakable. The smoke of the holy herb – nowadays claimed as an essential ingredient of West Indian 'culture' – hangs in a motionless mist.

Someone feeds the juke-box. The numbing, pseudo-portentous rhythm of the reggae pulses through the ganja mist. In one corner I notice a white girl, reading one of the many black publications now available in London. Elsewhere, a roughly dressed white youth, hunched into an oversized combat jacket, is striking a bargain with a dreadlock who, quite openly, holds up for his inspection a plastic bag that must contain at least a pound of marijuana. On the tables are scattered signs of holy herb usage – the broken stubs of unsmoked cigarettes pillaged for their tobacco.

'So, man, what can I do for you?' A hand falls on my shoulder. The accent is cinematic American hoodlum.

Resinous sticks of hashish are displayed.

'The best, my friend. From Pakistan.'

Isn't he, I ask, afraid of getting into trouble with the law? No . . . he has no fear of that. The police wouldn't dare come in there and make trouble. They knew what would happen if they attempted anything so foolish. I discover that he has already served a two-year prison sentence for burglary. A frame-up.

We are joined by one of his comrades. His stock of hashish is still to be cut into strips. He heats the blade of a penknife on the flame of a cigarette lighter and settles down to his task. Each strip will fetch £5. He will have about 20 such and would hope to sell them all that day: he conducts most of his business in the pub. As he works, he sips orange juice from a carton. Never touches alcohol. Never! He comes from Jamaica.

'Would you call yourself a Rastafarian?'

He does not cease his labour. 'I prefer to call myself dreadlock.'

'What's the difference?'

But he is not inclined to pursue the point. I ask if he has been to prison. He smiles enigmatically. 'Babylon is prison, man. Babylon is one big prison.'

'I take it, then, you're longing for the day of repatriation to Africa?'

He throws me a vague glance, sipping at his orange juice. I assume this to mean that, for the foreseeable future, Africa will have to wait;

that the Portobello and its environs are not about to be robbed of his presence. I watch the heated penknife blade slice easily through the block of hashish. The Babylonian captivity, at £100 a day, is sweetness itself, not to be lightly surrendered.

A third young man insinuates himself. He is lean and clean-shaven. Amphetamines are his speciality. His approach is more aggressive, tinged with suspicion and hostility.

'Are *you* a Rastafarian?'

The amphetamine salesman gazes levelly at me. 'All black men are Rasta.'

'How do you mean?'

No further enlightenment is volunteered. He wants to trade, not talk. Warily, I breathe in the cloying ganja mist. The reggae throbs.

'The true Rastafarian,' Lord Scarman wrote in his report on the Brixton disorders (or 'uprising' as it has come to be known in certain circles), 'is deeply religious, essentially humble and sad. . . . The dreadlocks, the headgear and the colours which he affects, are a daily reminder to him of Africa and a witness to the world of his belief that his exiled people must return there.'

The *true* Rastafarian. For more than a month, in Jamaica and in London, I had been pursuing this Holy Grail of authenticity. In that West London pub, I had reached the end of a wretched road.

* * *

Jamaica seemed the logical place to begin my search. After all, it was there that the cult of Ras Tafari had first seen the light of day towards the end of the 1920s; and, prophets not always being without honour in their own country, it is there that the movement – if it can be so described – has achieved its most widespread recognition and been accorded a respect that frequently verges on the idolatrous.

The funeral of the reggae singer and sage, Bob Marley, demonstrated the extent to which Rastafarianism had penetrated the national life. It was transformed into an affair of State. Orations were delivered by both the newly elected, capitalist-minded Prime Minister, Edward Seaga, and by the socialist leader of the Opposition, Michael Manley. The assembled multitudes smoked their ganja, grieved and grooved – and were not molested by the police. The only comparable event in the history of Rastafarianism was the visit to the island, in 1966, of the Ethiopian emperor, Haile Selassie, King of Kings, Conquering Lion of the Tribe of Judah, the God in human form destined to redeem his abused brethren, whose divine wrath would one day wreak its vengeance on iniquitous Babylon.

Between the visit of Haile Selassie and the funeral of Bob Marley a great deal had happened; a great deal had come to fruition in Jamaica.

Most portentously, the Rastaman had crawled out of the shadows of nightmare and been crowned a king: a phoenix risen from the ashes of the Black Power era. A new Jamaican, a new Caribbean man, had been born. He was not at all familiar to me. Gone was the genial, straw-hatted calypso type singing about rum and Coca-Cola and mothers and daughters compromising their virtue for the Yankee dollar. In his place had come the ganja-fed troubadours who sang about shooting sheriffs in self-defence; about rampaging 'rude boys' a-looting and a-shooting. The Caribbean black had undergone a sea change. He was beginning to acquire a style and a mystique peculiarly his own.

With the collapse of Black Power during the course of the Seventies, that mystique, that style, now in search of a fresh resting-place, would discover the Rastaman. His was a style that brought together and transcended all styles of black rebellion. Above all, with the international success of singers like Bob Marley, he made it glamorous to be oppressed.

*   *   *

RasTafari (Haile Selassie) is the living God – even though he is, according to the western Press, dead.

Ethiopia (sometimes construed as 'Africa' in a more general sense) is the black man's home.

Because Ethiopia is the black man's home, from which he has been cruelly separated by enslavement, repatriation to his origins is a necessity. His repatriation is not merely necessary but inevitable; it is foretold by Biblical prophecy.

White men are evil. Their treatment of the black man is adequate proof of this.

These are the four doctrinal assertions which the authors of a 1960 report at the University of the West Indies decided were common to all Rastafarians. A later observer expands the number to six, including in his list the propositions that White is inferior to Black and that the latter would one day rule the world.

No theology is more fluid, more elusive. There is no church; there are no scriptures; there is no ordained leadership. Each Rastafarian has his own version of the thing. You become a Rastaman by declaring yourself to be such – or, simply, by beginning to look like one. There are those who call themselves Rastafarian and who abhor ganja. Some reject the divinity of Selassie. The brethren can be 'clean-faced' or dreadlocked. Many are socialist and many are not. Some are primitivist in outlook, some drive around in sports cars and travel between continents by jet plane.

There are brethren for whom African repatriation seems more of a threat than a promise. Many appear to be neither deeply religious, nor humble nor sad. Quite a number of the brethren I have encountered are not – to disagree with Lord Scarman – 'scrupulous' in their observance of the law. Each Rastafarian is free to invent his own version of the creed. Each ordains himself. In that chaos of attitudes and posturings, the true cannot be separated from the false.

*   *   *

He was the most ferocious-looking Rastaman I had yet set eyes upon, a monument of a black man. Coal-black locks, thick and wild and spidery, framed a broad, beaten face. Speech, when it eventually came, was mangled, creeping out of his throat in a subterranean growl that was barely comprehensible. He reeked of ganja.

But, however unprepossessing, he was well known in Jamaica's Rastafarian circle, a blend of teacher and high priest. His claims to fame were substantial. He was one of the senior brethren who had instigated the 1960 University of the West Indies report on the sect; he had twice travelled to Ethiopia; he it was who had controlled the frenzied crowds gathered at the airport during Haile Selassie's visit to the island in 1966 – to him alone would the rabble listen, to him alone would it concede authority; and – his crowning glory – it was he who had first recognised the genius of Bob Marley, become a guru to him in the early days of 'struggle,' and even composed a song for him. I shall refer to him as the Elder.

Accompanying the Elder was an acolyte whose dreadlocks, by comparison, were embryonic. The acolyte was a journalist: he wrote a column about mainly musical matters for the *Gleaner*, Jamaica's major newspaper. He too, therefore, was not to be lightly treated.

'We do not call ourselves Rastafari*an*,' the acolyte remarked primly, glancing at the incoherent Elder. 'Nor do we like that word Rastafari*anism* either.'

'So what do I call you?'

The acolyte looked at the Elder. They exchanged knowing smiles.

'You may call us RastafarI.'

This 'I' language is one of the Rasta conceits. Most common is the 'I-n-I' doing service for 'we.' But there are scores of others: 'I-thiopia' (Ethiopia), 'I-vine' (divine), 'I-tal' (vital – a term applied to the vegetarian cuisine of some cultists), 'I-story' (history), and so on. It is a harmless affectation, but that, of course, has not deterred fanciful interpretations of its significance. There are those who see in it a profound self-assertion. Some go even further and talk about the birth of a new and revolutionary language. It is hard, nevertheless, to understand how talking about 'I-bages' instead of cabbages contributes to that process.

I was to be corrected again.

'RastafarI have no beliefs,' the acolyte said. 'RastafarI do not *believe* anything. The I-dren [brethren] *know*.' The I-dren knew, for instance, that they were living in the Last Days.

Later that evening, we went to the 'ghetto,' driving through unlit, litter-hazed alleys. I was escorted into a compound inhabited by two or three families. Under an open-sided shed lit by a feeble bulb some children were playing a dice game. A row of hens slept on the rafters. Reggae pulsed from a transistor radio.

We sat outside in the warm and windless dark. A pipe with a long stem and an oversized bowl was produced. Piously, it was filled with ganja. At the first inhalation, the Elder choked and coughed and spluttered. The hens up on the rafters were disturbed and stirred restlessly. In the still air, the smoke of the holy herb was overpowering, ascending in clouds which did not disperse. The Elder began to speak – about the Falkland Islands, about Richard Nixon, about Enoch Powell. He spoke about the First World War, the Second World War, the coming Third World War. He spoke about Hitler and about the Queen. It was impossible to grasp the logical structure of this discourse.

'Your English Queen know all about Rasta,' he said. Had she not been to Addis Ababa, holiest of cities? Had she not spoken with His Imperial Majesty? What did I think they had talked about? Was I not aware that at the coronation of His Imperial Majesty the Duke of Gloucester had been sent by George V to return to its rightful owner the golden sceptre of the House of Judah which had been seized from Ethiopia by Rome and from Rome by Britain?

He laughed. 'Your Royal Family know *all* about Rasta. They know *who* His Imperial Majesty is.' He rolled his reddened eyes at me. 'Now you have come all the way from England to find out about Rasta. You should ask the Queen!' He turned to his spellbound audience. 'This man has come all the way from England to see us. We always knew that one day the world would come to see us out. We predicted that one day Rasta would cover the world like an ocean. . . .'

*   *   *

'Everything's gonna be all right.' So runs the refrain to a well-known reggae song. Why everything's gonna be all right is not clear. But, clarity is not the point. The pseudo-portentousness of the beat is everything. Rastafarianism – as style, as imagery – has spread on the wings of its music. 'Music is an integral part of Pan-Afro Caribbean peoples' way of life,' says the *Voice of Rasta* (a North London publication), '. . . I and I have made a lot of sacrifices and compromises, but music and dance is something I and I won't sacrifice to please babilan.'

Such theology as is espoused by the London-based brethren derives almost entirely from the lyrics of Bob Marley. They have a dim perception of the Caribbean, most of them having either been born here or brought here at an early age. Victims of a double displacement, they have come to see themselves as, and be treated as, merely Black. Just being Black is enough. It is the saddest of denudations.

The Rastafarian creed – with its notions of Babylonian captivity and martyrdom, its racial emphasis, and its alluring denials of the Western world and Western achievements – is ideally suited to the circumstances. It makes it possible to be merely Black. No further effort is required of its disciples. The medium is the message. 'Soul' eats up intellect; rhythm replaces struggle.

His existence confirmed by the slack-jawed wonderment of his Babylonian audience, the Rasta-man is not required to justify either himself or his faith. Rastafarianism does not bring its devotees closer to self-comprehension. If anything, it has led them further away from understanding. At best, it gives the black a congenial image of himself. At its worst, it stimulates lethal visions of grandeur.

Rastafarianism transforms Blackness – being a Negro in a White Man's world – into a cultic experience. Allegory displaces reality. As Marcus Garvey said – the Negro does not know how to stop hurting himself. *(27.6.82)*

3.
Around the Island

The Pope at Canterbury
Hugo Davenport

Yesterday a Pope from Rome entered Canterbury Cathedral. And as John Paul II and Robert Runcie, Archbishop of Canterbury, walked together up the nave and fell simultaneously on their knees before the altar, the congregation burst into applause.

It was not the end of four-and-a-half centuries of schism, since Henry VIII broke with the Vatican, but the tremendous pageantry and carefully-planned symbolism of the reunion at Canterbury blocked the way back to ancient hatreds.

The ceremony in Canterbury was in sharp contrast to the sympathetic humanity of Southwark and the theatrical magnificence of Westminster Cathedral. It was almost oppressive in its solemnity.

Protocol had been weighed to the last speck of dust to avoid even the faintest suggestion of unequal status. The Pope and the Archbishop of Canterbury had identical chairs, identical lecterns, and their respective retinues of bishops. It was as if someone had placed a gigantic mirror along the east-west axis of the cathedral.

The clergy and lay dignitaries entered in three successive processions. The first two filed slowly into the soaring Gothic nave, and the first hymn rose to the vaults. Then there was a lengthy silence punctuated only by the echoed mutterings of a radio commentator.

At last the moment arrived. Canterbury and Rome stood together on the threshold of the west door. Dr Runcie was resplendent in his

Royal Wedding outfit, while the Pope, in white vestments with a scarlet cape, looked a little bent and frail. The congregation applauded noisily as the two leaders began their slow ascent to the High Altar.

At each stage of the journey they paused to mark their historic rapprochement by symmetrical tableaux. When they arrived, each kissed the seventh-century 'Book of Gospels,' whose open pages were protected by white ribbons.

For the watching journalists, the scene at the High Altar was framed by the stone canopy of a chipped and badly damaged tomb – perhaps vandalised by Cromwell's Puritan skinheads in what the Pope called 'the sad years of division' between the two Churches.

Dr Runcie, who began by greeting the Pope in nicely-pronounced Polish, rejoiced that 'the successors of Gregory and Augustine (the Pope and the missionary saint who founded the see of Canterbury) stand here today in the church which is built on their partnership in the Gospel.' The question of whether Anglicans or Catholics were the real successors, which has racked the conscience of generations, was not even mentioned.

The ceremony at Canterbury, the main ecumenical event of the visit, had three high points of symbolism. The Pope, the Archbishop of Canterbury and the Rev Dr Kenneth Greet, secretary of the Methodist conference, renewed their baptismal vows together, and then greeted all the cardinals, bishops and other church leaders with the 'kiss of peace.'

Then the leaders lit candles for Christian martyrs of different faiths – Dr Runcie for Cardinal Romero, the murdered Archbishop of San Salvador, the Pope for Father Kolbe, who gave his life for another at Auschwitz.

Finally, Dr Runcie and the Pope made their way to the spot where St Thomas à Becket was murdered on a hint from King Henry II in 1170, and knelt in silent prayer and reflection.

The Bible readings given by the two leaders – Dr Runcie's from St Paul's Epistles to the Corinthians, the Pope's from St John – were both highly involuted passages on the theme of unity within diversity. The labyrinthine phraseology seemed to reflect the extraordinary complexity of this attempt to bring the two Churches together.

It was only after these ceremonies were completed that the tension of the occasion seemed to lift, borne up by Sir William Walton's triumphant setting of the Te Deum.

That tension was also reflected in the security arrangements. On Friday they were efficient but relatively unobtrusive; yesterday they were tight to the point of strangulation.

Initially the Press were to be permitted necessary hand baggage, but after the discovery of a penknife in a visitor's bag, even briefcases had to be deposited with the police. More than 1,000 men from Kent Constabulary were on duty.

According to a detective, relations between the two groups of clergy as they changed for the ceremony fell a little short of fraternal.

'It's like two teams in a needle match at the Cup Final in there,' he said. 'You've got the reds on the left and the whites on the right, and they're not talking to each other.'

At midnight on Friday little knots of people had already gathered with sleeping bags and vacuum flasks, sheltering near shops or beside walls, to ensure a good view. Immediately outside the cathedral grounds several groups were installed by midnight.

The Pope had arrived in Canterbury by helicopter. The narrow streets were lined with good-natured crowds; although Polish groups waved their red-and-white flags all along the route, few of the other spectators seemed to be Catholic. The crowds were estimated by police at some 25,000, considerably fewer than expected.

A firmly Church of England woman had brought her family from Herne Bay because she liked the adventure. 'I saw him with the children on television today,' she said, 'and you could see he's a good man.' Most of Canterbury seemed to share that view. *(30.5.82)*

This is Your Life
Robert Chesshyre

In the sunshine the prison is open and unoppressive with plenty of sky, which is important in a place where a man might spend 20 years.

Apart from the sports field, where some indulge in punishing distance running, men move unhurriedly. Time is in plentiful supply. Exercise time is voluntary and, when the sun shines, is taken sitting down, or lolling about, chatting, playing cards. Only the occasional bad-tempered outburst gives a clue to the tensions.

There are no cameras or searchlights on the walls: the most visible signs of security are the dogs and their handlers. Although Maidstone, a category 'B' prison, often holds notorious men, most of them are 'doing their bird nice and easy,' by which they don't mean soft but without causing or giving aggravation. An armed robber said: 'If I found the front gate unlocked, I'd tell them.'

On Medway wing, which houses the majority of the long-term men, one is in his twenty-third year of imprisonment.

There were men playing snooker there, men sitting in cells in groups, men lolling over the upper landings, men watching TV, men who have lost the habit of mixing alone in their cells. Prison officers observed from each landing. It was strangely quiet for a place that contained so many people.

I felt the oppression of the hundreds of wasted years that these men's imprisonment represented stacked up around me. There was a glint of challenge in the eyes of some of the younger men, many of whom will be locked away from adolescence into early middle age. But the older men respond to the routine like trees answering to the seasons, their roots are so firmly in prison.

Forget the sports pitch, forget the lawns; long-term imprisonment at the end of the day – and there may be thousands of them – is to be locked away at a time when other men are taking a turn round their gardens or dropping down to the local, when children are being tucked up in bed. Some men prefer cells on the ground floor, so they can't see over the wall.

Maidstone's day starts at 6.40 a.m. when the first shift of uniformed officers parades at the gate. By seven, bleary-eyed men were shuffling along the landings, plastic pots in hand, to 'slop out.' Prisoners do not have to eat breakfast, but those who did that morning greeted it with a chorus of protest. It had been brought 50 yards from the central kitchen on a 'hot' trolley, but was said to be stone cold.

Work starts early, and men were soon straggling out, counted by an officer on a hand-held machine. The lucky ones, grabbing red arm bands from the office, to trusted tasks in library or canteen; the quite lucky to prison maintenance work and to constructive workshops like the print or carpenter's shop; and the unfortunate to 'miscellaneous' workshops, where they might pack toys or twiddle their thumbs.

The cells the men leave behind are as different from one another as such small places can be. Those without friends, relatives and outside money have the minimum of possessions, living in the stale, pervasive odour of unclean clothes and underwashed bodies. Their cell walls are almost bare, chipped where previous occupants have taken down pictures, bedding is discoloured, a few possessions – papers relating to a long-forgotten trial – are lovingly preserved in battered cardboard boxes. The atmosphere is one of overwhelming personal defeat.

At the other end of the scale there are immaculately wallpapered cells, with curtains, carpets, bedspreads, couches. 'These days,' said a senior officer, 'there has to be a very good reason why something should *not* be allowed.' Men team up; one pair used one of their cells as a 'workshop' for painting and cell hobbies, and the other as a sitting room, where there were small ornaments, a door curtain, and ornately framed family pictures – though each man actually sleeps in his own cell.

An oldish man was fooling around with officers, squirting water from a squeezy bottle, and being shot back from a water pistol. 'Outside you'd say "Why don't you grow up?" ' said an officer. In Medway anything that lessens the tension, however childish, is welcome.

'Charlie,' the man with the water bottle, is in for a 'domestic' murder, but the judge recommended that he serve not less than 20 years. He has done six. Despite his despair at the years ahead, 'Charlie' is clearly a survivor. 'Imprisonment isn't hard; there is nothing cruel or vindictive about it. The battle is against frustration and absolute boredom. The screws are no trouble at all: to get kicked, you've got to put your head on the line.' He is worried about deteriorating, saying that if he has to do his full 20 years 'they might as well keep me.' He's seen others go crazy.

He didn't express any remorse: very few prisoners do. The system fosters self-centredness: a man who is locked away sheds responsibility for providing for himself and his family; he becomes dependent, and that makes him demanding. Wives struggling on supplementary benefit are expected to supply all sorts of goodies: 'they' – probation officers, for example – are looked to for all manner of problems.

Most long-termers develop a survival strategy: some, like Charlie, play along with the system and earn their red bands. Others fight every inch of the way. I met one lifer going out after 14 years, much of it spent in tough jails like Dartmoor and Parkhurst, who didn't look as if he'd done a day: 'There are two ways of getting something in prison. You either creep or "perform." I bucked the system. Even small things, like refusing a haircut when you're ordered one, keep you going.'

Officially prescribed drugs can help. One prisoner said: 'I took the "do-your-bird" medicine, the happy gear. I didn't need it: I just got in on the act.'

Other drugs – particularly marijuana – are available in many prisons. One man swore he could get any drug I cared to mention within a few doors of his cell – he also said he could raise £500 in cash on the wing. Officers almost shrug their shoulders. There has been a tightening up on visits, but a man can bring pot in after a pre-release home visit with impunity, wrapped in a french letter in his bottom. Prisoners' orifices may no longer be searched.

The clue that a pot-smoking session is in progress is usually that a cell door is wedged and the spyhole blocked. By the time an officer has summoned a posse to push the door in, the incriminating evidence has gone out of the window.

The rise of pot as the prison fix has some benefits in that it has partially replaced hooch – illegally fermented alcohol – which can turn a man fighting mad and occasionally blind as well. An officer said he noticed the change four or five years ago at Parkhurst: Christmas was dead quiet. Basic alcohol is simple to make, and still on the menu: I was shown a ceiling where several gallons had recently been discovered.

There are said to be no 'barons' in Maidstone, men who run extortion rackets, though there are certainly men who get into substantial debt, and whose prison 'earnings' are committed before they have got them – everyone is entitled to between 95p and about £3, depending on his job, paid as 'credits' in the canteen. (This can be supplemented by 50p a week 'outside money,' and relatives can also pay for newspapers, and send in sports clothes, running shoes and cell furnishings.)

If there are no barons, there *are* 'firms,' groups of men who have known each other on the outside, and to some extent they maintain good order in a wing like Medway. They want no trouble, and trouble is anything that might interfere with the dodges they are involved in, such as brewing hooch or running a book. One man was being pestered by a homosexual: a friend let one of the firms know, and the homosexual was warned off. 'He was told to stick to his own sort.'

'Ronnie,' an armed robber, is a 'big boy' on the wing. He is in his forties, and has been to prison many times. He said he thought he had finished with crime some years back, but got into a financial mess. He was 'grassed,' and arrested by armed police actually on the job. He said that if he was let out tomorrow he wouldn't be back, and I was inclined to believe him.

But they won't let him out tomorrow, and he faces the years ahead with the philosophic resignation of the professional criminal, to whom prison is simply an unpleasant occupational hazard.

'The minute I looked down the barrel of that .38, I said to myself "it's a 15-stretch" [in fact he got 12]. From that moment I accepted it.' He said there was an attempt to make him turn supergrass and 'give bodies.' He glanced up at the small mirror in the corner of his cell: 'I could never look at myself again in that if a man was doing one day's bird down to me.' But his family photos are a daily reminder of the price he is paying for sticking to the code. 'What am I doing in prison at my age? I must be out of my brain.'

He started his sentence in Wandsworth, a prison he and most other

Maidstone inmates know well and hate better. It is a huge over-crowded prison with men constantly in transit, and has a reputation for firm discipline.

After Wandsworth, Maidstone 'has got to be the best prison possible. I couldn't settle for two months because of the differences,' said Ronnie, and I was told of other prisoners arriving at Maidstone who stood at their doors for several days, unable to believe the comparative freedom.

Ronnie spoke almost enthusiastically about the 'screws,' and, as if to illustrate his point, an officer who had brought me a cup of tea came back with another for Ronnie – 'and he's not doing that because you're here.' Almost everything is done to reduce the pressure of the years ahead: if there is a family crisis the assistant governor might well put a man through on the phone to his home.

Prisoners often form a very special friendship with one other man. Sometimes, though not in Ronnie's case, it goes further, and men become prison homosexuals, something that seems almost to be tolerated. One prisoner said: 'It's OK so long as they don't do it on the landings and frighten the screws.' Another prisoner referred to certain cells as 'married quarters.'

Most men find the mental turmoil involved in applying for parole difficult to handle. A young man doing a very long sentence, who had just been knocked back for the second time – although everyone at the prison thought he ought to get it – said he wouldn't try again because he couldn't cope with another refusal.

Perks like the very liberal visiting arrangements at Maidstone help to keep the lid on. Prisoners believe that serious misbehaviour would mean they would be 'on the island' – i.e., 'ghosted' to Albany or Parkhurst on the Isle of Wight – in the morning. The carrot has its uses.

Ronnie spoke about the fear that haunts a long-term man, that his wife is unfaithful. It is a worry prison officers tend to be rather cynical about, believing that the average prisoner is scarcely a model husband when he's out.

'Peter' is a far cry from the professional criminal, though he had been in prison as a young man, and more recently in a special hospital for mentally ill offenders. The murder he committed was bizarre and well-publicised, putting him out of the run of normal domestic lifers. He is now a comparatively old man with a trusted job.

'It's a wicked thing,' he said, 'to stand in a dark tunnel when you can't see a glimmer at the end. I spent the first eight weeks in a complete daze.' He is sustained by a number of prison activities: he has built himself a stereo in his cell, and is something of a celebrity for some writing he has been doing. He dreams of fishing and walking the

Pennine Way. His is not a complete life, but it is by no means totally unhappy.

Two much younger lifers sat in a cell, each about eight years into his sentence, and the years weighed heavily as their lives oozed away. One was very aggressive: he believed he had done enough time, and threatened that if he were not out soon, he'd eventually be reduced to taking a shotgun and robbing post offices. 'It would be *their* fault,' he said bitterly. In prison, violence as the solution to a problem is seldom far away.

He was one who refused to be friendly with officers. 'I can't sit chatting for half an hour with a man who's going to lock my door on me. The system is destructive. You feel yourself slipping into apathy. You have to fight yourself out of it. Why should I wash and shave? Where am I going? The only incentive to change your socks is when you can't bear the smell.'

Virtually every prisoner I met at Maidstone vowed that this would be the last time, but there is, sadly, plenty of evidence to the contrary. The Chief Officer, the prison 'RSM,' said: 'A surprising number of people really do volunteer for prison. They can't live unless their lives are structured, and society can't provide the structures.'

In the past I have seen inside overcrowded local jails, where the hopeless sweepings of our society are confined: I have heard (and believed) tales of prison violence and brutality: I have talked with men who, if they had done so much time in any other walk of life, would be in receipt of a substantial pension. In Maidstone I saw without doubt the more positive aspects of the system.

Prison life probably reinforces criminal tendencies. The same skills that are needed to be a successful criminal are needed to survive in prison. Few administrators or prison officers would claim that a man is reformed inside. It is usually an outside influence that is crucial. But in a prison such as Maidstone the opportunity is there for a man to improve himself: what makes him take – or reject – that opportunity must remain a mystery. *(9.8.81)*

Unemployment: The Real Victims
Robert Taylor

For the rest of the Eighties, Britain will have more than three million registered unemployed. Indeed, there seems little hope of any dramatic reduction in the numbers out of work in this country for the rest of the century, whatever any political party might assert.

The Manpower Services Commission estimates that as many as 3,500,000 will be registered out of work by 1986.

Who cares? The monthly official unemployment statistic has become the object of a sad ritual of accusation and counter-accusation. The TUC alleges that the 'real' jobless figure is now more than four million, while right-wing economists at the Institute of Economic Affairs like to play down the total, believing that only men between the ages of 25 and 54 without a job for more than six months should be judged as a 'strategic measure' of the size of the unemployment problem.

This grotesque numbers game may chill the blood or encourage complacency, but it does little to enlighten our understanding of what is happening in the labour market during the worst recession since the inter-war years.

Public opinion polls do suggest considerable concern about unemployment, but efforts by the TUC to arouse widespread protest have not proved successful. Union leaders are more likely to detonate agitation against Mr Norman Tebbit's tough new Employment Bill.

No doubt, cost-conscious civil servants at the Treasury are worried about the sheer financial waste of unemployment. It is estimated that it will cost Britain £14 billion in the next financial year. This represents over £9 a week for every working person, and it equals three times the entire borrowing limits of all the nationalised industries. Yet there are no signs at all that Mrs Thatcher's Cabinet is about to reverse gear in the coming Budget because of irresistible pressures over the length of the dole queues.

Even now, very few people are aware of the true character of our unemployment crisis. That overall monthly total – a snapshot of a moving stream – has mesmerised the opinion makers. Almost the entire effort of the Government has been concentrated on alleviating the problem of school-leaver unemployment. Mr Tebbit's bargain basement scheme for youth training will soak up £1,000 million by 1983/84, the lion's share of the Manpower Services Commission budget. But the fact is that our real unemployment crisis lies elsewhere, and next to nothing is being done about it.

By this summer, around one million of the registered unemployed will not have worked for more than a year. Nearly half the present jobless have been without employment over six months.

The manpower forecasters suggest that these figures will worsen over the next few years. The hard core of the jobless is growing at a frightening rate. In January 1980, 355,300 people had been without work for more than a year. By December of last year, that figure had reached 874,000. It will go on climbing into 1982 and beyond with no respite.

Who are these real victims of the recession? Four out of five of them are men, three-fifths are married and more than a third have children. Nearly three-quarters of them had manual jobs before they joined the dole queue: most have no skills or qualifications. They come in disproportionate numbers from the construction, manufacturing and basic industries. A quarter were made redundant. Many lost their jobs because of ill-health.

All ages suffer from long-term unemployment, not just the young. The number in this plight in the 25–45 year age group has doubled in the past year. It is especially hard for the older men, who can have little hope of finding a new permanent job after the age of 55. These workers did not price themselves out of work as a result of union power, whatever right-wing economists such as Professor Patrick Minford of Liverpool University allege. The facts show that the long-term jobless had work in low-paid sectors of the labour market with poor working conditions, few fringe benefits and often unsocial hours. Few have savings to see them through.

The Government has launched a Community Enterprise programme, designed to help the long-term unemployed, but it does not enjoy a high priority, with 25,000 places provided in 1982. But nobody has been prepared to give a guarantee to the long-term unemployed that they will be offered a job after a year on the dole or a place on a special employment programme. Few (if any) are likely to be able to take advantage of a training scheme, when so many skilled workers are now jobless.

Apparently, the long-term unemployed must wait for the upturn in the economy before they can expect to find work again. Yet unskilled manual workers are most unlikely to be in demand in sufficient numbers significantly to cut their numbers on the dole. By 1985, for the first time in our history, we shall have more white-collar than blue-collar jobs to fill. Manpower forecasters predict that the manual workers will suffer a further net decline in the late Eighties.

The Government is doing little to ease the pain of long-term unemployment. Earnings-related benefit will end this spring, and the flat-rate unemployment benefit will be taxed, adding to the squeeze on the living standards of those without work. For the hard-core the outlook is even bleaker. Labour in office and now the Conservatives have refused to put the long-term unemployed on long-term benefits like the sick and the disabled. After a year without work, they must manage on supplementary benefit. It would cost a mere £135 million in the next financial year to put the long-term unemployed on a par with the other disadvantaged. Contrary to popular myth, the overwhelming majority of the hard-core jobless are without work through no fault of their own.

The Child Poverty Action Group reckons that in the next financial year a married couple on supplementary benefits will have £5.39 a day (excluding housing costs) to provide for their needs and just over £1 a day for any child they may have aged less than 10.

A national obsession with the three million figure has diverted concern from the inner core of the truly disadvantaged, because unemployment hits our society in an unequal way. The deprived are almost inarticulate. Most have never been in trade unions. They show up in the statistics, but they often seem hard to find. We are creating a vulnerable under-class in Britain without any obvious future. They do not riot or cause the police much concern. Their plight is private, individual, almost invisible.

A civilised society has to act to help these people. We need to see job creation programmes for the long-term jobless; incentives for employers to take a risk and hire them; above all, a more general level of benefit after they have been out of work for more than a year. This does not mean an extravagant scheme that would lead to hyper-inflation. It might require a switch in priorities away from the school-leaver jobless to the long-term unemployed.

If we do nothing, the outcome will be grim. Britain in 1982 remains a rather callous, uncaring country, where the real victims of the recession go unheard. *(31.1.82)*

The Princess of Wales
Tom Davies

Love always has its reasons, but even seasoned analysts of the Welsh psyche are having trouble sorting out why the Welsh have fallen so abjectly and hopelessly in love with Princess Diana.

For three days and 400 miles last week, there was the astonishing sight of a whole nation having a nervous breakdown on rainswept pavements. Choirs sang, harps tinkled forth and grown men cried. One old man in St David's cried, pulled himself together, and burst out crying again.

Put two Welshmen together and you always get three points of view. But the general argument of the philosophers in the pub was that Princess Di never comes on 'posh' or 'above it.' In Builth Wells we watched her jumping around cleaning one of her shoes on the back of her leg.

This sort of behaviour makes her like 'one of us,' i.e. normal. If a pin was stuck in her, she would indeed bleed, but the real key to her success must be the way she can suddenly stop smiling in a crowd and look around with the purest terror in her eyes, as if a man in a peaked cap had just called saying he was going to turn off the electricity.

Welsh women, in particular, love this air of vulnerability and their dearest wish would be to take her home to administer many cups of tea, a mountain of well-meaning advice, and an aspirin to put her right.

Surrounded by one of the biggest security operations ever mounted in Wales, the Royal tour rolled across mountain and down valley, in triumphant serenity. Hour by hour they moved through the smell of chips and expensive raincoats, swooped into gloomy mansions and mayoral parlours. Children were kissed and babies poked as the Welsh, a radical race, re-lived the heady days of the Investiture.

The tour also proved what we had long suspected: Wales is two nations. During the early stages of the tour through rural areas, the response was warm but fairly restrained. Yet, as soon as it hit the valleys of South Wales, the traditional birthplace of British socialists, everyone – but everyone – went bananas.

Even when Princess Di spoke a bit of Welsh, sounding just like an English girl speaking a bit of Welsh, they were collapsed by the honour of it all. 'Speaks it like an angel, she does. Like an angel.' This ability should be of great help to her at another time since, as everyone knows, Welsh is the language of Heaven.

In the market town of Pontypridd, Princess Di was showered with enough flowers to start her own Chelsea Flower Show – or, if she preferred, a little gift shop, since the couple were also given a heifer, a ewe, sticks of rock, books of illuminated poems, even a plastic coat hanger. She also got advice from every corner. 'Don't worry about the rain, my love. It's good for the complexion.'

Even the unemployed lads in the pubs liked the visitors, but they were not going outside in case they got rain in their beer. Ponty's great characters, cleared out for the tour, are the sheep which roam the streets: filthy beasts with brown shaggy hair who pillage vegetable patches and, it is widely said and believed, are so inventive they climb on one another's backs to get over the fences into the gardens.

There was very little trouble anywhere except, it was later learnt, by a gang of youths on a shoplifting spree in Woolworths. There were some dissenting hiccups, but such was the hullabaloo that Princess Di seemed to have a touching inability to tell the difference between those for and agin her. She greeted them all.

Just before the royal party arrived in Cardiff on Thursday, a man was preaching in an empty rainy street and was, at one stage, surrounded by five policemen. They wanted to know if he would keep his voice down and the man was trying to explain to them that he was preaching in the Holy Spirit and, if the Holy Spirit wanted it loud, then loud it would be. He had no control over it. 'Why don't you grow up?' asked a policeman.

There was no keeping down the voices of the crowd when the royal couple turned up and, down in Splott, a suburb of Cardiff which even most Cardiffians avoid at all costs, the smiles were brightened when joined by the greatest smiler of them all, Jim Callaghan.

He smiled, and they smiled, and he smiled back in a sort of grand Eisteddfod of smirks. Such was the mood of celebration it was all rather as if Wales had been declared rugby champions of the world forever. For a land of radical socialists, it was something even more joyful than that. *(1.1.82)*

4.
A Troubled World

Shoot-out at Kandahar Bazaar
Nick Downie

I was woken at 6.30 for breakfast – which is to say, a glass of weak tea and a piece of stale, unleavened bread. Later, a chap turned up with a mule and a donkey to carry my gear and the ammunition to Kandahar, the second biggest city in Afghanistan after Kabul.

On the way we suddenly screeched to a halt, and everyone leapt out, displaying all the signs of that well-known military emotion, panic. 'What is it?' I asked, as they scrambled past. 'Tanks,' they said. I panicked too.

We leapt into a ditch, and I began to look for escape routes. However, it turned out that the tanks were about four miles away, across the river, and under attack. This was reassuring, even if the obvious military incompetence of my companions was not. We continued on foot, till midnight. The unencumbered Afghan moves at some speed, and I was left to pound along at the back, carrying my standard load of 40 lb. plus.

The morning of our fourth day, still feeling rather under the weather, I was woken with great urgency and told the city centre had been occupied and the fighting was about to begin. I now had to face one of those minor personal crises common to ageing war correspondents whose over-prolonged exposure to danger has left their nerves in tatters. Could I think of a solid reason for refusing the invitation? A blinding headache didn't seem a good enough excuse, and, as always on these occasions, the honour of both myself and the British Empire was at stake. Also, the event appeared to have been laid on for my benefit, and to decline would have destroyed all my credibility. Finally, I reflected that, willy-nilly, this was what I was being paid to do.

After a cup of tea, we set off in a horse-drawn cart, bells a-jingling. I confess that I've been to war in a wide variety of conveyances, but nothing quite as bizarre as this. We trotted straight up the now rapidly emptying main street of the bazaar, towards what I'd been told the day before was a government outpost. I remonstrated as forcibly as I could in limited Persian, but they paid not the slightest attention, and, twitching like a prawn on a hot-plate, I just had to hope that they knew something I didn't. As it turned out, they did.

We dismounted at the main crossroads, to a scene of indescribable confusion. Mohiedine were milling about in all directions, providing a beautiful target to any machine-gunner with a mind to loose off down the avenue. As I later found out, there was indeed an enemy stronghold 400 yards away, which had a clear field of fire. Why they didn't open up is beyond me. In the middle of all this was a chap sitting on a chair using a loud-hailer to challenge the Russians to come out and fight.

There then followed what must rank as one of the most unnerving half-hours of my career. I was carted off to a roof-top from which to admire the Kandahari skyline. It was a dangerously exposed position, but I did actually want a few pictures of this, so I rapidly filmed what was necessary, and then suggested we leave – immediately. 'No, no,' they said. 'From here you can watch the battle.'

My main objective was to get down to ground level, to find out what was happening, but these comedians were determined that we commit suicide by sun-bathing on the roof-tops. And, apart from that, there was nothing to film. The discussion became progressively more heated, and was still continuing as the first machine-gun crews spotted us and started to range in. At this point I took a unilateral decision and crawled off down the stairs (one had to crawl as there were large shell-holes in the external walls).

My peace of mind was not improved when we finally rejoined the main body. They were running around, apparently aimlessly, going first one way, and then in the opposite direction. Meanwhile the gunfire was increasing – it was heavy, close, and incoming. It didn't take much to work out that we were being surrounded. By now, having sprinted round it several times, I was becoming familiar with the geography of the bazaar, and I decided we were in the wrong bit – not that any part of it was exactly a rest home, but our area seemed particularly unhealthy. I had, somewhat haphazardly, become attached to a group of four or five men, and I prevailed on them to move elsewhere, which, to my intense relief, they did. We took up position in an alleyway which opened on to one of the main streets – and was therefore one of the potential assault routes.

At this point I will jump ahead slightly, and explain a few things that, happily, I didn't know at the time. There were some 200 Mohiedine defending the bazaar, of whom only 100 had arrived as an organised group – the word 'organised' being used in its loosest sense – and the rest just happened to be in the bazaar when it started, shopping, and so had no choice but to stay and fight.

We had no heavy weapons of any description, beyond about eight rocket launchers – light-weight devices like a bazooka that have to be fired from 50 to 100 yards against a tank. There was a shortage of rockets for the launchers. At the same time, the bazaar was rapidly ringed by troops, armoured personnel carriers, and tanks – sealing all exits. In addition, of course, the Government had fighter-bombers, gun-ships, mortars and artillery.

We hadn't been in our alleyway long, before we heard the sound that all infantry dread – the squeal of tank-tracks. There then began one of the most curious interludes of my misspent career. In our little group we had one rocket launcher and four rockets, one Kalashnikov automatic rifle, one light machine-gun with a single belt of ammunition, two ordinary rifles, and an anti-tank grenade (a thing about the size of a saucepan, range dependent on the strength of the man throwing it). None of this was exactly up to Stalingrad standards, but we were further weakened by the reluctance of both the machine-gunner and the Kalashnikov owner to stick their heads round the corner and actually open fire.

As the infantry were by this time beginning their assault, there was an obvious and pressing need for someone to do something. Luckily, the rocket man and a tall, rather splendid character called Jan Mohammad, were made of sterner stuff.

Incredible as it may seem, they beat off two assaults, although the tank never opened up with its main armament and neither did it come within range of our rockets. Judging by the general racket, this mind-boggling performance was being repeated all over the city. After two or three hours things quietened down, and we waited on events. The particular events I had in mind were a massive artillery barrage, a series of bombing runs, an afternoon's strafing by gun-ships, or a determined battalion attack down our street. The quite staggering thing is that absolutely nothing happened. We were caught like rats in a trap, and any self-respecting army would have wiped us out to the last man, but neither the Government troops nor the Russians did a damned thing.

I know I keep repeating myself, but Kandahar is not some remote and unimportant backwater, but the second largest city in Afghanistan. So, the question to which I have to try to find an answer is what the hell the Russians think they're doing in the place.

Towards evening the tanks made a final attack in another sector, and lost five machines in the process. At least, that's what I was told, although I could only see three armoured cars in the smoke. It was a remarkable scene. I filmed the burning wreckage at the end of the street, and then panned round to the alleyway opposite, which was jammed with about a hundred wildly cheering civilians.

As the tanks were some way away, I foolishly asked if we could get any closer, and some blithering idiot said: 'Follow me.' I did, for about a quarter of an hour, through a maze of back-streets. Finally he turned a corner and proudly pointed to a billowing, impenetrable cloud of smoke, which was quite useless from a photographic point of view. This in itself was unimportant, except that I'd expended a lot of sweat. More to the point, my battle antennae told me that we'd come too far. 'Where,' I inquired suspiciously, 'are the Mohiedine?' He gaily pointed behind us. 'And where are the Communists?' I asked, through gritted teeth. He indicated a spot 50 yards up the road. We had arrived slap between the opposing forces. I regarded him homicidally for a moment, and then set off at a brisk pace back the way we'd come, fighting the urge to sprint.

As darkness fell the enemy withdrew, and the Mohiedine assembled in the centre of the bazaar in a milling, chattering mob. The smell of unwashed bodies, oriental sewage, and hashish was heavy on the air. After a certain initial confusion, they then carried out – though it pains me to admit it – a well-organised night withdrawal, which is never an easy operation at the best of times. Score for the day: Afghans: three dead, three wounded. Government: eight or nine tanks and armoured vehicles, and maybe 30 or 40 killed and wounded. (The latter is my estimate – the Mohiedine claimed 300, which is pure imagination.)

The following morning, I set off for Quetta. It was an eventful journey: at one point, after a 15-hour march, the pack horse carrying half my valuable equipment fell into a canal; at another, we had to escape from a village under the eyes of a government tank patrol, trying to look like a bunch of locals out for a stroll. Finally, I was nearly driven (by mistake) slap into the biggest Russian base for several hundred miles.

So much for 16 days with the fearless Mohiedine. With luck I'll get eight or nine minutes of cut film out of this excursion. It really is a lunatic way of earning a living. There is no question, this is absolutely the last time. *(31.1.82)*

The Spirit of Winnie Mandela
Allister Sparks

Winnie Mandela, whose banishment to the small town of Brandfort was extended for another five years by the South African Government last week, remains undaunted by her persecution.

Mrs Mandela, wife of the imprisoned leader of the African National Congress, Nelson Mandela, was first sent here after the Soweto riots five years ago. Last Tuesday the Government extended her banishment, together with an order prohibiting her from meeting more than one person at a time, or from being quoted in South Africa, which was first imposed 20 years ago.

Although the Government has never been able to secure a major conviction against Mrs Mandela despite its extensive security laws, it has subjected her to a continuous series of restrictions, arrests, detentions and harassments for nearly half her life. She is probably South Africa's most persecuted person.

Since she married Nelson Mandela in 1958, not a year has passed without her being arrested on some pretext. In those 24 years she and Nelson have been together for fragmented spells totalling only four months. Otherwise one or other of them was in jail or he was underground.

They were even split up by an arrest before they could reach their own wedding reception, and Winnie still has her wedding cake, uncut, in a box at home.

For Winnie the banishment order has been the harshest restriction of all. It cut her off from home, family and friends in Johannesburg and dumped her in this one-horse town 300 miles away in Orange Free State province, the rural heartland of white Afrikaner conservatism, where blacks know their place. She could not even speak their local language.

She fears the experience may have permanently scarred her 20-year-old daughter Zinzi, who stayed with her for a time but is now in Swaziland.

Winnie herself is unbowed. She is a tall regal figure, one of Africa's great beauties, at 47 as enduring in her looks as Sophia Loren. She dismissed the renewal of the banishment order with a shrug when I called on her on New Year's Eve: blows like that have been part of her life for so long they have lost their impact.

If anything it is the townsfolk of Brandfort who are the more concerned, for life has not been quite the same since Winnie arrived.

She has stirred things up. She has pointedly ignored all their separate entrances and segregation signs. She has kept whites waiting while she uses 'their' public telephone at the post office: she has marched into the little dress shop and tried on dresses in the only changing room they have.

Worst of all, she has 'spoiled' the local black community. They grew up accepting subservience and they were wide-eyed seeing this black woman defy the age-old racial conventions and get away with it. Some whites complain that they, too, are getting 'cheeky'.

Brandfort even had a few small strikes last year, something unheard of in such a community. One was at the bakery and another by the 'night-soil removers' (not all the town has water-borne sewerage), who downed buckets for more pay. The young men are refusing to work for local farmers for 25p a day, as they had done for years.

'I have spoken to them,' admitted Winnie with a smile. 'They have been conscientised' – the vogue African nationalist word meaning politicised.

Strangely, there has never been a clash between Winnie and the local whites. They resisted her coming. Protests to the Government included one from the first President of the Republic, Mr C. R. Swart, who has a farm in the district and regarded her being sent there as a personal affront.

Once she arrived they did not confront her. Even when she broke the racial barriers, they kept away and did nothing.

'They seemed petrified of me,' said Winnie. 'There was this Communist come to live in their town. They just didn't know how to handle it.

'I seem to symbolise some terrible threat to them, to bring out the deep fear the Afrikaner has of his extinction. I never realised how deeply embedded this fear was in the Afrikaner until I came here.'

The whites put it a little differently. 'Yes, people were unhappy when she came here,' said Jurie Erwee, the mayor who runs a hotel and liquor store in the town. 'But we have got used to her. We accept her now.

'She is clean and well-behaved. She comes in here to buy things: champagne, Cinzano, stuff like that. I've spoken to her, and she's well educated.'

Winnie's life is devoted to the black community in the 'location', out of sight behind a small hill, where she lives in a three-roomed matchbox house, number 802. She was appalled by the malnutrition there, so started a gardening project. Now there are cabbages and beans growing around every matchbox house, and the community's diet has been transformed.

There was no clinic, so Winnie started a first-aid and baby care advice service. She is a qualified medical social worker. She has gathered all the 'location's' delinquent teenagers into her care. She visits them regularly, has provided about 30 with books and makes sure each day that they go to school.

Piet de Waal, the only lawyer in town, is one of the few whites who has had any kind of relationship with her. Under Law Society rules he was obliged to attend to her legal requirements if asked. He didn't much like the idea and called on the police to assure them he was only doing his duty.

Over the five years he and his wife Adele have succumbed to Winnie's charm and considerable personality. 'We have become quite friendly,' he admitted. 'I tell you, I've learnt a few things from knowing her, and I've come to understand her point of view on some matters.'

This has led to gossip around town that Piet de Waal is a *kaffirboetie* (nigger lover). Once when Adele's father, who has a brown Volkswagen like Winnie's, stayed for a week with his car parked outside, the story spread that Winnie had moved in with the de Waals.

The harassment has been constant. Winnie's banishment order restricts her to the house at night and over weekends, and prohibits her from receiving anyone inside the house other than her doctor and her lawyer.

To enforce this the police at first kept a 24-hour watch from a car parked outside: later they withdrew to the hill and watched through binoculars.

Winnie is a devout member of the Anglican Church, but there isn't one in Brandfort. Each week either Father John Rustin or the Bishop of Bloemfontein, the Rt Rev. Frederick Amore, motors 40 miles to Brandfort to celebrate Holy Communion with her – in the road outside number 802, because they are not permitted inside. One gain is that this particular clause has been relaxed in the renewed order.

For the rest, all Winnie has to look forward to are the periodic visits to Nelson. She is allowed to see him twice a month for 45 minutes: there is a glass panel between them and they talk through a monitored telephone connection.

Because of the cost of flying – the authorities will not allow her to go by train – she cannot go that often.

'I look forward to the visits so much,' she said, 'but the trip back is awful. I feel so empty. Look, I'm confident he will come out one day, I have no doubt about that. But I can't help thinking of all these years of our lives that are going down the drain – our best years.

'Nelson is 63 now, and I am like a young girl, still longing for the experience of married life.' *(3.1.82)*

A Conspiracy of Silence
Jacobo Timerman

In a glass case in one of the galleries of the Lohamei Hagueatot (Fighters of the Ghettos) Museum at Haifa, I recently noticed a small piece of white paper.

Dated the summer of 1944 in Budapest, and signed by Raoul Wallenberg, it was a telegram sent to London and Washington begging the Allied Press to notice what was going on in Hungary. The message was brief. It ended with the words: 'Public opinion always helps.'

Most journalists and media people then, not to mention those engaged in military strategy, would have thought otherwise. Adolf Eichman was in Budapest arranging for the transport of Jews to Auschwitz. How could a few newspaper articles in the Allied countries hinder this implacable butchery?

But Wallenberg was no day-dreamer. During the months when he worked as a Swedish diplomat in Budapest he saved the lives of some 100,000 Jews. He was a skilled organiser: calm, imaginative and daring. He knew how to buy off Nazi officials; he learnt how to frighten them with threats of future judgment and how to tranquillise them with promises of future refuge after the war. He found clandestine ways of buying Portuguese passports, and passports issued by Central American republics. He rented offices, which he turned into sanctuaries protected by the Swedish flag. He became skilful at paying ransoms for those already in the hands of the SS.

And he never forgot the importance of world public opinion.

I believe there should be a copy of Raoul Wallenberg's brief telegram posted up in every single editorial office of every single newspaper in the civilised world. It was one of his last testimonies before Soviet troops entered Budapest and he himself vanished for ever into the infinite twilight world of the Gulags.

Exactly 32 years later, in Buenos Aires, the military rulers of Argentina reached the same conclusion as Wallenberg about the importance of public opinion. But whereas for Wallenberg it implied the need for a permanent shout of protest, for Argentina's military men it meant, on the contrary, an absolute need for silence. The reason is simple enough: Wallenberg saved 100,000 lives; the Argentine colonels, in the years after their seizure of power in 1976, oversaw the murder or disappearance of 30,000 people.

The crisis confronting the world in these early years of the Eighties is no different from that which confronted it at the beginning of the Thirties. During those years, appeasement evolved into a new form of politics. In our present decade, silence occupies the same position. And it performs the same function: it annihilates man's natural predilection to live together with his fellow men, whatever their differences, in peace and individual freedom.

In the United States, the Reagan Administration has converted silence into an ideology. As evolved by the US Ambassador to the United Nations, Jean Kirkpatrick, and right-wing savants Norman Podhoretz and Irving Kristol, it seeks to explain that violation of human rights in Argentina, Chile, South Africa or South Korea does not affect the vital interests of the world's democracies, and that those interests should prevail over all other political or moral considerations.

In the Soviet Union, silence is a weapon of foreign policy. The Russians denounce the violation of human rights in Chile, with whom they don't have diplomatic relations, but not in Argentina, their principal trading partner in Latin America after Cuba. In Russia, as in other Communist countries, silence has become the cement of nationhood, the touchstone of patriotism. Criticism of the regime is synonymous with treason; or, when it is publicly expressed, insanity.

Silence is used to bring hope to the hopeless. It is used to blackmail those in fear. The mothers of Argentina's *desaparecidos* – those who have vanished after their arrest by the armed forces – are informed by the Government that a prudent silence might lead to a solution of their problems. It is the same kind of blackmail as the White House applies to members of Congress when it assures them, in considered official tones, that if they remain silent and approve military loans to Argentina, Chile and Uruguay, they might thereby obtain the liberty of a few of those imprisoned without trial and without being charged.

Silence is imposed on Palestinians. If they are seen to make contact with sympathetic groups in Israel, then, they are warned, they will never get their own State. Or they will be assassinated. Silence is imposed on Israelis. If they speak out, especially abroad, about the right of Palestinians to have their own form of Zionism, that is to say a

Palestinian nation of their own, they are told – I have been told – they are imperilling the security of Israel; Israel will disappear.

The Communists propose that we should silence our attacks on the repression of free speech in Nicaragua, because the young republic is threatened by an imminent invasion organised by the United States. In fact the only way Nicaragua can defend itself from that invasion – and the danger is a real one – is by counting on the support of genuine democrats in the rest of the world.

The Communists resort to silence on the pretext of imminent peril. By doing so they are simply mirroring the ideology of the Reagan Administration, which urges the democracies of western Europe to keep quiet about the crimes being perpetrated in El Salvador, Guatemala, Argentina, Honduras, on the grounds that Communism is the more dangerous threat.

If we allow this great conspiracy of silence to enfold us, then the Third World War – the final war to end all wars – may explode, not merely because of the accumulation of nuclear weapons, but also because of the accumulation of so much immorality and ignorance, so much stupidity and hypocrisy. That is how wars are really unleashed.

Until a few years ago, silence was a nightmare. Now it is a conspiracy. Some days ago in London I attended a remarkable denunciation of that conspiracy: the publication of the fiftieth edition of the 'Index on Censorship.' Here, in these pages, are all the denunciations of all the silences. The conspiracy of silence is made visible, it is clearly exposed. And revealed here, too, is the immense, sustained, brave battle against that conspiracy.

Perhaps this time we may be able to fulfil Wallenberg's plea. Maybe we can see to it that the voice of public opinion is so powerfully heard that no war, no violation of human rights, will be possible. Mankind can survive – if it can make its will to live heard above the conspiracy of silence. *(6.12.81)*

Sharon's Kingdom
Gavin Young

Visiting the West Bank of Jordan almost exactly four years ago I was reminded of G. K. Chesterton's little detective-priest, Father Brown, as he contemplated an Oriental dagger at the scene of an apparent suicide. 'It's the wrong shape,' he said. 'The wrong shape, if ever I have seen it in this wicked world.'

Things have changed for the worse, Israeli attitudes and sweeping population shifts have made the shape of the disputed West Bank 20 times more wrong, and the prospect for Israeli–Arab peace looks very dead indeed. Last week a serious Israeli friend, out of tune with Mr Begin, said: 'In practical terms, total and unshiftable Israeli dominion over the West Bank is now a political fact.' A fact that probably means war in our time.

Of course, the leadership of Israeli politics has plunged into impatient extremism. The Israeli air strike against residential Beirut was a grim symptom of this. Yet it is not what happens in Lebanon but the shape of the West Bank that will determine peace or war in the Middle East for the rest of our lives.

Last week I heard a 'hard line' Israeli in the Knesset telling me: 'We are certain eventually to annex Judea and Samaria (the West Bank),' and (outside the Knesset) a chorus of Israeli voices flatly stated: 'The land is ours. The Arabs here can stay on our terms or go.' An Israeli diplomat reminded me that in order to manoeuvre Begin into the peace agreement at Camp David, Carter and Sadat were obliged to cut, like an 'expletive deleted' from the Nixon tapes, all mention of 'self-determination for Palestinians.'

So, for one extreme (the PLO), the only acceptable future for the West Bank is based on that unmentionable self-determination. For extremist Israelis it is outright annexation. The Camp David agreement talks of an alternative: 'autonomy' for the West Bank Arabs – which now could mean only local (and limited) self-government in the patches of Judea and Samaria not newly settled by the Israelis. That alternative has been drowned by the wave of new Jewish settlements. Mr Begin has very nearly created his own New Palestine; and it has a distinctly colonial aspect.

Returning there, you find that in four years you are no longer in the landscape you knew – the one Egyptian, American and European bureaucrats imagine they are discussing in their meetings in Geneva, Haifa or Alexandria. You can find new – and startling – maps in the office of General Ariel Sharon, the new Minister of Defence and the 'Other King of Israel', as Israelis call him (Begin is *the* 'King').

Sharon's mission is to encrust the West Bank with Israeli settlements with all the Supermanly vigour with which he punched his way across the Suez Canal to divide the Egyptian armies in the 1973 war.

Sharon hardly seems real. As described by the *Jerusalem Post* recently, he is a 'human juggernaut'; he exemplifies 'intemperance, ruthlessness, deviousness and general unstoppability.' And although, as the paper added, 'The contempt he has shown for democratic parliamentary procedures has earned him fear and loathing,' one out of every two Israelis says he is the man best qualified for the job.

Sharon likes to slap 'facts' down like nuclear bomb shelters and then challenge all-comers to uproot them. Maps and a guide from his office disclose some startling 'facts' – new Jewish townships – in stone, metal and cement which are clearly designed to defy uprooting by President Reagan or anyone else.

My guide spouted a few 'irreversible facts' at me as we went from new settlement to new settlement. (Sharon himself shepherded thousands of Israeli voters in brain-washing driveabouts, called jokingly 'Sharon's Tours,' during the recent election campaign. 'Imagine,' he told them, making their tender floating-voters' flesh creep, 'If Yassir Arafat is allowed to put a rocket here, he would close Tel Aviv airport. I'm the one to see he never does!')

Before Begin, the guide said, there had been about 30 settlements on the West Bank (excluding East Jerusalem). Soon – say, in 1984 – there should be 108, or even more. At the same time, the earlier ones would be doubled in size and the Jewish population expanded to nearly 200,000. (The Arab population is now below 700,000.)

At Maaleh Adumim settlement on the Jericho road, new blocks of flats crown the hills like white honeycombs. 'It'll be as big as the Old City in Jerusalem,' my guide cried exultantly. A huge industrial site has mushroomed there, too; other large population concentrations straggle down to Jericho, each one with asphalted driveways, playgrounds with Donald Duck swings, wire fences and watchtowers.

'The Arab areas of the West Bank,' said my guide, 'will be like two kidneys, one north, one south of Jerusalem.' The kidneys will be joined to Jordan only by one narrow exit pipe, through Jericho.

'There was nothing in the Jordan Valley before we filled it with settlements,' he said. 'Only bedouins and a desert.' Surprised, I thought of the age-old green trees and gardens of Jericho. 'Look at these,' he said in Ramallah, pointing to some modern Arab houses. 'Built for political reasons with money sent by the PLO.' But the money had been hard-earned in Dubai or Jeddah by West Bank Palestinian doctors and engineers in exile.

Near Nablus is the zealot-inhabited Israeli settlement of Elon Moreh, from which, at night, an illuminated Star of David shines down on the neighbouring Arabs. Here, a tight-lipped, attractive young woman denied the star was provocative, and added sternly: 'We intend to create a city here, to watch Arab Nablus down there. A city of 60,000.'

Over coffee and cakes, she fleetingly compared the PLO to Hitler and said: 'We have to get enough Jewish families onto the West Bank. I mean hundreds of thousands. We should have annexed all this in 1967. Give the Arabs here anything – autonomy, for example – and they'll ask for more and more: an army, land, finally a State. The sooner they see we're here to stay forever the better for them. *The land is ours.* Arabs who want to stay, let them stay; otherwise they can go.'

The Israeli security areas – purple stains on the government map – now cover the whole Jordan Valley and the eastern third of the high ground of the West Bank. With another stain Sharon obliterates a wide strip on the western third. A broad purple arm springs west from Hebron. With another, Arab East Jerusalem is cut off from Arab Ramallah. Yet another divides Ramallah from Nablus. In these purple areas, Arab villages sit like small isolated communities marooned by flood-water. Autonomy will avail them little.

An Israeli political opponent of Begin who lives in East (formerly Arab) Jerusalem said: 'There is already a mass of Jewish communities, not intermingling in the least with the Arabs. The Arabs will be dependent on the new Jews for work, but they will not have equal rights. They will simply be cheap labour for the Israelis and still effectively under Israeli military rule.'

Defence and foreign relations would be in Israeli hands. Arab areas would remain subject to the unchallengeable whim of Israeli Military Security. Even some hard-line Israelis complain that 'autonomy' would mean, in effect, the perpetuation of an Israeli colony. They give this as their reason for favouring annexation.

East Jerusalem, with its population of 100,000 Arabs, has, of course, already been (illegally) annexed. It is practically unrecognisable. Vast suburbs of highrise flats have sprung up north, south, east and west. Like tentacles of concrete, they clasp Arab East Jerusalem to the Israeli State, and now they push into the surrounding West Bank. The expansion has been so quick, so extensive, that, without a glimpse of the famous golden dome within the walls of the Old City or the tower of St George's Cathedral without those walls, you might wonder where you were: Singapore? Casablanca?

North-west of Jerusalem, 50 Arab homes were destroyed because they would have overlooked the huge, new Israeli-subsidised township of Ramot (security again). Close by, plans include 2,000 flats and supermarkets for Israelis only, and a highway linking other new Israeli townships.

The Israeli Air Force had just bombed Beirut when I passed through the Old City on my way to visit Meron Benvenisti, a liberal intellectual and a former Israeli deputy mayor of Jerusalem. At the Fifth Station Souvenir Shop in the Via Dolorosa, Israeli and foreign tourists side-stepped Arabs on white pack mules, or clustered round handsome touts, or pointed out unshaven Israeli soldiers with sub-machine guns.

In Beirut, I suppose, rescuers were at that moment still taking civilian bodies from the rubble. In Galilee, Israeli families, in cellars with fused lights, could hear the Palestinian rockets from Lebanon cutting water-mains, hitting a maternity home.

Where I was standing was the nub and cause of it all, and Benvenisti said: 'When will the world realise that there's no difference now between East Jerusalem and the West Bank?'

The West Bank, Benvenisti says, will never again be independent, because 'the burgeoning Israeli military infrastructure – bases, depots, training, testing areas – cannot make do with pre-1967 Israel. After the Sinai withdrawal, the generals need the new space we occupy here.'

He thinks military government, dispensing ham-fisted decrees, is bad for all concerned. He advocates an Israeli civilian authority in the West Bank responsible to the Knesset; free speech, and full academic freedom for the Arabs; free municipal elections (the Israelis put a stop to them last year, when they foresaw the results would be pro-PLO).

The Israeli occupation of the West Bank is now 14 years old: nearly two-thirds the period of the British Mandate, almost as long as the Hashemite Jordanian era. And occupation, it is well known, corrupts occupiers as well as occupied.

Palestinian youngsters are dropping out of school to work on construction sites – a reversal of the Palestinians' traditional drive for educational excellence that has made them the élite of the Arab world. And now the frustrations of a long alien occupation are driving some youngsters to seek solace in the bigoted xenophobia of Muslim extremism.

Israelis claim the level of Arab 'agro' has diminished very noticeably in recent years due to a new tough Israeli approach. This is probably true, although in one week recently, the local pro-PLO paper, *Al Fajr*, reported the following incidents: 'Four people sentenced to 18–27 years for placing explosive charges in Haifa. . . . A curfew on El Bireh's main street after an Israeli bus was stoned. . . . Four held following the killing of the Israeli Military Governor of Rafah. . . . Two bombs dismantled in Nablus. . . . A bookseller arrested for selling banned books. . . .' And the Israeli *Jerusalem Post* said: 'A brand-new Mercedes belonging to a resident of East Jerusalem was set alight. . . . The security forces believe the owner was suspected of collaborating with the Israeli authorities.'

Those are symptoms of hostility latent after 14 years. But there is nothing here like Ulster; nothing, surely, that the overwhelmingly strong Israeli security force could not cope with almost casually. Yet,

there seems to be an astonishingly high rate of Israeli military harassment of West Bankers. Gabi Baramki, the acting head of Bir Zeit
College, the biggest of the three Arab universities, a quiet, unaggres-
sive man, though a Palestinian nationalist, tells of a non-stop series of
Israeli humiliations that seem designed to provoke Arabs.

These include interference in the curriculum; scrutiny of lectures
months in advance; the banning of books ('The Merchant of Venice'
and John Steinbeck's 'The Moon is Down' about the Nazi occupation
of Norway, are two predictable ones); the deliberate withholding for
months – 'without rhyme or reason,' says Baramki – of work permits
for visiting professors.

Respectable members of the faculty are picked up by security forces,
he says, often slapped or kicked, insulted, arbitrarily deprived of their
identity cards.

Many students report casual beatings, terrifying arrest and deten-
tion without charges. Shouting soldiers force their way into houses at
gunpoint and at random. They even storm on to the Bir Zeit campus,
rough up students and staff, break fixtures. Non-violent student
protest is broken up with tear-gas. Stone-throwing is met with real –
not rubber – bullets. (Baramki's daughter had her leg shattered by a
bullet recently. She wasn't even demonstrating.) In Ulster, where
British soldiers and police face death from bombs, bullets and Molotov
cocktails from hour to hour, such use of real ammunition would be
profoundly shocking.

Shouldn't there be conscious efforts to conciliate, not provoke, the
Arab population, whether Israeli policy favours autonomy and peaceful co-existence – or annexation with votes for Arab fellow citizens? Is
such crude Army behaviour betraying the high moral traditions of
Israel – indeed of all Jewry? These are questions liberal Israelis are
asking with growing anxiety. And in asking such questions they
certainly do not intend to condone shooting outrages by Arabs against
Israeli civilians – like the murderous attack reported recently on a bus
outside Jerusalem.

In Jerusalem recently, I told Israeli friends of a tour of Israeli
settlements I made in 1968. Then, I said, I found young Israeli
conscripts seriously worried about the implications of the new military
occupation of the West Bank. 'It is not our moral role,' they had said
earnestly, 'to lord it over Arabs or anyone else.'

Alas, there's been a change here, too. The other day Israelis told
me: 'It's a sad fact that after 14 years Israeli youth – the Occupation
Generation – is used to it all. This year, two-thirds of our Army boys
voted for Begin or further right.'

In Nablus, the Arab mayor, Bassam Shakr, one of three West Bank mayors whose cars were bombed (he lost both legs), had just returned from treatment in London. His sticks leant against the wall. He is now allowed, he said, by the military authorities to travel to any other town on the West Bank. He hobbled to his office and is a hero to West Bank Arabs. His attackers have not been brought to court.

His female lawyer, a famous Israeli called Felicia Langer, was in his office by chance, a vigorous blonde in white sleeveless blouse and a blue denim skirt, clutching a briefcase. 'I'm going to the High Court,' she said, 'about the continued intimidation by the military of Bassam's wife and 14-year-old son. Isn't it enough that he lost his legs and no one was arrested for it? The police didn't even question him as part of a so-called investigation. Imagine that.' She said she had sent Begin a letter complaining of police inactivity in the case: no answer. Israeli extremists are widely suspected. So is a Government cover-up to protect them.

Recently, an Israeli writer – a political scientist and Kibbutnik – wrote in the *Jerusalem Post* that once Israelis wanted their State to be 'a light unto the nations,' but that now 'religious nationalism,' a 'cult of darkness,' a 'new tribalism,' has replaced that humanistic vision.

Perhaps that is a major reason why the chance of self-determination for Palestinians has been quite overwhelmed by the certainty of Israeli supremacy either in the form of annexation or a spurious autonomy.

Right-wing Israelis were indignant when I suggested that Israel's domination over the West Bank was comparable to France in Algeria or Britain in India. 'The difference,' they snapped, 'is that the land is *ours*!' Yet that colonial similarity will persist as long as the Arabs are equally convinced that it belongs to *them* and must passively watch more Raj-style enclaves inexorably hemming them in.

'King' Sharon has now become Begin's Defence Minister and set his throne on the West Bank. On the other side of Jordan, a real king, Hussein (who will have nothing to do with an imposed West Bank autonomy), has warned for years that 'Israel can have peace or land – but not both.' But in Jerusalem the unheeding shout grows louder and more insistent: 'This land is ours!' Why, one wonders, should there *ever* be a peaceful solution there? *(9.8.81)*

Memories of a Vanished Land
John le Carré

The PLO's representative in London was a washout. He didn't answer my letters and in the end I had to winkle his phone number out of someone in the know. I rang and got a man, then a girl with a pretty Arab-American accent, then the man again, as if he had taken the receiver from her hand. We made a date for Monday, at the egregious hour of half past one.

To reach the lobby you stand in a kind of glass tank while they look you over. At the front desk, closed-circuit television screens show the street outside and the office of your host upstairs. There is logic to this, for his predecessor was shot dead in his chair – does anyone remember who by?

I had confirmed my appointment by letter but he stood me up anyway. I asked for the owner of the pretty voice but she was away too. A lot of people were loitering in the street when I left; most of them had been loitering there when I arrived. I imagined my own back, in fish-eye distortion, disappearing from the closed-circuit television screen. And yet another muddy photograph of myself, entered in some far-off Whitehall file.

*   *   *

I flew to Beirut for New Year. I arrived in the dark and was met at the airport by three boys who practised their English on me between checkpoints. One of them would have preferred Spanish: he had studied in Havana. The other two hoped to study later. So what do you do now? I asked. Fight Zionism, they said.

I woke early and saw the light coming through the bullet holes in the curtains. I lunched at the flat of a wealthy Palestinian executive and his wife, and we could have been in Monte Carlo. Two of their sons had been to Cambridge, the third to Harvard. They had a Christmas tree like a cedar, with lights that went off and on in series. On the walls, among other glories, hung several Roberts watercolours of Palestine. My hosts had seen more plays in London than I had.

When lunch was over, a Palestinian guest remarked that, whatever happened, he personally would never return to Palestine: 'This would represent too great a drop in my social and economic lifestyle,' he explained, as if he had been listening to the Open University. Nobody suggested he might never get the chance to find out.

*   *   *

Fatah's offices were less sophisticated. The street had been wrecked by an enormous car bomb, which the Palestinians said was Israeli. A ring of cement-filled barrels closed off the entrance. A group of boys lounged nervously outside holding their machine guns by the spout. I hate lifts but the stairs were out of bounds.

The Commander wore a fur-lined raincoat like a cape, even while he sat at his desk. 'We are exiles,' he said to me simply, between frustrated efforts to reach someone on the field telephone. 'Therefore we have only our country to love. The Jews have stolen our country. Therefore they have only the Palestinians to hate. They live on a guilty conscience. That is why they must kill us.'

He had finally reached someone. He spoke cryptically and was cut off before he had finished. If it takes him so long to make a phone call, I wondered, what does he do in a war? 'The deep instinct tells me: violence solves nothing,' he said, as he settled again to wait. 'The deep instinct also tells me that the peaceful path is an illusion. Their aim is genocide. Please return to your hotel. You will be contacted.'

It was dusk and cool and there was a brazier burning at the first Palestinian checkpoint. The fighters sat round it as if it were a campfire to keep away the animals, and some looked old enough to remember Lawrence.

*   *   *

Getting there is still a blur. Dead of night. A succession of brown Volvos with whip aerials, hurried changes in little courtyards, the wet rattle of machine-guns as the guards hopped in and out beside me. The smashed night city, buildings holed like cheese-graters, the swift, apologetic body searches, another car and suddenly we are a convoy of three or four.

Enter a building, climb a staircase lined with fighting men, everyone is smoking and the windows are heavily curtained. Now we are in a ruin, now in a Hilton-style L-shaped drawing-room with orange nylon carpets crackling with static. In the smaller part sits Arafat at his desk, signing letters, and the air is clean at last because no one smokes.

He wears a white *khefya* and a khaki shirt and a silver pistol in a holster of plaited brown plastic, and he does not look up as we enter. I sit at a long English-style reproduction table, to the right of the carving chair, and a sense of theatrical timing overcomes me: his.

Briskly he rises from his desk, comes towards me, a busy statesman to his fingertips. He is neither thin nor fat, his body has the floppiness of unuse and the whiteness of something kept underground. It is said he never sleeps in the same bed twice, that he manages his own security arrangements, that he is abstemious in everything except in his love of Palestine and her people. A bold lady journalist had recently asked him whether he was homosexual. He replied urbanely that he was married to Palestine.

Recently also, according to the rumours, the driver of his car had been killed in an attempt on his master's life. But the man who had done the deed, said the same rumours, was now a treasured member of his bodyguard.

But the less fanciful stories were the more impressive: of his durability, his dedication, the undeniable love he enjoys among his wretchedly abused people, his talent for diplomacy. And what other Arab leader – I was asked repeatedly – could talk to the Saudis, the Russians, the Libyans and, *sub-rosa*, to the Americans within the same week, and hold the ring?

His hand was light and soft, the creases of his tunic were razor sharp. He smelt just a little of baby powder: I remembered someone telling me he had an obsession with hygiene. But all this was trivia beside the mobility and extreme swiftness of his perception; the brown eyes that stayed on you, reading you as he talked.

His first clichés are like sighting shots as he takes your measure: 'Sir, I am a man of history. . . . Sir, I believe in the justice of our cause. . . . Sir, I am not anti-Semitic, I am anti-Zionist. . . . Mr Begin tells us that in order to fight we must hate, but Sir, I fight for love – for love of Palestine.'

His spoken English, like his manner, was soft and painfully considerate. After an hour of it, his concern for his syntax began to overcome his concern to communicate. His surge of interest in me waned, he stopped altogether and, unbothered by time or silence, gave himself over to some private and seemingly agonised contemplation.

*   *   *

The procession to mark the seventeenth anniversary of the Palestinian Revolution starts at dusk and is crammed by the thousand into the canyon of a narrow brilliant street. Pipers and flagbearers lead. A loudspeaker bellows slogans, a stationary band strikes up a beat, the plastic-covered photographs of Our Chairman Arafat hang down like washing from the electric cables strung above the pageant.

A place is somehow cleared, a ring of girl dancers begin a *dabke* with a Kalashnikov, tossing it to one another above their heads. The rain stops, a skirmishing warm wind runs like an explosive blast down the street, flattening the posters. Suddenly the podium is flooded with men, Arafat's white *khefya* just visible at their centre.

Then it happens. Without warning, the whole street explodes to the sound of shots and ricochets. Bright green smoke belches over the heads of the crowd, followed by blood red: the firework display in honour of Our Chairman has begun. The coloured smoke swirls upward, its density makes a perfect screen for any sniper to shoot and slip away, but this is not Our Chairman's day to be shot. He stands still and diminutive, his fingers raised in the victory sign while the speechmaker pounds on with his slogans.

The procession continues: small children with toy guns, big children with real guns, veterans and pretty girls in combat gear. Someone has handed Arafat a long-stemmed brass cup. He sets its bowl alight. Other hands transfer the cup to a giant plate mounted like a holy relic on a wagon. Our Chairman has lit the flame, but the fierce wind whisks it dangerously into the overhead cables, threatening a fresh disaster.

Our Chairman is saluting again – this time a special contingent of orphans, known as the Children of the Martyrs because their parents have already died in the fight for their homeland. They hold, instead of guns, green cold-burning neon torches which light when you open the packet.

As I left, I met my Commander in the sheepskin raincoat. He was pale and tired out.

'One bomb,' he said in despair. 'One bomb.'

*   *   *

The house in Sidon had a tangerine orchard at the back and an old, tired Labrador bitch who sunned herself while she fed her puppies. Sitting on a bench, one of the guards told me in halting English about an old man he knew of, I think his uncle, who one day, after 30 years of exile, decided he would go home.

He was old and sick of waiting and he wanted to see his village again before he died. Besides, he still had the deeds to his house, given to him by the British during Mandate times. So he packed up a few things and set off across the Jordan, armed with the deeds to his house. Nobody stopped him, and the last that was seen or known of him, he was being driven away by an Israeli patrol, still waving the deeds to his house in their faces.

*   *   *

Rashidiye camp is famous for its football team. The camp in its day has been the all-Palestine champion in chess, basketball, handball, pingpong and tennis, but football is its best sport without a doubt.

At the age of eight the boys join the Ashbal, or boy scouts; at 14 they are considered fledged fighting-men. They study hard and place great weight on academic excellence. But somewhere in the middle of this busy programme they still put time in at football, though the pitch is often bombed. Their silver trophies are kept in a special room, with sticky labels on them to record the victory. Behind them on the walls hang the dusty photographs of martyrs who were in one or other team before they died.

The football ground itself is a big dustpatch with an UNRWA school one side and an American-built cluster bomb on the other, which is really no more than a great cylinder to hold 800 grenades and a few thousand steel nails, though this one is empty. Since 1970, according to the secretary of the camp, Rashidiye has seen around 700 attacks from air, land and sea.

'Sir, is there a people in the world without land, except us?'

I tried the Armenians but it didn't work. I tried the blacks of South Africa but that didn't work either.

The purpose of the bombing, he explained, was 'to kill us and stop the development of our culture.'

The air raid shelters had no lights and were too shallow. On the road to Tyre, a cow was picking rubbish out of a bombed car. We passed bullet-spattered seaside houses and children splashing in a water-logged bomb-crater.

'I promised myself I would never kill in cold blood,' my host remarked as he drove. 'It's different now. If I were a young man again, I would not hesitate to take the violent path. When we are rejected by Europe, lied about by America, betrayed by our brother Arabs, murdered by Zionists, is it not tempting to pull the world's ears by an outrageous act?'

In Sidon, also, he took me to the prison. I think it is Crusader built, but it didn't seem the right time to ask. The interior is a huge stone silo with balconies to the sky, and it is where refugees take refuge when they have been bombed out of their refugee camps. Fresh white paint gave an illusion of hygiene.

The cell doors stood open as if for hospitality; the figures inside appeared at first motionless. They were 10 and more to a cell and the children moved with great economy. The symmetry of the clothes-lines suggested the competitive pride of the villages. A woman I spoke to had one son left. The Zionists had the rest. As we left, Israeli spotter planes were still circling overhead.

The last time I saw Arafat, he was accompanied by most of his high command, at a school for hundreds of orphans on a hill above Beirut. He was dancing with the children, swinging the bobble of his *khefya* to the music, stamping his feet while they clapped and cheered. He wished me a Happy New Year and asked me only to report what I had seen. 'I am a man of history. Justice is on our side,' he said.

*   *   *

On the day before the invasion, I went with an Israeli friend to the northernmost kibbutz of all, called Misgav Am. It stands on a wild spur which looks into Lebanon on three sides, and straight downward at Haddad-land. It is a place carved for Jews by Jews, from Arab territory, first established as a strongpoint in the war of independence and later settled by sabra pioneers.

The air raid shelters have crazy paving over them and funny drawings on the doors; the lush lawns are fed by sprinklers. There is a big indoor pool. Ezer Weizman gave the children here a present of an old aeroplane, and it stands not far from the dormitory where a group of young Arab terrorists held a siege until they were shot. In the course of it, one child and one adult died. The story has long entered Israeli legend, and a hundred trees have been planted in their memory.

The following night, I went to a Jerusalem party and was lectured to by a gentle Israeli ex-Ambassador of distinction. The bombing of Tyre, Sidon, and Beirut, not to mention Rashidiye Camp, had been continuing round the clock. We have yet to learn its effect, but likely estimates put the Palestinian dead in the thousands. The Ambassador was trying to explain to me, by a series of delicate loops of Middle East logic, why it was quite impossible for the Palestinians ever to make peace.

*　　*　　*

I cancelled my ticket home and stood in Jerusalem's military cemetery, watching the funerals of the first three Israeli dead soldiers to be returned from Lebanon. An Israeli journalist I knew stepped out of the crowd and greeted me. He had lost a son in the war of '73, and was here because he knew the family of one of the dead men. He was in a state of almost manic grief.

'In '73, we fought for the peace that was round the corner,' he told me. 'What do we fight for now? It goes on, and on, and *on*.'

The invasion of Lebanon was supposedly sparked off by the attempted murder of Mr Shlomo Argov, the Israeli Ambassador to London. Nobody I spoke to in authority in Jerusalem would hear for one moment that Argov was not attacked at the behest of the PLO. They should have waited, for it seems a hit list has been found, and one of the other names on it is that of the PLO's own representative in London, the man who doesn't answer his correspondence.

*　　*　　*

The attack was a monstrosity, launched on speciously assembled grounds, against a people who on the Israelis' own admission constitute no serious military threat. It is as if we British had lost our temper with the IRA and decided to punish the entire Irish people once and for all – convincing ourselves at the same time that when we had done so, we would hear no more of their troubles.

Too many Israelis, in their claustrophobia, have persuaded themselves that every Palestinian man and woman and child is by definition a military target, and that Israel will not be safe until the pack of them are swept away. It is the most savage irony that Begin and his generals cannot see how close they are to inflicting upon another people the disgraceful criteria once inflicted upon themselves. It is worse still that they have so far taken the Americans with them. *(13.6.82)*

The Murder of Solidarity
Neal Ascherson

As the snow vanishes from Poland, so do the outer signs of martial law. The armour has long gone from the streets, the rare armed patrols are hardly noticed, and the most obvious remaining sign of the 'state of siege' is the 11 p.m. curfew. But the clear light of spring also reveals all the country's old problems – many worse than ever.

Martial law has so far cured nothing. The only optimists in Poland appear to be the interned Solidarity leaders. Those outside the wire and the walls suspect they are living in a dream world. While the economy moves towards another terrifying downwards slide, the political situation appears deadlocked. It looks as if martial law and government by a semi-military directorate under General Jaruzelski will remain for a very long time to come.

Many senior party and State figures who supported martial law are now bitterly disillusioned. They hoped that, behind the military shield, some economic reform on market principles could be introduced; the desperate prospect of industry, food supply and financial credit now make this almost impossible.

They hoped that the West – bankers and treasuries especially – would understand their attempt to end the paralysis of the Polish State and were staggered and enraged when it was taken as a Soviet-inspired *putsch*.

They hoped that the Church and the workers would come to be

grateful for the removal of a handful of demagogues, but they are not.

They hoped that the military shield would also allow the party to recover confidence and unity: the signs are that, deprived of the power monopoly, the party is actually disintegrating more rapidly than before.

So the general and his colleagues, civil and military, are digging in. The slogan 'Winter is yours, spring will be ours,' seen on walls in January, has turned out to be nonsense. Active resistance is still weak and disorganised. The political problems are the passive but unyielding hostility of the population, and the chaos within the Polish United Workers Party. Both condemn the Military Council for National Salvation, which hoped to be transitory, to carry on indefinitely.

The party is still not functioning. The central committee has met once since December and the regional committees meet, but the main machinery remains suspended. The hardline faction, powerful in the security services, seems to control much of what is left of the party apparatus. This means that the small group of party men who still hope for 'dialogue' with society and who form the civilian side of the Jaruzelski team – Mieczyslaw Rakowski, Hieronym Kubiak, Kazimierz Barcikowski and others – would be swept aside, with their moderate policies, if the party were given back its 'normal' leading role in society.

The chances of 'national understanding,' broadening the regime's base, remain poor. The working class remain steadfastly loyal to Solidarity and Lech Walesa, though they might accept a limitation on the union's political activity. The party is still split on how and whether to restore trade unions.

For the Church, the most worrying symptom is the campaign against intellectuals. On the one hand, the Polish intellectuals have mostly refused to co-operate with the new regime. On the other, a purge is slowly gathering pace. Usually politely conducted, the 'verifications' have none the less decimated the journalists and are now extending to publishing, the judiciary and the academic world.

Purging has its own dynamic: if vice-chancellors fall, then lecturers, then headmasters, eventually schoolteachers will be sacked for Solidarity sympathies. Rakowski, in particular, seems opposed to anything on that scale, but it remains to be seen whether the 'directorate' can bring their hunting dogs to heel.

Organised opposition to military rule is still forming. Regular local bulletins proliferate, mostly under the aegis of KOS (Committee for Social Defence) which in turn is related to regional Solidarity groups and to 'groups of five' organised in factories.

But Solidarity underground has so far no central direction or clear strategy for the future. Quarrels and suspicions inevitably divide these groups, uncertain whom to trust.

At the extreme, young students are beginning to play with explosives and arms – in the Polish tradition of symbolic politics, a boy last week tried to blow up a Wroclaw monument to the police. Most opposition workers regard this sort of thing with horror, as useless action which only provokes repression.

None of this, by itself, threatens the regime. In Krakow last week, I saw 'Solidarity lives and will live' posters, the glue still wet. But the core of opposition at present is the extraordinary moral solidity of the industrial workers, taking no extreme attitudes but calmly telling any inquirer that they still support Solidarity. In this sense, the confident mental world which Solidarity created in 1980 still survives.

It is the menacing gulf of economic crisis which cuts off every political road. For a visitor, matters at first seem better than before martial law: there is more in the shops, queues are shorter, order has replaced the petrol chaos, power supplies have improved. But this is largely deceptive. Shopping is simpler because the huge February price rises threaten Polish incomes. Many people are living on savings or on lump sum compensation payments, which will run out.

For the first time since 1970, it is sheer poverty rather than shortages which Polish working-class families are just beginning to experience, and every calculation one makes on family incomes against the cost of living comes out on or below the solvency line.

It is at the parish churches, where foreign parcels come, rather than the shops, that the queues now form. Bishop Domin of Katowice told me that although the Church had received as much food aid in the first two months of 1982 as the whole of 1981, this still amounted to only just over a pound weight per Pole. The case for the price rises was economically unanswerable. But the fact is that ordinary people do not know how they will manage.

Major economic reforms – introducing factory independence, a degree of free market and workers' control into industry – seem doomed. The condition of industry is simply too serious. Though most of the Press now is either vapid or vicious, excellent economic journalism still is licensed, and the papers predict a fall in Western imports of about 50 per cent, a fall in national income of over 20 per cent and a fall in real wages of around a quarter.

The cause of all this is the Polish debt and the refusal of Western banks and governments – for reasons more financial than political – to extend more credit. Deprived of Western raw materials and parts, Polish industry is simply stopping: the figure of 40 per cent of industrial capacity unused is being put about.

In this situation, it is Soviet deliveries which keep some wheels turning. Some industries are sacrificing their Western markets to form long-term contracts with Comecon countries. Only coal is raising production. This is no moment, in short, to introduce free-market principles.

At first, most Poles regarded what was done on 13 December as a national tragedy, the total destruction of 16 months of hope and energy. Now the loss seems less total, the situation more familiar. A torrent of jokes – nobody can remember so many – suggests that military rule is the same old muddle conducted by other means. The news that a militia patrol was bribed to let people queue for meat after curfew was almost welcomed. If the crisis does not end in real hunger, strikes and bloodshed, a *modus vivendi* may be found with this regime – though never a relationship of trust.

The longer this queer semi-military regime lasts in Poland, the greater its significance for our times becomes. A Communist State is being ruled with the party only a participant, and the soldiers especially – and some Ministers – begin to feel that for all their unpopularity and failures, they are making a better job of it than the party did alone. The more the military find out about how Poland was really being run in the last decades, the angrier they become.

It begins to seem just possible that – with Jaruzelski winning firm Soviet support earlier this month in Moscow – there may be no return to orthodox party rule at all. If the economic crisis can be weathered, an orderly Poland which does not riot and rebel may be better guaranteed by an authoritarian block of officers, selected politicians, perhaps eventually some lay Catholics and non-party professors, than by the power monopoly of the Polish United Workers Party which has so shatteringly failed.

In a back-handed, undemocratic way, one of the things that Solidarity began to fight for in 1981 would have been achieved. And the history of all Eastern Europe would enter a new stage, with new possibilities.

As for the Poles themselves, this generation has entered the awful darkness which fell in turn on their fathers, their grandfathers, all their ancestors since the nation was first partitioned almost two hundred years ago. The cycle revolves again: 1981 recalls the Rising of 1944, the military coup of 1926, the tragic insurrections of 1863 and 1830 and 1794.

Before the Hel Peninsula came Auschwitz and Pilsudski's concentration camps and the Russian citadel at Warsaw and the convoys of men and women making for Siberia in chains.

All we can be certain of is that this generation knows how to hold itself now that its turn has come, that it will invoke these ancestral spirits to retain its courage, that the Poles can never believe that Poland is lost, while they are alive. *(28.3.82)*

5.
Some People

Life with Margot
Lord David Cecil

No one I have ever met or read about in history or fiction was more extraordinary than Margot Asquith.

She looked extraordinary enough. Beneath a bony, witchlike head, with a big hooked nose and sharp dark eyes, moved and attitudinised a small skinny restless body, dressed usually in the height of fashion. I say 'usually' because for other purposes she might adopt a different style. I remember when she had a fancy for learning to drive a car – luckily for her own safety and for that of others, this fancy did not last – she appeared dressed in riding breeches and flying helmet. Since by this time she was close on 70, this costume was too young for her; so also were many of her fashionable dresses.

This was not a consideration that would have occurred to Margot. Not that she was vain; she did not admire her own looks or expect others to do so. But she always behaved as she felt. She dressed young because she felt young. Her demeanour was of a piece with her appearance. It is impossible to be less inhibited than she was. She always said what she thought, regardless of the impression it might make on the person she was talking to. An acquaintance who bored her once asked Margot to call her by her Christian name. 'I couldn't' replied Margot. A moment later, feeling she had perhaps been unnecessarily unresponsive, she continued, 'Oh all right then, Ermyntrude or whatever your name is!' The lady's name was not Ermyntrude.

Margot's actions were as demonstrative as her words. On my arrival on my first visit to The Wharf at Sutton Courtenay, she immediately gathered me into her arms and gave me an affectionate kiss. Since I had met her only once or twice before and then in a crowded room, this startled me; what may be called 'social' kissing was not so common a practice then as it has since become. In fact, Margot's was not 'social' kissing. Puffin, her son, had told her that I had become a great friend of his and that was enough to make her, regardless of convention, enfold me in a loving embrace. Her feelings easily and frequently found physical expression. If excited, she clutched one's elbow; if amused she squeezed one's arm; and, like a very young child, if she wanted to engage one's attention she had a habit of seizing one's wrist and keeping hold of it till she finished what she had to say.

This could happen sitting next to her at a meal; the consequence was to hamper one's use of knife and fork. If Margot's feelings were touched – and they were easily touched – she might lay her head on one's shoulder. This too could happen at meals, thus adding even more to the difficulty of eating. At such emotional moments, her eyes would fill with tears which soon began to trickle down her cheeks. It was, however, an April shower. Within minutes, even seconds, all was sunshine again, the causes of her tears forgotten, and she was discoursing gaily about her youthful adventures in the hunting field or expatiating with eloquence and severity on the weaknesses of the political colleagues of her husband, Lord Oxford and Asquith, the former Liberal Prime Minister. I suppose this was a sign that her feelings were on the superficial side. But it also showed they were genuine and spontaneous. For myself, I found her comic and disarming and winning. She cried as easily as a child and forgot as quickly.

Indeed she was in many ways childlike, with a child's naïve unthinking egotism and lack of inhibition. And she had the imaginative child's inability to distinguish between reality and fancy. She lived much of her time in a daydream world founded on her experience of the real world so altered by her sense of the dramatic as to bear only an intermittent relation to it.

She was like a little boy who, because he would have liked to kill a lion, tells you he has done so; like the little boy, she believed her own stories. She used to relate with zest and conviction how on the evening of 4 August 1914, when the Government met in 10 Downing Street to decide whether or not to go to war with Germany, she lay overcome with agitation across the threshold of the door into the Cabinet Room in which the Ministers were making their momentous decision. Even as a youth of 19, I found it hard to believe this sensational piece of autobiography. Surely some other observer would have noted that the

Ministers could not get in or out of the Cabinet Room without stepping across the prone form of the Prime Minister's wife! But Margot believed it, in the same way as the child believes his tale about the lion.

Margot was a brilliant talker and in a unique fashion. Hers was an imaginative, not an intellectual, brilliance. Her mind, incapable of consecutive thought, worked by sudden intuitions that could penetrate to reveal, as by a flash of lightning, the essential characteristics of a scene or a person. Further, she recorded them in phrases unforgettably vivid and original, in particular in images both apt and extraordinary that seemed to have arrived in her mind as by unbidden inspiration. These images were often caricatures but, like all good caricatures, each exaggerated in order to bring out better the essential characteristics of their subject.

Here are some examples. Presented with an impressionistic, very slight water-colour sketch: 'It is like a mouse's sneeze.' Complaining that modern sermons tended to be too secular in tone: 'It would be as suprising to hear God mentioned in one of them as to find a fox in a bus!' Describing the unflagging vitality of Ettie Lady Desborough, a famous social figure of the times: 'Ettie is so strong; she will be made into Bovril when she dies.'

Lady Desborough came in for a lot of criticism at Margot's hands, inspiring some of her most memorable phrases, as when she said of her flattering tactfulness, 'Ettie tells enough white lies to ice a cake.' She considered Lady Desborough's taste in decoration philistine, made more so by the fact that the walls of her house, Taplow Court, were hung with trophies of animals killed by her husband, a famous sportsman. 'When I went to stay at Taplow,' Margot said to me, 'I was greeted in the hall by a stuffed rhino holding azaleas in one paw and visiting cards in the other.' Lady Desborough's food pleased her no better than did her furnishings – 'fussy and over-elaborate,' she called it. 'You know the kind of thing – the salad was decorated with the Lord's Prayer in beetroot!' This last phrase is a striking example of Margot's gift for imaginative caricature. Though a wild exaggeration, it hit the nail exactly and dazzlingly on the head.

Such remarks made one laugh and were intended to. But Margot's images were often employed less to amuse than simply to express her feelings as forcibly as possible, so that, if her hearers laughed at them, she could even be surprised. I recall her claiming to have invented the safety habit for women riding sidesaddle, as they did in her youth. 'Before I wore a safety habit,' she exclaimed, 'I had picked up every turnip in Leicestershire with my teeth.' When this provoked a laugh, she looked bewildered. On another occasion, when I came down late for dinner, she turned to me and said, 'David, do not be so unpunctual;

it makes me sweat at my kneecaps.' I was flustered to be the cause of so disagreeable a symptom of nervous agitation. All the same, and to her surprise, I could not help bursting out laughing. Some of her images were even more startling. She held strongly that Arthur Balfour, the Conservative statesman, for all his surface kindness of manner, was lacking in true compassion. 'Arthur Balfour has no womb!' was her unusual way of expressing this view.

Much of Margot's conversation was surprising without the assistance of strange images: it was what she said that astonished, not just how she said it. 'The secret of health,' she once told my uncle, Hugh Cecil, 'is to have all your teeth out and drink a glass of brandy five times a day.' Harold Baker, a dignified middle-aged barrister staying at The Wharf, was once woken at one in the morning by a knock on his bedroom door. He opened it to find a footman – these were the days of footmen – who said, 'Lady Oxford says will you stop that hooting, she can't get to sleep.' In fact the noise had been made by an owl. One wonders what wild train of thought had led Margot to think that a middle-aged barrister was spending the small hours of the night standing at his bedroom window imitating the cry of an owl.

The thought of the Royal Family had an especial power to stimulate these flights of fancy. So far as I know she did not know any of them well; I imagine they would have found her unacceptably eccentric. But though far from being a snob in any servile sense of the word – Margot treated persons of all ranks the same – she did like to people her daydreams with romantic figures, such as kings and queens, and to claim intimacy with them. 'We mean to live very quietly,' said Margot when her husband fell from power, 'only seeing the King and a few friends.'

Her admiration for King George V led her to be critical of the people around him and in particular of his doctor, Lord Dawson of Penn. She felt so strongly about him as once to say to me – this was in her old age – 'Lord Dawson was not a good doctor: King George V himself told me that he would never have died, had he had another doctor!' This was the most surprising statement ever made to me by Margot – or by anyone else, for that matter. *(20.12.81)*

Acton in Aspic
Maureen Cleave

When Sir Harold Acton was an Eton schoolboy 60 years ago, tea was the predominant meal, and for it his mother would send from Florence white truffles; 'an acquired taste,' he wrote, 'which few others shared.' Even as a schoolboy he was outside the common run and so he continued to be, vital to his generation but always somehow on the edge of it: in Florence when they were in England, in China in the Thirties while they were cultivating their leftist sympathies, in India during the war.

He feels himself, he has said, entangled in the past, and his semi-isolation from changing times has preserved him *en gelée* and lent him the interest of an historical personage.

Yet he knew everyone, certainly anyone who now tempts a biographer, a Sitwell, a Sackville-West, a Cunard, and letters arrive once a week at his house in Florence asking what he can remember of so-and-so.

'A man writing *another* book about poor Evelyn [Waugh]. Not a very interesting life; a charming, witty, original person, a good writer, one of our *best* writers, but not a fascinating life. He could be very disagreeable, made no effort ever to be polite. Then a man I don't know, Mr Chapman Pincher, wants to know about Roger Hollis. This Pincher thinks he was a terrible traitor. I remember him as rather agreeable, rather drunken. . . .'

Harold Acton, the writer and historian, lives alone in the house where he was born, the famous and beautiful Renaissance villa of La Pietra, just outside Florence. The approach is a long thin avenue of cypress trees running through an olive grove. It was Sunday, a misty day, and the sounds of the city below were no more than the barking of a dog and the chime of a church bell, making us lonely dwellers in the time and space of the vast house. It contains his father's massive, richly varied and unpredictable art collection, and it seems to accommodate this rather than human beings. It is difficult to imagine children in La Pietra and Sir Harold said his father had hated them. He himself had never been childish, indeed had never really been young.

He is a big man in his seventy-eighth year with imposing looks and clear, curiously round brown eyes that seem to belie seriousness. He is invigorating company, with conversation that leads from one thing to another in the most delightful way, a sense of decorum that must be Edwardian, and charm enough to disarm a bandit. The charm is tinged with apology: you lead such a grand life, he supposes, that nothing short of the best is good enough for you.

'I wish,' he said, 'I had asked some of our picturesque Florentines to meet you but you said it was to be a tête-à-tête. Would you like tea, coffee, some sort of drink? What can we get to stimulate you? It will soon be lunch. The house, as you see, is a big one and we have domestic difficulties; I am much reduced and take what I can – macaroni and that sort of thing. It is very frustrating because my mother was extraordinarily particular and we had a long tradition of the best table, the best of everything. Ah the butler I had! The baskets of fruit with which he would decorate the table, the leaves of box, petals of petunia and azalea! I was spoilt!'

Princess Margaret and others of the same stamp are still prepared to take what Sir Harold calls pot luck in La Pietra, and it turned out to be the most delicious duck for lunch, served to us by a footman in white gloves.

Sir Harold prodded it with his fork. 'Duck,' he said with a sad little shake of the head, 'I don't think there's very much on it. I'm afraid it's touch and go.' We ate beneath the rather stern gaze of very early Madonnas, four to a wall; there were leather footstools under the table for your feet.

He adores gossip about grand people – 'Gossip,' he says, 'is the food of history,' but the same powerful curiosity that keeps him alert crosses all social barriers.

He doesn't sound completely English, but takes exception to this being pointed out. 'The English one hears nowadays seems strange to my ears. I went to Eton not long ago to see a play of Anouilh and they were all talking cockney. They acted with enthusiasm, but their accents defeated me.'

His voice is almost singular and, though never raised, rich in drama. He spoke of some columns that had recently toppled over in the garden: 'Calamity! Calamity!' he cried, and his voice had a dying fall. D. H. Lawrence was dealt with in the same way: 'Crude! Crude! Still, he had the prophetic air, you felt his words were *pearls*; and Frieda, fat, bossy, red-faced, *intense* with a capital "I." Everything had a double meaning, *rooted* in sex!' His enunciation was most clear.

His opinions are not always predictable: Prince Rainier and Princess Grace he described as *really good sorts*.

He was born with many options and he took up a great number of them. He has been a poet, a teacher, a writer of fiction, an historian, a translator from the Chinese and, always, an aesthete. He sticks to the label despite its limp-wristed connotation; an aesthete, he says, is a lover of beauty and he has been one from birth.

His childhood in La Pietra fed the senses. He set out for England, aged eight, with a phial of attar of roses in his luggage and it says a great deal for his character that this sissy nonsense was not stamped out by a damp Berkshire preparatory school. Not a bit of it. He entertained them with the story of his seduction by a huge American negress, 'her velvet skin, water-melon mouth, ivory teeth and tongue like liquid coral . . . Afterwards she would give me a heart-shaped lump of ice to cool me off.'

In no time he had them running round producing a magazine of art and fashion, and collecting objects for a private museum. It was the same when he went to Eton and when he went to Oxford: he was exotic and stylish, a leader to be followed. This, he said, was because he had never been young.

'I have always felt the same age, never young. Evelyn always treated me as if I were the elder. People listened to what I said.'

It was his rooms at Oxford, harmonium, elephant's foot and so on, that Evelyn Waugh used for Sebastian Flyte in 'Brideshead Revisited,' his habit of reciting poems through a megaphone out of doors that he attributed to Anthony Blanche. 'I don't like the book but it's very factual: we were outrageously voluptuary, the food we ate, plovers' eggs and things like that, and as for the megaphone, I used to read poems all the time from my terrace in Meadow Buildings – rather unusual rooms, not fashionable. Once I recited the whole of "The Waste Land" at a League of Nations garden party. The *Oxford Magazine* wrote an attack – this awful rubbish read by this affected aesthete – and a lot of elderly women walked out in protest. One was a descendant of Wordsworth, I heard.'

But Waugh did his old friend a bad turn because the rest of Blanche's reputation for low living and seedy practices stuck to Harold Acton with serious consequences. When war broke out and he joined the RAF, he hoped to be sent to China where he felt he might be of some use, only to stumble across a reference to himself in a secret file as a scandalous debauchee, followed by the conclusion that he should on no account be allowed to proceed to China.

He never got over this disappointment, and he wrote his autobiography, 'Memoirs of an Aesthete,' to dispel the notion that he had spent his life in low dives and opium dens.

'I was very hurt, I will confess. People wrote to me about it saying "This is you," and "This is you," and I suppose the character was sufficiently like me to be plausible. It was my rooms, my furniture, but I was not this Blanche' – Sir Harold pronounced the name in French – 'Brian Howard, poor fellow, was much more in Evelyn's mind. My own life has been utterly unsensational.'

He does remember delivering Blanche's warning lecture on the dangers of English charm. 'Evelyn always fell for it, blonde colourless women with very sharp tentacles. As they grow older they become infernal and the charm is pickled, usually in alcohol. By the way, it is very striking to us who live in Italy the colossal consumption of alcohol in England.'

How the gin and whisky emptied when the English came to stay, he said. An old, old friend, a famous beauty, came to stay and downed whole glasses of vodka, so that Sir Harold feared she would fall over the furniture. But to return to Evelyn, though he thought it better if he chose his friends' wives for them, Waugh had married happily enough in the end.

'He used to feel arrows of temptation but he never succumbed. Susceptible, don't you know, but very disciplined. He used to say that had he not been converted he would really be a fiend. Religion saved him from every point of view.'

Waugh must have expected him to get his own back because when he heard about Acton's proposed memoirs he said: 'Good-bye, this is the last time we shall speak.' 'I laughed it off,' Sir Harold said, 'but I knew he had a conscience. He thought I would say something frightful.' He did not and their friendship survived. He has a little story about Waugh being too small to clamber out of the giant baths in La Pietra but he didn't tell it to me.

He got his own back on Violet Trefusis, whom he loathed, in a subtle way, not by what he wrote but by the photograph he used in one of his books of her with her French maid. The French maid is most elegant in furs, while Violet looks a ninny, gauche and plain. 'Wasn't it wonderfully well-chosen?' Sir Harold cried. 'A ghastly woman, I hated her. She had many friends in spite of her wickedness, and wicked she was. Mrs Keppel, her mother, was an angel, charming, witty, kind-hearted, motherly. The King was an old man by the time they met and nothing much happened.' He added some interesting details about Mrs Keppel's investments.

He moves with a distinctive gait on the balls of his feet, doubtless in a lifetime's effort to remain upright on the highly polished wood and marble floors of La Pietra.

His senses had been engaged since childhood, but what of his affections? Two volumes of autobiography and nothing but a glancing reference on page 120 Volume I to kindling flames in Elgin marble breasts! He smiled. 'Ah, you spotted that! My emotional ties have been with countries rather than with people. There have been ephemeral passages of emotion, but can they be called emotion? Rather part of a flowering of the senses when one is young. My passions have been devoted to the arts and to a few people – the people on the highest sublimated scale.

'I could never have been a good novelist because I don't know enough about people; I have been educated by objects and books. Never to have had any really close intimacies, that has been my life; and whether or not it suits me I don't know.'

In old age, objects had the edge on people. 'Objects are eternally young. When I am in London I always pop in and see the Piero della Francesca in the National Gallery, the Madonna and Child under the little roof, the clear lucid colours, the sculptured forms – eternally young.'

He triumphed over a severe illness and friends suspect this is because he was enjoying life too much to give in to it. It was a bore to look after one's health and he was not at all afraid to die, to join what he called the happy majority – indeed he never thought of it – but he was most anxious to stay alive. 'I want to be aware in the world,' he said, 'I want to be *à la page.*' (21.2.82)

The Man who Lost his Tribe
Alan Road

A chicken's foot hangs starkly in the wire netting that protects the beleaguered home of Gerry Fitt in Belfast's Antrim Road. Thrown there by one of the nocturnal patriots who regularly attack the house, it was probably intended as some kind of contemptuous symbol. But chicken Gerard Michael Fitt most certainly is not. The Independent MP for West Belfast proved that beyond any shadow of doubt in the Commons, when at the beginning of the Maze hunger strike he launched an outspoken attack on the IRA.

A few nights after his Westminster speech, the Fitt home was besieged by hundreds of demonstrators who stood ominously silent looking up at the windows. Many carried flaming torches and every five seconds someone beat a single stroke on a drum. The whole performance was carefully orchestrated to intimidate, and such things certainly take their toll, Fitt admits. His wife, Ann, a chronic asthma sufferer, has spent long periods in hospital, and Geraldine, the last of the five daughters dubbed by their father the 'Miss Fitts', failed to do as well as expected in her A-level examinations.

When the hunger strikers began to die, petrol bombs were thrown at the house. Fragments of them still remain among the half-bricks, chunks of breezeblock and other missiles scattered in the front garden. The Fitts' decaying Georgian house in this once-genteel Belfast road was on a list of preserved buildings. A friend asked what that really meant. 'Well,' said Fitt, 'you have to get planning permission before you blow it up.'

It was no laughing matter, however, when on the anniversary of the introduction of internment, scores of hooligans kicked down the front door at 4am and surged up the stairs to the bedroom where Fitt, his wife and daughter were sheltering. The intruders' mood was ugly, but the MP, dressed only in vest and underpants, recalled a book he had read about the French Revolution, which stated that at any given moment the man at the front of a mob is its leader.

He pointed his gun at the nearest hooligan and hoped that if he could intimidate him, the others would also be scared. Fitt and his friend Paddy Wilson had always said they would never carry guns, and then the Catholic Senator was found one night with his throat cut. Now Fitt was glad to have his Browning automatic.

By this time his wife, who was having an asthma attack in the bedroom behind him, was begging Fitt not to shoot, and the leader of the mob was shouting 'He's got a gun!' In a moment, Fitt recalls, the intruders were falling over one another to get back down the stairs and out into the street. It still rankles with the MP that despite repeated calls to the security forces, it was 25 minutes before assistance arrived in the Antrim Road. 'It was the longest 25 minutes of my life.'

Today the front door, with its one-way peephole, is made of steel and the padlocked windows are bullet-proof plastic. After dark, spotlights shine down on the doorstep which is scanned by a television camera set high under the eaves. At the back of the house there is another steel door and the whole yard is enclosed with wire netting like a cage at the zoo.

Such fortifications are the price one pays for becoming what Gerry Fitt calls de-tribalised. 'If you leave one tribe in Northern Ireland, you're lambasted for being a traitor and having sold out, but the other side still view you with suspicion,' he says. 'It is very cold out there if you are de-tribalised.'

Wherever he goes out there, he is accompanied by an armed police bodyguard. Recently, when he took his wife on holiday to recuperate in Jersey, they were trailed by four plainclothes officers even on the beach. On Sundays the MP has to consider carefully which mass to attend. The early service, with its sparse congregation, might provide an ideal opportunity for a would-be assassin, while the crowds at a later one could provide perfect cover for a terrorist's getaway.

In recent years, Gerry Fitt says, he has carried the coffins of almost 100 terrorist victims – Catholics and Protestants – to cemeteries. 'I have a running account with a florist who sends wreaths for those who have been murdered,' he adds with chilling resignation.

When, following his attack on the IRA, Fitt lost his seat on Belfast Corporation which he had held for 23 years, it was a bitter blow: a rejection of everything he had worked for. Admittedly, he was unable to conduct a normal election campaign. 'Who would have delivered election addresses?' he asks. 'Cars would have been hijacked and my supporters kneecapped.' On the eve of polling he issued his only statement: 'A vote for me is a vote against the gunmen.' The electors chose his hardline Republican opponent and Fitt lost two-thirds of his support, ending up with only 541 votes.

'Since then I haven't met a single person who voted against me,' he says wryly, and as he deals with the problems of the stream of unfortunates who arrive on his doorstep each day, Fitt would be less than human if he did not wonder from time to time whether it is all worth it.

Not that circumstances have changed the MP's central beliefs. 'I would like to see a united Ireland,' he says. 'I don't believe Ireland should ever have been partitioned and partition brought continuing tragedy.' But having said that, Fitt recognises that Ireland cannot be united by bombing and murdering people. 'If it could, you would just be transferring the problem from Belfast to Dublin.' The IRA would be replaced by Protestant killers. 'It is no use removing the geographical border while the border in people's minds remains,' he says. 'I'm more for uniting people than uniting land.'

Gerard Fitt, the third in a poor Catholic family of three boys and three girls, was born in 1926 in Walbeck Street, a cul-de-sac of small terraced houses just around the corner from his present home. As a boy he used to run messages for the lady who owned it. When he was eight, the boy lost his father, who had been a labourer with Belfast Corporation. Times were hard and Mrs Fitt supported the family on the half-a-crown a day she earned in domestic service and 17s 6d a week outdoor relief.

It was about this time that young Gerry saw his first politician, Harry Midgeley. The maverick MP was addressing a street-corner meeting and Fitt recalls the scene vividly. 'The women were wearing shawls and some of the kids had bare feet.' Children were playing with a pony, but Fitt had eyes only for the man who was speaking from the back of a trap. 'I got the feeling that there was someone the people loved,' he says. 'Some day', he thought, 'I'll be up there and helping these people.'

That day was to come in 1958, when Fitt was elected to Belfast Corporation as an Independent Labour councillor. In 1962 he entered Stormont and in 1966 he won the West Belfast seat at Westminster and has held it ever since. At one stage he was a member of all three bodies and took an impish pleasure in speaking at all of them in the course of a single day. Fitt has an irreverent sense of humour and once for a wager shook hands with John Kennedy 27 times during the President's visit to the city.

At 55 Gerry Fitt does not seem the stuff heroes are made of. He is balding, bespectacled and nursing a duodenal ulcer. He stands, on the rare occasions when he is standing still, with hands thrust forward into the pockets of his raincoat. When he leans towards you in a bar to emphasise a point, you can feel the Browning automatic slap against your leg. His rolling gait is a relic of his seagoing days. Two other reminders of those days are the tattoos Fitt bears on his forearms: on the left a representation of Mother Ireland and on the right 'A Sailor's Grave' with a lurid picture of a sinking ship.

The MP's abhorrence of violence probably springs from his teenage experiences as a merchant seaman on Murmansk convoys, when destroyers and U-boats fought deadly duels with torpedoes and depth-charges. 'Germans were out there trying to kill me and Royal Navy ships were trying to kill them,' he recalls. But at least in those days one did not know the enemy and whether he was married or had a family. 'Here you get your enemy's blood on your hands,' he says with distaste. The Protestant Shankill Butchers, for instance, stuck knives in their victims' throats, he says, and the IRA killers do the same sort of thing. 'The IRA have put off any hope of reunification with the Republic by what they have done.'

Whatever the pressure on Gerry Fitt, he will be fighting the next general election. 'I never ran away from a fight yet,' he says. In the meantime he has to carry on this twilight existence of a public figure. 'The one big thing I miss is not being able to go anywhere I like and talk to people.' Sometimes he avoids his police shadow. 'I tell him I'm not going out this afternoon and then I go for a walk along Royal Avenue and shake hands with people. It does something for me.' But always there is that heavy weight in the raincoat pocket to remind Fitt of the realities of being de-tribalised. 'It only needs one madman with a gun,' he says. 'And as you know there are an awful lot in Northern Ireland.'
(20.12.81)

Nott the Defence Minister
Simon Hoggart

In February this year our Defence Secretary was dining in Italy with the Head of the Security Services. 'You see, Mr Nott, I know everything about you,' the swarthy spymaster remarked. The Minister paled slightly and a forkful of food paused in its passage between plate and incisors. 'For example, I know that today is your fiftieth birthday. May I congratulate you? It is a fine age for a man. When a woman says "Yes" he is flattered, and when she says "No" he is relieved.'

Sadly for Mr Nott, the woman who rules his life has lately brought him neither flattery nor relief. In the perplexing court politics of Downing Street he was being slowly shifted, as it were, from the bedchamber into the passage outside. If this were Russia, he would find his picture razored out of Pravda's May Day coverage. Nott, they said, was 'erratic.' He could not always be relied upon. She had been heard to suggest that he lacked loyalty to Sir Geoffrey Howe, whom he hoped to replace.

Then came the Falklands.

Nott was born in Kent to a West Country family; his father was a grain broker from Devon. He was sent to Bradfield College in Berkshire and later became a Gurkha officer during the Communist rebellion in Malaya. Here he lived the same life as his men, so gaining their lasting loyalty and conveniently saving his European food allowance. The money helped him to go on to Trinity, Cambridge, where he read law, economics and (of course) became President of the Union.

Before entering politics – he became MP for St Ives in the 1966 election – he was a merchant banker. But he always claims his real roots are in his Cornish farm. People need roots, he says, and must cling to them; some of his critics have alleged that until a month ago he spent rather too much time rooting in the West Country and not quite enough at his desk.

The farm is no smoothly computerised agro-tech food plant. To put it bluntly, Nott's side of things (his Yugoslav wife grows flowers, quite efficiently) is chaotic. A neighbour says: 'If the Task Force had been run on the same lines as John's farm, it would have been off the coast of Alaska.'

This is an important clue to Nott's character. His public image – to many Tory MPs as well as the voters – is of a desiccated accountant, calmly slicing up the once mighty Royal Navy because the set of figures in the red column doesn't match those in the black. In fact, Nott is a highly emotional man and often scatter-brained as well; nor has he the essential ability of successful Conservatives to keep a civil tongue in his head. If someone says something particularly stupid to a Tory Minister the response is supposed to be: 'Y-e-e-s, I hadn't quite looked at it that way before . . .' Nott says: 'What a particularly stupid remark that is.'

Every fortnight since February Nott has met the officers of the Tory backbench Defence committee, an important and influential body, in his tiny ministerial room at the Commons. Every fortnight the meeting has begun with a blazing row between Nott and Winston Churchill over the subject of defence cuts. They sit, or even stand, bellowing at each other across the tiny strip of carpet. Nott is actually one of those rare politicians who really doesn't mind what he says.

Very shortly after the Falklands crisis began, he held a crucial meeting with the officers of the Defence, Foreign Affairs and 1922 Committees. It was an important meeting because these people's goodwill was essential for the Government and for Nott's personal future.

He began with a moving plea for loyalty, loyalty to the Government and to him personally. Then he added: 'We *shall* win, in spite of the soft underbelly of the Conservative Party.' It was a peculiar and rather silly thing to say, because at least half the people in the room, whose loyalty he was beseeching, regarded themselves as part of the soft underbelly, and knew that he meant them. 'John's problem is, as they say in the North, that he sleeps in the knifebox. He's too clever by half,' another colleague says.

His predecessor at Defence, Francis Pym, used to go to great lengths to take his junior Ministers with him; there would be detailed meetings and a strategy for the whole Department was laid out. But when Nott was put in to sort out the admirals and balance the books, he simply announced his policies and told those beneath him to get on with it.

'The point about John is, believe it or not, that he is the Tory version of Michael Foot,' one of his friends says, if not in a very friendly way. 'He's clever, a super debater, highly emotional, very kind-hearted and completely disorganised.'

This internal chaos left him utterly shattered after the Argentine invasion, and led to his making one of the most disastrous parliamentary speeches since the (last) war. Yet his very emotional turbulence ('up and down like a bloody yo-yo,' one less than admiring colleague says) carried him up to make a sturdy, confident quarter-deck speech a few days later – a speech that guaranteed his survival.

Like so many of Margaret Thatcher's Government, he made his reputation by falling out with Ted Heath, with whom he was once on reasonably close and friendly terms. Towards the end of 1973, when he was a junior Minister in the Treasury, Nott began to get worried about the rapid growth in the money supply, the consequent inflation, and the prospects for a Tory victory in the next election, which was then expected in late 1974. So after long thought he decided to approach Heath, and bearded him politely in the Lobby. Could he have a word after the Division? he asked. 'If you want to resign, put it in writing,' Heath said curtly, and turned away.

Heath's friends say it must have been meant as one of Ted's celebrated mirthless jokes; Nott says it was serious. In any event, the row over monetarism led to a permanent and bitter rift. After the defeat of February 1974, Nott made several scantily disguised attacks on Heath's leadership. When Mrs Thatcher won in 1975, Nott's economic philosophy and political track record guaranteed him preferment. He started in her economic team, where Denis Healey said he was much the most impressive spokesman the Tories could put up against him. The following year he became shadow Trade Secretary.

Nott is a good debater with a sharp knowledge of what passes for wit in Parliament. For example, he awarded Sam Silkin the Order of the Clay Cross, a gibe which stuck. Mrs Thatcher likes good Commons performers, particularly if, like Nott and Norman Tebbit, they have a thuggish streak. When he became Trade Secretary in 1979 it was widely predicted that he would be the next Chancellor.

Yet Nott has never been a true, born-again monetarist. In July last year, in the celebrated meeting at which the entire Cabinet except Sirs Keith and Geoffrey defected, Nott joined the wets. He once remarked that we should boycott French wine because it was 'overpriced'; an absurd *non sequitur* to a free marketeer. But then Nott has always been closer to the emotions and the soil of England than to the austere academics of Chicago. *(2.5.82)*

6.
Some Places

An Indian Journal
Sue Arnold

'And how do you find Kashmir?' asked Mr Kumar politely, as we glided over the dark green grass of the Dal lake at Srinagar in a sort of tented gondola called a *shikara*. Disconcertingly like Surrey, I wanted to say. No wonder homesick British colonials came flocking up here for their holidays. All those larch-lap fences skirting neat gardens and prim little houses with attic dormers could comfortably transfer to Camberley without raising a single Home Counties eyebrow. When the dying Mogul Emperor Jehangir was asked to name his last earthly desire, he opened his dimming eyes and whispered, 'Kashmir, only Kashmir.' I suppose 'Frimley, only Frimley,' hasn't quite the same ring.

Mr Kumar offered spiced Kashmiri tea, excellent, he said, for headaches, heartburn, influenza and dysentery. We sipped cinnamon tea. Somewhere a sitar moaned, peacocks strutted on the far shore and a faint whiff of incense wafted over the lapping water. So far so perfect. Three weeks of Indian delights lay ahead. We had letters of introduction to two maharajas and a brigadier, and to this end had packed crêpe-de-chine dresses and gold dancing sandals. The plan was to spend two days in Ladakh on the borders of Tibet visiting Buddhist monasteries on a quick Karma crawl, and then go back to Delhi and all those romantic places – Agra, Khajarho, Jaipur, Jaisalmer, Jodhpur. . . . Mr Kumar blew his nose over the side of the boat.

'How long do you stay in Srinagar?' he asked. We said we had tickets to fly to Leh in the morning, and had even packed a cardigan apiece because Ladakh in early winter could be chilly at night. Mr Kumar looked surprised. There was no aeroplane to Leh in the morning, he said. The winter schedule had begun and the next flight was in five days, the very date we were due at the Lake Palace in Udaipur, maharajas and all.

So we went by bus. It was a B class bus. The A class bus only ran on Sundays. B stands for Basic Bus. It had four wheels and a ferocious fume-spewing engine and somewhere, somehow, above the wheels and behind the engine, sat the passengers, goats, chickens, babies, sacks of rice, rolls of carpet and a flotilla of ever-burning kerosene stoves brewing up char. The journey to Leh takes two days with an overnight stop at a one-yak town called Kargil. The road crosses three majestic mountain passes, Zoji La, Fatu La and Namika La, all pushing 14,000 feet into thin air.

Did I say road? There is no road. There is a narrow ledge strewn with boulders and the corpses of lorries along which our Sikh driver plied his merry way at breakneck speed. There is no comforting barrier between the ledge and the edge, so that when I opened my eyes, just once (for the Srinagar Leh road is justifiably dubbed The Most Spectacular Road on Earth), I could look straight down on to the wrecks of vehicles in the ravine 14,000 feet below.

We stopped at a military checkpoint. As this is a sensitive border area, the army controls the entire route. An officer peered in through the window. 'Only two overseas ladies,' he asked suspiciously. 'No gents accompanying?' 'No gents,' we whispered weakly. The two unaccompanied ladies passed the night on the mud floor of the Dreamview Hotel at Kargil, a bucket being the 'attached bathroom', and on the morrow proceeded to Leh, taking in as many inaccessible monasteries perched high on crags or buried deep in gorges as their light summer footwear would allow. They tasted *tsampa*, the staple barley diet of the monks, drank tea laced with rancid yak butter, and heard lamas in strange yellow bonnets chanting mysterious chants. And at last they reached Leh airport on Monday morning for the 10 o'clock once-weekly flight to Delhi, for they had vowed that come hurricane or hellfire they would never *ever* travel the Most Spectacular Road on Earth again.

At 11 o'clock the booking clerk announced that due to engine failure the flight had been cancelled. When was the next one? Same time next week, he said. With heavy hearts the two unaccompanied ladies headed for a taxi to take them back across Namika La, Fatu La and Zoji La. That night they slept in a village called Drass, and early next morning it began to snow. By lunchtime 15 feet of snow had fallen and four taxis, two B class buses, nine lorries, 50 army trucks, two unaccompanied ladies and a goat were stranded on the Most Spectacular Road on Earth somewhere in the Himalayas.

'It is no use,' said a soldier. 'The road is blocked both ways. You will sleep tonight in the trucks. It may take a week to clear the road. If it is not cleared by the 10th (it was now the 3rd) the road will officially close until the end of May. I am sorry.' So were we. I was glad I'd brought my cardigan.

We divide into two groups. The eight elderly Americans from Ohio and their 43 pieces of luggage are winched into the back of one truck, the rest of us clamber into another. It is 4pm, cold and getting colder, dark and getting darker and the snow keeps falling. My feet in dainty sandals are beginning to look and feel like raspberry ripple ice-cream, but rummaging in my bag I find two plastic carrier bags (thank God one is from Harrods) and put them over my tights and under the socks borrowed from Larry, a bearded anaesthesiologist from LA. I can now get out of the truck to pee without fear of frostbite.

Larry (who has seen a lot of those survival movies) speaks. 'OK you guys, we gotta make a plan. We gotta pool our resources. How many sleeping bags we got, how much food? And since we gonna be here some time, we better get acquainted.'

Huddled in a circle, knees covered with old sacks, backsides frozen on the wet, metal floor of the truck, we introduce ourselves. There's Larry and Maryanne from Laguna Beach, Dieter, a Lufthansa pilot and his blonde, giggly girlfriend, Bernard, an elderly French tax inspector, Pierre, a Belgian schoolteacher, Hervé de Monès Delibouix, a lanky Parisian student, Andrea, an Australian nurse, my companion Mrs P, Irish but living in St Anton, and one British ace reporter with a Harrods carrier on her left foot to prove it.

We pool the food, two biscuits, five walnuts and some cheese, not much if we're going to be here for a week. I feel sorry for the Australian nurse. It's always the nurse they eat first in those survival films. Three soldiers climb in with us and brew tea in a kerosene drum. They say the temperature drops to minus 20C at night. Larry gives us all sleeping pills called qualudes, which he says are all the rage in LA. They give you a buzz like cocaine before you drop off. We swallow our qualudes, start giggling maniacally and eventually fall asleep in a jumble of arms and legs.

The Lufthansa pilot leaves his size 11 feet in Mrs P's stomach all night. In the wee hours the soldier on my right attempts to share my sack in a less than platonic fashion. Should I protest at this shameless impropriety or be grateful for the extra body warmth? We compromise. At dawn we are woken by a strange dripping sound. Icicles are melting on to our heads. I crawl over 13 bodies, lift up the flap and look out. Snow, snow, thick, thick snow. More landslides, two trucks are buried.

Mrs P and I empty the contents of our luggage and wear them. I am now lumpily clad in three pairs knickers, two prs tights, three T-shirts, a silk dress, dungarees, a cardigan, one pr carrier bags and a shirt wrapped round my head to shield my ears from the icy wind. A soldier returns with grim tidings. We shall not be moving over Zoji La pass to Srinagar for at least another three days. A peasant wrapped in a blanket and a goat across his shoulders passes. Where is he going? 'To Sonemarg, the village beyond Zoji La', he says, on foot. Hervé says he's going too. Mrs P and I opt to join them; we're still hoping to make the Lake Palace at Udaipur by Friday. The others are taking it in turns to squat under the truck.

Two kilometres on, the snow is up to my armpits and we give up. We are now at the front of the convoy and seek refuge in the front of a civilian lorry with two drivers and an Indian hitchhiker. At least it's warm. We drink tea and eat dal and the Sikh driver tells us his uncle went to London for an operation on his kidneys and came back in a box with his name on a brass plate. It was a very fine box, he says. Night falls. The smell in the cab is pungent and I produce my bottle of Joy by way of room freshener. 'I love French perfume,' says the Sikh emptying £22 worth on to his turban. He rolls us all a joint. They too have run out of food. If we're to be hungry we might as well be high.

Another day, another night. Every morning the driver lights a kerosene stove under the fuel tank to defrost the diesel in case we can move on. On Thursday evening we are told the road will not be cleared and we must return to Drass, 30 kilometres back and, according to the records, the second coldest inhabited village in the world. The first is in Siberia. Hervé, Mrs P and I are loaded into the back of a military truck carrying scrap iron. Five miles before Drass we hear a strange cater-wauling. We peer out. Eight elderly Americans from Ohio are stand-ing, sobbing, vomiting, praying by the roadside next to their 43 pieces of luggage and a broken down army truck. Can we give them a lift? We heave them in on top of the scrap iron, ripping fox-fur jackets, smashing Nikon cameras. It has started to snow again.

Mrs P and I have stopped looking for trucks with chains on even one wheel to lessen the danger of crossing Zoji La. We have given up scrounging food. We have abandoned all attempts at hygiene and we have now turned to prayer. One reason for coming to India was to find a guru who would clue us up about enlightenment. Well, we're certainly getting enlightenment. We want to go home soonest to try it out. We never want to set foot south of Haslemere again. Enlightened Rule One – Foreign Parts are for Foreigners.

I may as well tell you about Drass. It has one street, three dwellings loosely classified as hotels and no women. Yaks, dzos, goats, dogs, men in shaggy blankets yes, but no women. I read somewhere that in the interests of birth control polyandry is common in Ladakh. Having lived in Drass I can see why, though where the lucky women were I never found out.

I ran into the Chief of Police one morning standing beside his yak.

'Do you think I might borrow a typewriter anywhere?' I said.

'You must ask the office manager of the Drass Development Corporation,' he said, indicating a squatting, blanketed figure next to another yak.

'Please may I borrow your typewriter?' I said.

The office manager of the Drass Development Corporation considered the question in silence.

'How long for?' he said.

'An hour?' I said.

'Fifty minutes,' he said.

'Thank you,' I said.

We went to a concrete building with a mud floor and a ladder. We climbed the ladder and found an ancient machine on the floor. Five male secretaries, also in blankets, appeared to be guarding it. The office manager shouted orders in Hindi. Two secretaries carried the typewriter to a table, another brought a chair. The rest watched. I sat down. They waited.

'There is just one thing,' I said timidly. 'May I have some paper?'

'You did not ask for paper,' said the office manager accusingly.

This was true.

'You see, I can't really type without paper,' I explained.

'I have no spare paper,' said the office manager.

'Only a few sheets, say four,' I pleaded.

'Three,' said the office manager and unlocked a big tin cupboard.

I began to write a letter home. I told the children where I was and why, and how treacherous the road over Zoji La would be. I said I might not be home till the spring because in five days' time the road closed officially until May. Over my shoulder, the secretaries watched the letter grow. It was when I got to the part about doing their homework that I began to sniff. My glasses misted over, the words jumbled up. The sniffs became snivels, the keys jammed. It was no good. I abandoned all restraint, threw my head down and howled huge, heaving, choking, gasping, soggy sobs. The secretaries waited. After about 10 minutes I stopped. 'You are weeping because there is something wrong with the machine?' asked the office manager.

Every morning we asked the captain if the road was open and every morning he said it was too dangerous for civilians. On the fourth day Mrs P and I sneaked out to the army camp and begged a lift. No permission, said the soldiers. I began to snivel anew. 'I have never seen an English lady weep,' said a soldier with interest. 'OK, get in, but you must lie down and stay quiet because I am carrying explosives and it is forbidden to take passengers. Please do not smoke.'

I can't tell you much about crossing Zoji La because I was lying in the back of the truck face down on top of a crateful of grenades covered by old sacks. It took eight hours to drive five vertical kilometres. Whenever we ran into a half-buried, defunct truck we squeezed past it, our chainless wheels inches from the edge. At midnight we reached the village of Sonemarg. The proprietor of the Dreamland Hotel locked us in our room because, he said, an English girl had been murdered here last month.

The flight from Leh to Srinagar takes an hour. We had been on the road for eight days. In the taxi to the Oberoi Palace Hotel I removed the two plastic carrier bags which I had been wearing over my feet in lieu of socks. Imagine Pandora's Box full of mature Stilton and last year's slurry and you will know the score when I removed the bags.

'Susan,' said Mrs P, running her fourth bath. 'Promise me that if I ever mention foreign travel again you will say one thing to me – Zoji La. OK?'

'OK,' I said. *(10.1.82)*

Land of the Closed Anemone
Katharine Whitehorn

If you go to Japan stuffed with pretty images of stone gardens and kimonos, Madame Butterfly and paper fans, the first shock of Tokyo is the absolute hideousness of almost everything you see. For every elegant fountain there are two clattering overhead railways, for every pretty temple there are 10 tasteless blocks of flats. You turn up at what is plainly the back of a building and it turns out to be the front.

But I suppose I can have no aesthetic sense to speak of; for after a day or two I was simply bowled over by the fact of being in a town where everything *works*. Telephones aren't out of order, people keep appointments on time, taxis arrive; their Underground is a dream and they even have the decency to put the names in English lettering.

People give you information that's correct and they always seem to be trying to help – I never got lost once without being rescued by someone with a bit of English.

The prevalence of English dates from the American occupation; but you see signs of Westernisation at every turn. A schoolgirl in the street wears a tartan skirt and carries a bag with Peter Rabbit on it; except that her socks are spotless, she could be English. The models in the shop windows, the faces on TV, are western; the bridal advertisements in the buses say 'My Wedding' in English (often, with unintentional humour, flanked by the Buddhist stork). If you have to hold on, the telephone may break into 'Annie Laurie.' They fly out Ian Thomas, the Queen's dressmaker, twice a year, and dress labels are in English even where every stitch is local.

Mills & Boon titles are advertised on TV, all Shakespeare's plays have recently been done both in the theatre and on the box – an agent who lives there treasures the memory of Lady Macbeth in a kimono, playing the cello with the leaves falling; they've even shown Monty Python with an actor explaining the jokes.

I was warned before I went that Japanese set much less store by actual words than we do: that when a man says 'yes' he means 'I have taken in what you say,' not 'I agree.' Professor Suzuki, a kind psychologist, explained the process to me: 'I will say what I think you are thinking; you will say what you think I want you to think.' The idea is to arrive at a consensus, but it makes a conversation more like a pavane than a handclasp; they have a terrible time keeping their phone bills down and an interview with the doctor ('We feel very impolite to ask questions') can be an agony of non-communication.

Go into any workroom or office and you'll see little meetings and group discussions going on: endless attempts to arrive at 'harmony', with everyone feeling comfortable about what is agreed. This makes for a lot of smiles and surface tranquillity, but it's no way, of course, actually to get anything done. So after work they all go off and drink together – ostensibly to cement a deal or to celebrate their work friendship; in fact to get just drunk enough to say what they really think, sometimes quite rudely.

There is a sweet convention that no one can be held responsible for what he does when he's in drink; next morning the salient points will be remembered, the pugnaciousness carefully forgotten. It comes as something of a shock to the westerner, starry-eyed about those perfect, much-vaunted industrial relations, to realise that, without whisky, the system simply wouldn't work at all.

This has its drawbacks. One of them is the number of totally tanked-up citizens you see propped against the station walls in the evenings – only a small proportion end up in the new 'capsule hotels', where you get a space that's like a coffin only comfortable, or in the 'tiger tank' at the local police station. Another snag is the irritation of wives, left at home in the evenings.

The fact that business life continues so far into the evening presumably accounts for Tokyo's interminable red light district. Like Tokyo itself, it seems to go on and on and on, street after street, until the tired tourist begins to think there can't be that much lust in the whole world. Brothels are illegal, but bars proliferate, where they have progressed from 'topless' waitresses to 'bottomless', and from the phrase No Panty to simple No Pan. Proper geishas still exist, of course, but they are far more of an undertaking than an evening in a risqué bar, which in any case seems more modern.

I met a girl who'd worked as a bar girl: 'They kept asking me "what colour is your pubic hair?" in English. I always said "green".' Greatly hung up on pubic hair are the Japanese; it's the one thing it's illegal to show in photographs.

A good deal of a bar-girl's work has nothing directly to do with sex – lighting cigarettes, pouring whisky, smiling, it's just a female version of Japan's almost universal overmanning. A train hurtles past a level crossing; there is a man to wave it on with white gloves and a little flag.

You go into a big department store and it's just like one in London or Chicago – except that instead of having to light a small fire to attract attention, you find someone smiling and bowing when you're barely off the escalator. In a set-up where a good many firms take on their employees for life, they are still avid for the latest labour-saving technology; so they use up their spare people on presentation.

Nothing since Okinawa has irritated the Japanese as much as the words of a Common Market official, that they are a nation of workaholics living in rabbit hutches. The trouble is that they *are* desperate for space; never mind the bonsai trees, they even keep expensive cockroaches as the world's smallest pets. Their very behaviour is subdued by it; one full-blooded Neapolitan – or even Samurai – gesture would crash through about three streets of modern Tokyo. And it's made much worse by modernity: traditional quilts can be rolled up by day, as western beds cannot; chairs take up more room than flat floor-cushions; and then there are all the gadgets and transistors and TV sets, and frequently a piano as well.

I stayed for a couple of nights at an inn, a rikoyan, in Kyoto. The tiny alley leading to the inn was a garden: stones, plants, ferns – the whole thing only a couple of feet wide; across shining wooden floors I followed the woman to my room, changing slippers at every turn. The room had a sliding window looking out onto a river; a floor-level dressing stand and a TV set; the bed was two quilts beneath and one above.

As I lay there like a hamburger in my bun, with the strong acrid smell of the tatami straw in my nostrils, I began to feel a little of that calm, that sense of inner space which is what seems to keep the Japanese sane: 'A Japanese child is taught from an early age to be private inside himself,' I was told; I could well understand that someone from the city might come back to such an inn almost as a retreat.

Then there was the question of the bath. In Japan you wash and rinse first in cold water before getting into a tank of hot water that is shared (successively, thank God) by all. It was brim full; presumably the small Japanese, I thought, don't displace much water, but if I get in . . .? In the end I hung on the sides by my forearms, but later I was told that was quite wrong: 'Shooshing the water out onto the floor is half the fun!' they said. 'Why, a sumo wrestler can empty the whole bath!' I didn't care for the comparison, exactly. But it did remind me that I scarcely saw a single fat woman all the time I was in Japan; evidently they restrain themselves even in eating.

I was taken down to the sea to walk about through the small houses of a fishing village, to visit a little shrine where you pull on a bell-rope to alert the guardian spirit, to watch the local people digging around the rocks for mussels, for sea-slugs, and for some of the nastiest-looking spiked worms I ever hope to see.

There were also anemones; and they seemed to symbolise a basic difference between the Japanese way and ours. We are the open anemone; we have all our fronds out, always trying to make contact, to impinge, to touch, to hold. The Japanese are the closed anemones, with all the feeling nerve-ends tucked away, trying at all costs to preserve a smooth glistening exterior, to hold the tensions and press-ures all inside – inside yourself, or at very least inside your home.

That this may lead to a terrible build-up of pressure within your home, that it may make women 'the shock absorbers of society', is undeniable.

Japanese women take a lot of flack from foreigners about their alleged docility and there certainly seems to be a lot of it about: They no longer actually walk two paces behind their husbands, but they often serve his meal without sharing it; waitresses approach ground-level tables on their knees; kimonos, and the tottery gait required by the relevant sandals, are a common sight, especially on Sundays. Even in the disturbances of the late Sixties the girls apparently carried the stones for the male students to throw.

A nicely brought-up Japanese woman is still expected first and

foremost to know how to arrange flowers, never to make the first pass
in love and above all how to do the Tea Ceremony.

It is necessary to explain that the Tea Ceremony has about as much
to do with tea as Holy Communion has to do with knocking back a
decent bottle of claret; which is just as well, since the stuff tastes like
boiled lawn-mowings. At first sight it seems to combine the worst
features of both opera and cricket: a terrible slowness, and a set of
minute differentiations meaningful only to the initiated. Those who
are to partake kneel in a row, while the girl who is to do the ceremony
tittups in, using special mincing steps; she kneels down in a special
manner, picks up a special box with a special gesture, lifts the lid *so*,
dips in the spoon *so* . . . eventually you are passed the cup, which you
accept, murmuring admiringly about the grace of the woman, the
delicacy of the cup, even the excellence of the taste.

Every object used in the Tea Ceremony is very beautiful, very
expensive and is usually kept wrapped in a cloth, in a bag, in a box.
Those who do it regard it as a sort of spiritual discipline, like transcen-
dental meditation or yoga: so to subdue your thoughts, so to control
your movements is to pour tranquillity upon your soul, not just to pour
hot (well, fairly hot) water on green tea.

The Tea Ceremony is a symbol of all that's traditionally been
expected of women in Japan. Different societies want different things
of their women: Italians want warmth and emotional generosity;
Kikuyus are keen on a willingness to work; a Japanese woman is
supposed to be in charge of the happiness of her household, to create
calm and beauty and a soothing order, a haven from the awful
pressures outside. They have a saying about the six enemies a man has
– two bosses above him, grinding him down; the two men beside him,
keeping him up to the mark; and the two beneath him, forever after his
job; he mustn't come back to a seventh enemy at home.

So whatever she is feeling she must control; she is not supposed to
present him with any jagged emotions of her own and if she happens to
be feeling wretched she must just put as good a face on it as she can.

One way or another, quite a few marriages hold together on terms
which Western romantics would find unacceptable – 'a good Japanese
wife packs French letters in her husband's suitcase,' I was told (she can
buy them in any supermarket); a husband posted overseas won't
necessarily take his wife with him, and a husband doesn't ring to say if
he'll be late home from work. I found this hard to believe, and asked
one working mother if her husband rang. She laughed. 'He only rings if
he's going to be home *early*,' she said. 'To be sure dinner's ready.'

The Japanese educational system makes Manchester Grammar
School look like a holiday camp. The tots start kindergarten long

before the official school age, they work longer hours than we do with only a month's holiday in the summer; and in addition most of them go to a *yuka* (crammer's) in the evenings and/or weekends. The school pressure's intense: there are over 700 school-age suicides a year; and with father out several nights a week drinking with his workmates, a woman can all too easily turn into an 'education Momma' who lives only for her children's success at school.

But I doubt if the married women of Japan are about to erupt; and I would not have the impertinence to feel sorry for them. For this is the great snag of going to a country and asking about The Women. You see the statutory women's leaders or the Prime Minister's wife, the local feminists, if any; and you get just about the same story wherever you are: 'No, we are not yet liberated but we are making progress' on the one hand; and 'Ah, but traditional women have a lot of power' on the other. You hear this, whether you're talking about somewhere like Iran, where the women have a family network and enormous subterranean clout, and pity the poor Yemeni women as slaves; or somewhere like Somalia, where sentimentality about 'traditional femininity' is somewhat marred by the knowledge that the girls have their genitals sawn off.

It seems to me Japanese women have one traditional strength they would be idiots to throw away – and I don't mean being bossy about the house, or even having control of the family's finances, though they have (and a flourishing trade in fake pay packets has grown up, to help men keep back some yen for themselves). There are two ways of being strong, and when it comes to mastery over other people, the Japanese woman is plainly not doing so well. But there's another way.

A Japanese woman has immense mastery over herself; she has what they call *gamman*: the quality of being able to put up with things, to endure. It is the ability to consume your own smoke, in Rose Macauley's phrase; or in the Emperor Hirohito's, 'to bear the unbearable.' I have heard an African woman say: 'We have to know that we are stronger than those who oppress us' – the Japanese women do. With luck, they may be a bit less oppressed as time goes on; but I doubt if there's anything so safe or shining about our times that she would be wise to abandon her inward armour.

Solzhenitsyn said: 'If you want to change the world, who would you begin with – yourself, or other people?' Most of us would think it far more fun to begin with other people. But in a society where the pressures and strains aren't likely to change at all, control over yourself may be the best way of surviving. *(26.7.81)*

No Fear of Flying
Clive James

I like airports and airliners. This is not a case of frankly admitting to myself, as with my fond feelings for television, an enthusiasm that was always there but masked by intellectual snobbery. There was never any hope of generating enough intellectual snobbery to cover up my keenness for the airways.

I was already enslaved when the old compound-engine Douglas DC-6Bs were shaking my house to pieces back in the early Fifties. The house, situated in the Sydney suburb of Kogarah, lay among the approach lights to what was then the main runway of Kingsford-Smith airport – or aerodrome, as it was always called in those days. Before attaining long trousers I could already identify, from the engine note alone, the DC-4, every variety of the DC-6, the Lockheed Constellation, the Convair 240 and the Boeing Stratocruiser. They all rattled the crockery but the DC-6B could crack a Pyrex casserole dish.

When the first Stratocruiser arrived via Hawaii, to the accompaniment of a tremendous publicity campaign from PanAm, I had already been camped for two days in the sand dunes about a hundred yards from where it was due to touch down. Other members of my gang were hollow-eyed from hearing me tell them all about the wonder plane's double-bubble pressure hull, but they looked appropriately awestricken when the huge machine descended right in front of us with gouts of flame from the exhausts of its Twin Wasp radials. Essentially a B-29 bomber nine months pregnant, the Stratocruiser was far from being the world's most elegant airliner, but it seemed to me aesthetically pleasing beyond anything I had ever known, and even today I can hear the pained squeal that the tyres of the main undercarriage made as they hit the tarmac and started rolling at 100 m.p.h. plus.

Those old piston-engined airliners would have fascinated me even if they had never left the ground, but the thought of such beautiful mechanisms actually travelling through the sky was almost too much to take. In those days, flying was an activity for grown-up, fabulously wealthy people with deep voices: to my knowledge nobody in short pants had ever been allowed the freedom of the air. But one could haunt the airport at weekends, and one did.

All through my early teens I was down at the airport on Saturday afternoons making myself indispensable to the cleaners sweeping out the planes. Although I was careful always to wear an old leather flying helmet in order to blend into the ambience, somehow my daydream of being asked to replace a sick co-pilot ('Think you can handle it, son?')

never came true, and indeed I was not to get airborne until many years later. But I saw the flight-decks of most of the piston-engined airliners up to and including the Super Constellation, a version of the original Constellation which had been so often 'stretched' that its shadow going over our house perceptibly lowered the air temperature.

Older now, the proud smoker of several cigarettes a day, I was there again in the sand dunes when the first Boeing 707 landed, ushering in the intercontinental jet era that should have begun with the de Havilland Comet but tragically did not. My theoretical allegiance was to the British designers, but emotionally there was only one thing to do about the 707 – gape in wonder. Kingsford-Smith's old main runway was not long enough to take the new plane, so the transverse strip was extended out into Botany Bay, thereby preserving our house from the cataclysmic effect of the twice-weekly PanAm 707 flights from Los Angeles. In fact the 707, though noisier than the later wide-bodies, made nothing like the racket kicked up by the piston engines of all those stretched post-war classics that had been fragmenting my mother's china for the previous decade. Jet roar has no throb in it – it can howl but it doesn't hammer. Nevertheless, the good people of Kogarah were glad to be no longer in the blast path. All except me.

Farewelling an early girl-friend on her PanAm 707 flight back to America, I stood heavy-hearted as the plane took off, not because she was going without me but because she was going instead. The aircraft looked powerful enough to reach the Moon. The wheels came up, the flaps retracted, and you could see the flexible wings take the weight as the plane went spearing up through the heat-wobble. Imagine how it must feel. Alas, imagine was all I could afford. When I left for England the means of transport was a rusty old ship that took five weeks to get there. Then there were two or three years in London when I scarcely earned enough to catch a no. 27 bus. But eventually I found myself getting airborne, not – emphatically not – because I had become rich, but because air travel was expanding to embrace the poor.

The Sixties were the great age of the charter flight. Before the wide-bodies had even been invented, mass air travel was already underway. You could get to Milan, for example, for a very small amount of money if you were a student. The planes were ageing Britannias and even older Douglas DC-7Cs belonging to unknown airlines operating from tin sheds at the wind-swept edges of Gatwick or Luton, and most of your fellow students turned out to be 90-year-old Calabrian peasant women in black clothes carrying plucked chickens.

On my first flight I was already petrified when we took off, largely because I had made the mistake of looking out of the window at the moment when the pilot arrived by Jeep. He was wearing an eye-patch, walked with a stiff leg and saluted the aircraft with what appeared to be an aluminium hand. Around his neck the silver brassard of a Polish award for bravery gleamed in the weak sunlight. But in the air I was too busy to be afraid.

The ancient dwarf nun in the seat beside me – one of my fellow students – had never flown before in her life except when dreaming of the Last Judgment. Her rosary clattered in her gnarled hands like a football fan's rattle and when the plane tilted to avoid the Matterhorn she sang a brief excerpt from a Donizetti aria before being sick into her plastic carrier bag full of new potatoes. I got the job of holding her hand while the heavily loaded plane crabbed sideways on the wind and hit the runway between the two long lines of gutted old DC-4 which in those days told you that you were landing at Malpensa, Milan's second best airport. At Linate, the first best, we would probably not have been allowed to land even if on fire.

Other early flights were equally hair-raising, but somehow I never seemed to mind. There was a way of flying to Paris which involved a long bus-ride from London to a grass-strip airfield terminating at the Kentish cliffs, an even longer bus-ride from the French coast to Paris, and an incredibly short hop across the Channel. The airborne sector of the trip was accomplished in a high-wing twin-engined British airliner whose make I will not specify, lest you take fright and cancel if you ever find yourself booked on one of the few surviving examples. No doubt it is a perfectly good aircraft in normal circumstances, but with a full load including me it took so long to get off the ground on the British side that one felt one might as well have stayed on the bus. Once again I made the mistake of looking out of the window, this time as the aircraft was pitching and yawing over the bumpy grass and dodging between sheep at full power towards the cliff edge. A rabbit popped out of its hole, looked at me, and overtook us.

But it was worth it just to be enskied, even if that particular flight rose only just far enough over the English Channel to clear the upper-works of Greek oil tankers steaming towards each other. I used to spend all those early flights with my nose squashed against the window. Nowadays I have learned the trick of always asking for an aisle seat, so that if you have a drunken Bulgarian hammer-thrower sitting beside you, at least you won't have to climb over him to get to the toilet. But in those days I wanted to see everything happening outside, even when what was happening outside was too close to the inside for comfort.

You never knew when there would be a revelation. At night the cities were like jewelled cobwebs on black velvet. Coming back from Venice on a BEA Comet 4 night flight, I was one of the only two passengers aboard and got invited to the flight deck just at the right moment to see the lights of Paris. Stacking around Gatwick in a chartered Britannia while the pilot negotiated through an interpreter for permission to land, I saw an old Elizabethan – one of the loveliest aeroplanes ever made – slip out of the cloud 1,000 ft below us. I presume our aircraft waggled its wings out of recognition rather than surprise.

I finally got a trip on a Boeing 707 at just the time it was about to go out of style, because the first wide-bodies were already proving their routes. But it was still a thrill, not least because the destination was Boston – a long way from Europe. Over mid-Atlantic a BOAC VC-10 going the other way went past a few miles to our left on my side of the aircraft, and a mile or so above. The condensation trail came out of the cobalt blue distance like a spear of snow. Letting down into Boston, I watched the magic suitcase of the Boeing wing unpack itself, the flaps jacking out and curving down to turn the aerofoil into a parasol.

It was a long time since I had bought *Flight* magazine every week and memorised the contents, but I was still clued-up enough to be aware that the same wing had held the B-52s up in the sky while they split the ground of South-East Asia and drove a lot of little children crazy just with the noise. There is good reason for thinking we are alive in a particularly shameful stretch of history, the only era in which the innocent have ever been obliterated on an industrial basis. But on the airliners and in the airports I found myself unable to pretend that I did not enjoy living in the twentieth century.

You will find an extermination camp in the seventh book of Thucydides. People have always destroyed each other on as grand a scale as the prevailing technology allowed. But powered flight has all happened within a single lifetime. Last week I had dinner with a man who remembers crossing the Atlantic on the old *Aquitania* in 1906, the year the Wright brothers first flew at Kittihawk. Even Leonardo, who could do anything, could only dream of flying. And here was I, without even a licence to drive a car, riding down out of the sky into Massachusetts after having crossed the Atlantic in a few hours, a king of infinite space.

Then the wide-bodies came in and the age of mass aerial migration was on for young and old. By those who flew them the wide-bodies were known as heavies and the name was soon in use among such non-practising pilots as myself. The DC-10 I found hard to love at first, especially after one of them crashed near Paris and killed a lot of people, including someone I knew. The Tri-Star I found disconcertingly hard to tell apart from the DC-10, until I learned to remember that the DC-10 was the one with the third engine half way up its tail.

There was no difficulty, however, about spotting which of the three principal heavies was the winner. Nobody with a proper appreciation of the Boeing 747's looks will ever call it a Jumbo. The 747 is so suavely proportioned that it doesn't even look very big except when it happens to taxi past its ancestor, the 707, whereupon you feel that a mackerel has given birth to a mako shark.

Loved by pilots for its handling qualities and seemingly infinite reserves of getaway, the 747 flies like a fighter and at first glance even looks like one. In fact it looks a lot like the old F-86 Sabre, with its flight-deck bulge perched right forward like a Sabre's bubble canopy and the same proud angle to its tail feathers. On the ground the 747 is perhaps a bit fussy underneath, like a house being moved around on a lot of roller skates, but when it gets into the air, cleans itself up, and pours on the 100,000 horsepower of its turbofans, there is nothing less awkward or lovelier aloft. Unless you had been told, you would never think of it as having 400 people on board. It looks as if there is only one man in there, having the time of his life.

The greatest number of heavies I ever saw in the one place was at New York's Kennedy airport after a storm. There are almost 400 747s in the world and it looked as if half of them were queuing to get away. Unfortunately, I was in one of them, so didn't get a very good look.

The airliners haven't shrunk the earth. Going all the way around it still feels like a journey. But they have turned it into one place. Beyond the airport boundaries, each country remains odd enough to satisfy anybody's thirst for strangeness. Meanwhile the airports hint at a peaceful world. My only regret is that I will probably be too old for space. I have done my best to snare a window seat on an early space shuttle but so far they are being niggardly with the tickets. To go up so far that there is no down is still one of my dreams of heaven.

Meanwhile, as always, there is poetry enough in the here and now. All I do for a living is put words beside each other but I have been shown wonders without even asking. With raw egg dropping from chopsticks into my lap I have looked down on the North Pole. In the Persian Gulf at midnight I have seen the oil rigs burning like the damned. Best of all, I have found that every way you fly leads home. Crossing the paralysed red rock ocean of Australia's Dead Heart as the sun comes up, Qantas flight QF2 lets down over Sydney Harbour before the morning glare has burned the pale blue summer mist off the silver water. Over there on the right is my house, the sideboard now full of intact crockery. There is time enough to think about the misery we have caused and how much we have destroyed. For now, look what we have created. Only a few minutes ago we were in the cave. Whatever next? *(10.1.82)*

7.
That's Entertainment

Seeing in the Dark
Michael Holroyd

When the bank manager sent me a new bank card, he explained that I must have been waving the old one near a television: that would account for the power having gone out of it. I mentioned this in some amazement to a friend, but she merely added that 'because of radiation' I had better keep eight feet away from any colour set myself or the power would go out of me too. After this I began to feel differently about television. It is not something, I realised, we look at and control, but an eye that watches us and eventually controls the way we see ourselves.

If we see ourselves in a hostile light we do not blame television. Television is friendly, one of the necessities of life, a periscope that can show us, as we huddle below, all the world's wonders. It is our passport to go anywhere, our encyclopaedia to know everything. Yet its friendliness is deceptive. We are free to travel everywhere so long as we don't move, to find out anything without a thought. Television has begun to swamp us with this illusion of freedom.

Freedom was a word used very persuasively by Mr Peter Jay in his keynote address on the future of television at last year's Edinburgh Festival.

Dazzled by the romance of the machinery, he imagined new freedoms of fibre optic technology that could create a magic grid connecting every home in Britain and producing an eternal revolution of multitudinous programmes. 'Theoretically, there could be as many programmes as there are viewers', he said.

It was a blinding rather than an illuminating vision, and reminded me of a perpetually lit library where I had once worked in America. You could switch the lights there from 'bright' to 'brighter'; and then to 'brightest': but you could not switch them out. These lights turned night into day, burning away all traces of privacy and acting (it was explained to me) as a wonderful deterrent to burglars.

In America, where I have recently been waking up to morning television, there is a wide choice of early programmes – sport, yoga, religion, perhaps a soap opera in Spanish and at least three versions of the news. The great majority of Americans watch the 'less demanding' programmes and this has provided a useful recipe for the 'popular mix' we would have to offer in Britain.

As a medium for information, television is inferior to radio. Like travel, television narrows the mind. Shakespeare did not need to go to Denmark to write 'Hamlet.' Experience derives from what we feel, not what we see – which may become a substitute for feeling.

In the same way, television has made us extraordinarily well in-formed on subjects we know nothing about. Pictures often determine the selection of news on television and current affairs programmes that, growing increasingly over-simplified, give us the illusion of understanding more. But if we really wanted more information we would give more money to radio. The more television news we are persuaded to see at the expense of radio, the less actual information we are likely to receive.

Radio was conceived in a more decorous age. In the old Savoy Hill days there would on occasions be no news. Big Ben would strike nine, the announcer would come to the microphone and inform the waiting public that nothing important had come to his notice that evening. He would then play a little encouraging music. It was unsophisticated, but unpretentious. Today there *has* to be news and tomorrow there will have to be *more* news.

What is bad news for the human being in the street is often good news for television, for the individual is always outnumbered by the audience and it is the requirement of spectators rather than partici-pants that wins currency. It is not that we, the viewers, support the bad guys against the good. Nor is it that television, in any obvious sense, is a Great Persuader. It is merely a blank cheque. Whatever we see endorses our prejudices, helps to grow a cuticle of insensitivity, pays us dividends in virtuous indignation. We need a new Orwell to expose this illness within the dictatorship of democracy.

The most effective literary censorship in the world is the habit of not reading. Many writers have come to feel that, however well they may write, they can affect nothing. This is the belief of the *Spectator*'s television shock-horror critic, Mr Richard Ingrams, who divides writers into two categories: those who entertain him and those who are 'boring.'

In a sense he is right; that is, he accurately reflects the standard of the day, becoming (like Mr Tony Benn) a celebrity largely through his attacks on the fashionable celebrity cult and (like Mr Malcolm Muggeridge) a successful part of the media he is criticising.

Television has become the chief vehicle for a love-hate obsession with 'personalities' that, T. S. Eliot prophesied, might lead to the cultural breakdown of the twentieth century.

'I will become the most famous teenager in the world,' claimed Marcus Sargent who, having been rejected by various groups, let off some blank shots on television near the Queen. 'I wanted to be somebody. I wanted to be famous.' He was rocketed from obscurity into the news.

Whatever moments of excellence it achieves, television is a natural enemy of the other arts and has almost overwhelmed them. It has taught us to be impatient. We almost want the pictures in our galleries to *move*; want our theatres to fill accustomed slots with television characters and natural breaks; we do not want a cinema industry because, as Sam Goldwyn once said, people cannot be bothered to 'go out and pay money to see bad films when they can stay at home and see bad television for nothing.'

The difference between television and literature is fundamental. When we read a book we enter into a secret intimacy with the author, an intimacy (as Henry Green called it) between strangers. We form our own images in our heads. But when we watch television we all plug ourselves into our sets and collectively receive identical images. Words, action, images-in-colour, music and a firework display of technicalities: everything is supplied instantly and on a flat screen that does not allow us (as in the theatre) focus or perspective.

There is little left for us to do: we are merely receivers of received pictures, in danger of becoming less like human beings and more like extensions to the set. We watch for much the same reason that we drink – to be rid of ourselves; to switch life onto automatic pilot. We use televisions as we use Valium – to keep ourselves quiet, to keep our children quiet.

Television is a desert in which we sit happily sunbathing. And as we sit there the desert spreads. Do we want to make the whole world a desert? The answer is: yes, we do. Only more of it, we pretend, can obliterate the lack of real nourishment. We are addicted.

Television has fallen too far into the hands of those who are contemptuous of words and see the future of television as part of a non-literary culture. It would be best perhaps if television were wholly silent, leaving the supply of words to the viewers.

We are often told that television stimulates reading. The argument is simple, not to say simplistic. The best-seller lists are choked with titles that have featured on television and some of them are classics. But many viewers of 'War and Peace', 'Pride and Prejudice', 'The Mill on the Floss' must have turned into disappointed readers: the 'reading' had already been done for them on the screen. One bookshop has accommodated Nicola Paget while she signed copies of 'Anna Karenina'; the next step surely is to ask Robert Powell to autograph the Bible.

Pulled into the force field of television, literature and the theatre rotate like dying worlds without the energy to establish independent life. They have come to rely on television for money: and money, which should provide freedom of action, has imprisoned them.

Modern television feeds on electricity and on ourselves. We give it the best place in the room; we give it our most flattering attention; we give it our vitality and our capital. This must be the meaning behind that sudden failure of my bank card. *(10.1.82)*

In Defence of Television – a Reply
Melvyn Bragg

Michael Holroyd's article 'Seeing in the Dark' will, I fear, have done precisely what he despairingly accuses television of doing when he wrote that it 'endorses prejudices, helps to grow a cuticle of insensitivity, pays us dividends of virtuous indignation.'

It is important to attempt to answer his case, since the understandable disenchantment which he articulates could exacerbate that distrust of television which exists among some of those who see themselves as the guardians of a culture threatened and neglected by the upstart one-eyed monster.

If such a divide were to become the accepted wisdom – on the one hand literature and the fine arts which preserve the best, on the other television which promotes the worst – then television in this country would be encouraged to slide down the slipway into the delta of American sludge.

The only model we have for breakfast television is across the Atlantic and it is easy to deride the game-shows and old films which sprawl across the channels: not as easy, though, to dismiss the news programmes. The world news is always well represented, the main points of the domestic news well covered; reaction to the newest author/actress/celebrity to be interviewed varies according to taste – but the whole package serves a useful purpose in a nation without national newspapers.

Holroyd diminishes television as a 'medium for information' by comparing it with radio. He could go on to diminish radio by comparing it with the more substantial newspapers and magazines and, further, diminish *them* by a comparison with longer essays and books. Television's greatest single liability has always been scarcity of space. That crucial factor has led to far too many compromises and sometimes they cannot be defended. Nevertheless a system which, on a single ITV channel, can maintain a weekly strike of the analytical 'Weekend World', the investigative 'World in Action', the roving 'TV-Eye' and the reliable 'News at Ten' with its evening off-shoots and the regional supplements, cannot be dismissed out of hand.

Holroyd distrusts the medium. It is traditional that all new forces are disdained by those whose allegiance is to an established form. In its early days the novel was dismissed as a coarse arriviste; so was the cinema. But the truth is that the medium is not as important as what is said through it. On television I have seen plays, documentaries and comic programmes which have stayed with me as long as many contemporary poems, paintings or novels. Television is merely an instrument. There are those who have used it with great skills; to assume that those who have watched it have not been able to discern these skills is both a massive underestimate of the general intelligence and an uncharacteristic act of snobbery on Holroyd's part. Nowhere in his article does he give even the impression that he has considered the achievements of such works as Potter's plays, for example, or of 'Horizon', 'Chronicle', 'Monty Python', etc.

It is as if he has decided to shut his eyes and in the process shut his mind. 'What is bad news for the human being is often good news for television,' he writes. But is television alone in reporting on 'bad' news? Disruption of order is the basis of 'news' in journals, on radio and on television. Why has he singled out television for this fault?

The burden of his case rests on the phrase 'television is the natural enemy of the other arts and has almost overwhelmed them.' Both parts of that statement seem to me demonstrably untrue. 'It has taught us to be impatient,' Holroyd writes. 'We almost want the pictures in our galleries to *move*: want our theatres to fill accustomed slots with television characters.' I don't. I don't know anyone who does. I don't really believe Mr Holroyd does. It is no more than a reductive fantasy masquerading as an argument.

'We use television as Valium,' he claims. No doubt some people do – just as many people read a few pages of a book to 'help them get to sleep'. Some find music 'merely soothing'. But there are those who find music, books and television stimulating. The passive viewer is a derogatory figment of Mr Holroyd's unresearched prejudice. The relationship many people have with television programmes is often far from passive. In a way this comment – with the loaded choice of the word 'Valium' – is not far from that pre-twentieth-century conviction among many educated men that the 'sheeplike masses' should not be given the vote because they were too stupid.

It is true that 'the difference between television and literature is fundamental'. Even admitting, as he seems to, the success of television adaptation of novelists as literary as Henry James, he still has a case. The author's voice, the quintessence of the work, has eluded the grasp even of such a practised and faithful adaptor as John Mortimer with 'Brideshead Revisited'. But that does not mean that television has failed literature. It can be argued, I think, that television plays, over the past 25 years, have produced a body of work which can be compared not unfavourably with the novels, films and stage plays of the period. Indeed several of our finest stage dramatists – Osborne, Pinter, Stoppard, for example – as well as several good novelists – Fay Weldon, William Trevor, Ian McEwan – have delivered for television a quality of work which is not less than their acknowledged quality in their more usual fields.

And with series on painting, on music, on ballet or opera, television again and again has attempted – sometimes successfully, I think – to bring in the traditional arts. Nor can television be justly accused of 'almost overwhelming them'. How has the RSC been overwhelmed by television? Transmission of some of its productions and of documentaries such as the 'Nicholas Nickleby' feature have left the company intact, as far as I can see, with the satisfaction of knowing that its work has reached a larger audience. Were the great galleries 'overwhelmed' by Lord Clark's 'Civilisation'?

It would be disturbing if Mr Holroyd's untypically shallow outburst were to assume the status of accepted intellectual wisdom. If a section of the intellectual community merely throws up its hands and refuses to think or analyse what is good and what is bad about television, then television will be much poorer than it need be. *(17.1.82)*

Revisiting Brideshead
Martin Amis

This buxom new paperback of 'Brideshead Revisited' – now, apparently, 'a major TV serial' – recommends itself on the cover as Evelyn Waugh's 'best-loved' novel. The claim may be accurate, but 'Brideshead' is Waugh's most hated novel too. Equally enthralling and distasteful, it is a problem comedy, like 'Mansfield Park' – worrying, inordinate, self-conscious, a book that steps out of *genre* and never really looks at home with its putative author.

Snobbery is the charge most often levelled against 'Brideshead'; and, at first glance, it is also the least damaging. Modern critics have by now accused practically every pre-modern novelist of pacifism, or collaboration, in the class war. Such objections are often simply anachronistic, telling us more about present-day liberal anxieties than about anything else. But this line won't quite work for 'Brideshead', which squarely identifies egalitarianism as its foe and proceeds to rubbish it accordingly.

Of course, the modern world, 'the age of Hooper', has now arrived, and even the most well-adjusted vandal – the most helpless product of junk food, adult videos and mangled cityscapes – must find plenty that is cheerless in his new surroundings. Yet the present age will be lamented in its turn, like the last. The good is gone, the bad is all to come: this theme is as old as literature. What a writer does with it is simply a matter of style and tone.

The novel is littered with countless, often laughable asides on the Great Falling-Off. One thinks of such moments as the *ubi-sunt* passage on the decline of the English bathroom (where the chrome tap? where the carpet?); the escape from Lady Marchmain's cluttered parlour into the main rooms of Brideshead and 'the august, masculine atmosphere of a better age,' under 'that high and insolent dome'; the painful meal with know-all, know-nothing Rex Mottram in Paris, where the burgundy 'seemed a reminder that the world was an older and better place than Rex knew, that mankind in its long passion had learned another wisdom than his' (Ryder must be a simple soul, by God, to be so elaborately solaced by a glass of wine).

These are minor follies, perhaps, pitiable but innocuous. Try this, though, for authentic hatred of the common man and the common age: 'These men [Lady Marchmain's brothers] must die to make a world for Hooper . . . so that things might be safe for the travelling salesman, with his polygonal pince-nez, his fat wet handshake, his grinning dentures.' Or this, after the disclosure that Rex is a divorcee: 'Round the argument circled and swooped like a gull, now out at sea . . . now right on the patch where the offal floated.' Offal, eh? But then Rex (or 'people of Rex's sort') is someone 'that only this ghastly age could produce,' in Julia Mottram's ringing phrase.

Waugh's snobbery is revealed here as a failure of imagination, an artistic failure; it is stock-response, like sentimentality. This brings us to the second main objection to the book, one that is closely connected, in my view, with the vulgarly romantic version of Catholicism which Waugh chooses to celebrate. There is something bare-faced, even aggressive, in the programmatic way that the novel arranges for its three most unregenerate characters – Sebastian, Lord Marchmain and Julia – to claim the highest spiritual honours. Sebastian, whose life has been impartially dedicated to shiftlessness, whimsy and drink, becomes a holy fool, shuffling among the lepers and sleeping in his 'monk's cell'. Lord Marchmain, who likewise has done nothing in his 70 years but follow his own hackneyed inclinations, snatches salvation in the last second of his existence. 'I've known worse cases make beautiful deaths,' says the priest, rubbing his hands after Marchmain has jeered him from the sick room. And Julia. . . .

For the first two-thirds of the book, Julia doesn't constitute much of a departure from the standard vamp/heartbreaker/scatterbrain of Waugh's fictional women, who are presented as brisk embodiments of philistinism, will and appetite, cynical *in the heart*, above all. Quite what qualifies Julia for her moral jackpot in Book 3 remains unclear. Her roll-call of worldly infamies is dourly stressed – she has her 'vicious' escapade in New York, she 'lives in sin' with Ryder. And yet here is her curious epiphany, a two-page 'tumult of sorrow!' complete with semi-colons and telltale adjectives:

> . . . never the cool sepulchre and the grave clothes spread on the stone slab, never the oil and spices in the dark cave; always the midday sun and the dice clicking for the seamless coat.

Ryder's love for the Marchmains, it would seem, is aroused not only by their noble blood but by their congenital holiness. Whether the reader feels much uplift during Julia's voluble trance is more open to doubt. What the reader senses, I suspect, is the fat wet handshake and grinning dentures of bad art.

Bad art is, of course, a major theme in 'Brideshead Revisited'. The book would be without much of its staying power if Waugh hadn't hedged his bets in this way. Ryder's artistic talent is seen in terms of his infatuation with Brideshead itself – in terms of connoisseurship, of English 'charm'. 'It was an aesthetic education to live within those walls,' says Ryder. 'This was my conversion to the Baroque.'

It was Waugh's conversion too, but to the Baroque in its decadent, bastardised literary form. 'I have been here before': the opening refrain is from Rossetti, and much of the prose reads like a golden treasury of neo-classical clichés: phantoms, soft airs, enchanted gardens, winged hosts – the liturgical rhythms, the epic similes, the wooziness. Waugh's conversion was a temporary one, and never again did he attempt the grand style. Certainly the prose sits oddly with the coldness and contempt at the heart of the novel, and contributes crucially to its central imbalance.

'Most of the reviews have been adulatory except where they were embittered by class resentment,' said Waugh in his 'Diaries' (written while drunk). In his 'Letters' (written while hungover), Waugh refers to 'Brideshead' repeatedly as his 'magnum opus' – 'a very beautiful book', 'my first important book.' In a touching letter to his wife Waugh tenderly scolds Laura for not taking the 'Mag. Op.' seriously enough; it is almost a whimper of neglect. Later he confessed himself 'greatly shaken by its popularity in USA.' 'I re-read "Brideshead Revisited",' he wrote to Graham Greene in 1950, 'and was appalled.'

Perhaps Waugh would regard *this* review as a product of class resentment, the complaint of a Hooper who doesn't know which fork to use, and who says 'Rightyoh' and 'Okeydoke'. I think it unlikely. Waugh wrote 'Brideshead' with great speed, unfamiliar excitement, and a deep conviction of its excellence. Lasting schlock, the really bad good book, cannot be written otherwise. 'The languor of Youth. . . . How quickly, how irrevocably lost!' The novel had its origins in this regret, the more keenly and confusedly felt by someone 'beginning to be old.' But then all this had somehow to be turned into art, and that is where the real trouble started. *(25.10.81)*

James and Nora
Edna O'Brien

James Joyce was the first surviving son of two people for whom marriage was an escalating disaster. His mother died of cancer when he was 21. And though he knew her to be a victim and cursed the system that made her so, he would not ease her dying throes by kneeling.

For the large and motherless family it was a case of flits by moon-light as they moved house again and again to avoid the landlord and bailiff. They lived on credit loans and the sale of anything saleable. Their diet was tea, fried bread and dripping, their arguments fired by hangover, their repartee quick, unaffectionate and bitter.

At that time in Dublin prostitution was carried on as publicly as in Algiers. The clientele were sailors, British Tommy army officers, and privates who went in closed cabs at night. No doubt the brothels did not have the flamboyance or carnival fevers that Joyce later wrote about, but there he found his much-desired abasement. The one Joyce singled out to immortalise in 'Ulysses' was run by Mrs Bella Cohen, whose main ambition in life was to send her son to Oxford.

Yet not there in Rings End Road, permeated with fog, was the essence of his being laid bare. He longed to copulate with a soul. What we long for, it seems, we eventually get. It was June, June the tenth. Barnacle day. Nora Barnacle. He saw her in Nassau Street and they stopped to talk. She thought his blue eyes were those of a Norseman. He was twenty-two, she was twenty. A country girl who worked as a chambermaid in an hotel. They made a date and arranged to meet the following day at Number One Merrion Square, outside the house of Sir William Wilde. On that corner Joyce had the dubious advantage of being able to see in four different directions, of being able to catch sight of her either walking towards him or alighting from a tram. We all know the trepidation, the ingrained despairingness of these waits. He was no exception. She did not show up.

He wrote to her that night and said that he had looked for a long time at a crop of reddish brown hair and had to concede that it was not hers. Might they have another appointment? His tone was light but no doubt his intention determined. In this jaunty, fairly illiterate girl, whose plumpness might have appealed to Rubens, Joyce was to seek and find the earth mother, dark, formless, made beautiful in moonlight. Joyce was a Dubliner, Nora was from Galway. She was to bring in her jingles, her stories, the echoes of her ancestry, the other half of Ireland – soil, gloom, moon-grey nettles and muttering rain.

He tried to be her, to know her as she had been in her convent days in Galway when the Sisters of Mercy prepared her for First Holy Com-munion; her scallywagging days when she and her friends made dates with a man in the church and then devoured the box of chocolates he had given them. Nothing was to be kept from him. In her company he left aside his jeering contemptuous nature.

For entertainment they walked. They could not afford to do any-thing else. Yet he was not blind to what he saw – the watchtowers, the murmuring waters, the fishful stream, and the empathy of the mighty dead. He was not to assign it to paper until long after he saw and noted it all.

She wrote to say that in his company she always felt herself to *be*, her spirit took leave of her body in sleep, and the loneliness which she felt in his absence faded away in his presence. Joyce, who scrutinised every living thing, recognised at once that these were not the words of a girl who invoked charms and made beds and emptied chamber pots for a living. He guessed rightly. She had copied the letter from a book of etiquette of the time. Possibly he loved her even more – God becomes man becomes fish becomes barnacle goose becomes feather bed mountain Nora.

Joyce applied for a teaching post in Zurich in a Berlitz school and was accepted. It was then his cadging began in earnest and he asked a friend, Starkey, to get from his father's shop one toothbrush and powder, a nail brush, a pair of boots, a coat and a vest.

When they set out from the docks on their clandestine adventure it was shrouded in secrecy and possibly dread. When they arrived in Zurich there was no vacancy, and so they went to Trieste where there was none either, and finally they settled in the naval town of Pola. Soon a letter to his brother Stanislaus tells how Nora is lonely whenever he is away, and how her boot pinches.

He earned two pounds a week by teaching English, mostly to officers of the Austrian Navy. He looked forward to the day when he could get a new suit and have his teeth fixed. They rose at nine and partook of chocolate. They lunched in a locanda opposite, surprisingly had dinner at eight, and then on to a café to read the French newspapers. Very soon Nora became pregnant. They quarrelled, but then they would make up.

There was a less sunny side to her. There was the helpless exile who lay in a dark room and cried. She was afraid to go out into the street without him, for fear of being insulted. She spoke 30 words of Triestine dialect, could not learn French and disliked Italian cooking, thinking it too sloppy. The Director of the Berlitz School said, upon meeting her, that she was not worthy of Joyce.

They spent nights of horrible melancholy, one of which she salvaged for him by quoting a line of his poetry – 'O sweetheart hear you your lover's tale.' She had misquoted it but her very utterance had miraculously revived his flagging belief in himself as a poet. Also, their estrangements were a spur to their lusts.

They had reckoned that their first child was due in August but, not surprisingly, they had miscalculated the event. Joyce was about to go bathing when Nora was struck down with a pain that seemed remarkably like indigestion. Their landlady summoned the midwife. Six hours later, when he heard that he had a son and heir, he took it in his arms, hummed operatic airs to it and predicted that it would have the singing voice of its father and its grandfather. This was a hope that he never forsook.

Years after, James Joyce believed that a mysterious malady had caught hold of his children when they were very young. In fact, he believed that he and his wife had not loved them enough. In a sense they were still massively in a state of love with each other. Joyce was only 24 and caught up in the double exhaustion of teaching and writing. His wife and he were still physically besotted. But poor.

They moved to Rome, where Joyce had taken a position in a bank, a task to which he was constitutionally alien and unsuited. Bethelemites was how he termed them. There was not a day that they were not in search of a room, in search of an inn, in search of a meal, in search of a pupil. He was fond of his son, he said, but his own spiritual barque was on the rocks.

He would rage and call on God to change his luck. He would stay too long in the tavern and come home to a disgruntled wife, flapping like a rag in a breeze. He said he would not be surprised if she didn't unload a second male child for the dynasty. Genius and parenthood make bad bedfellows.

When they looked for lodgings they would be turned away because of having a small child. Nora would wait first in a café and then in a cinema while he arrived late at night with the money just received for the private lesson. They would have dinner and then search for a room where the tariff suited their means.

They slept head to toe to avoid the risk of future Joyces. The next morning he would go to the bank, Nora and the boy, Georgio, would vacate the room at noon, go to the cinema and re-wait in a café for him to arrive with the money from the private lesson so that they could do the exact same thing.

If only she had kept a diary. Of what was she thinking? Her loneliness? Galway? Her family? Their future? She even delivered a complaining letter to him at his bank, but all he could do was blow his nose in it. Sealed in a world of intellect and language, he could imagine what he did not have, but for her there was no such outlet and there was no money, no girlfriends, no chatter and no clothes.

His dislike of Rome caused him to hand in his resignation in a burst of pique. He toyed with the idea of going to Marseilles except that he did not have the money for the postage stamp to apply for a position there. Despite sleeping head to foot, Nora had again conceived. So it was back to Trieste. He taught, he wrote articles and soon he fell ill with rheumatic fever. This he believed he contracted from his many encounters with the gutter. First we feel, then we fall.

While he was in one wing of the hospital, his daughter was born in the Paupers' ward and he insisted that she be named Lucia after the Patron Saint of eyes. When Nora was discharged from the hospital she came home to a small flat, a noisy son, an overworked brother-in-law and her own depleted self. Not the stuff of heady love.

Writers are a scourge to those they cohabit with. They are present and at the same time they are absent. They are present by the fact of their continuing curiosity, their observing, their cataloguing minds, their longing to see into another person. But the longing is discharged into the work.

The photographs of Nora with her growing children show us a solemn woman with an unreadiness to smile. She loved clothes and he indulged her in this, but clothes are a poor substitute for the first flush of undivided attention. Most of his time was spent in a semi-dark room with a rhyming dictionary, maps, street directories of Dublin, different coloured pencils, engrossed like a sizar and lost to the outside world.

Yet for all his scathingness and despite his unremitting intellect, Mr Joyce was a romantic when it came to women. It is said that he made two jaunts into clandestinity. One with a pupil, Amalia Popper, a daughter of a Jewish merchant, and the other with Marthe Fleischmann, an aristocrat, a pagan Mary, the very antithesis of his robust Nora. But neither wrenched him from the family hearth. His intense, obsessive, solicitous overlove had transferred itself to his children, particularly to his daughter, Lucia, who resented her mother.

Mr Joyce and his wife are said to have sexually – though not of course emotionally – severed when she was 39. Her third child, born prematurely, had died and that had taken the revelry out of sex. Her daughter was her replacement. The mother – seeing, resenting and having to accept – 'You're changing accooshla, you're changing from me. Or is it me is . . . A way, a lone, at last, a loved a long a.'

By the time he wrote that, he had already repudiated love and said that when he heard the word love he felt like puking. His repudiation was a gigantic bitter and perverse leap, but it was inevitable. It has in it all the trademarks of the sons and daughters of the Roman Catholic Church.

The Joyces moved to Switzerland at the outbreak of the Second World War. Shortly after he was taken ill, and with a body writhing like a fish he was brought to hospital. Upon operating it was found that he had had a duodenal ulcer for several years. He asked that his wife's bed be put next to his, but the request was refused. Mother and son were sent home and that night Joyce died.

Nora survived him by a long number of years, but when she died there was no room on the hill next to him in the Fluntern. The blunders that attended their elopement, the births of their children and all their wanderings had not forsaken them in death. *(24.1.82)*

Guys and Dolls at the National
Robert Cushman

It is about time the National Theatre got round to staging the real classics; and having finally taken the plunge with 'Guys and Dolls' (Olivier) they have surfaced with a production that for sheer brazen pleasure is unequalled in London. They have done the show proud; but then it has done the same for them.

The show has the primary mark of a post-war musical: a story that the authors obviously believe is worth telling, and to which all other elements of the show are subservient; on this level it is the tightest job of its time.

What sets apart Abe Burrows's book and Frank Loesser's score is a total lack of solemnity; in spirit and setting the show returns us to the raffish, unbuttoned New York musicals of the Thirties. It is the closest Broadway has ever come to getting the best of both worlds.

Damon Runyon mythologised the seediness of Times Square and district in his prose, just as Cole Porter and Lorenz Hart did in their lyrics. It is indeed amazing that nobody thought earlier of turning one of his stories into a musical. But there is a little difficulty here. This Runyon is a joy to read, and there are some other scribes who take a delight in imitating his style as soon as they are asked or maybe sooner. But when he sells his stories to the movies the flow of the narrative is much hindered by his loquacity and the pictures are generally stinkers; and while Damon is content to take the money, it causes his friends no little grief.

But this Abe Burrows is a smart guy, and though he allows himself one paragraph of strict Runyonese (rather screwed up in the National production), he generally sticks to quick-fire gag-writing. He offers his own equivalent of Runyon's affected innocence; when Nathan Detroit satirically announces that he will hold his floating crapgame in Radio City Music Hall, Benny Southstreet faithfully inquires, 'how you gonna fix the ushers?'

The show is, besides, beautifully, indeed classically structured, with the crap-shooters looking forward to their game, the Save-a-Soul missionaries to a make-or-break prayer meeting, and the fate of both gatherings hingeing on the bet made by gambler Sky Masterson to take mission sergeant Sarah Brown on a date to Havana.

Meanwhile Loesser's lyrics preserve spirit and style. You know you are home when in the opening 'Fugue for Tinhorns' Nicely-Nicely Johnson sings of his favoured racehorse, 'I tell you Paul Revere – now this is no bum steer – It's from a handicapper that's real sincere.' The triple rhyme gratifies the ear; the juxtaposition of the slang 'bum steer' with the orotund 'sincere' is in the best traditions of both Runyon and Broadway. For the comic short story and the theatre lyric live under the same threat: one false word and both are dead.

Obviously the National production offers the attraction of straight actors essaying song-and-dance. But this only becomes blatant in a tap routine occupying a limbo between closing number and curtain-call. Otherwise we are constantly aware that these are *British* actors; but that is a bonus. Cast and audience conspire together to animate a myth with which both are familiar, but to which neither is native.

And Richard Eyre's direction has the subsidised theatrical virtue of respect for the text. There are no crass modernisations; it is not only the comic dialogue that is cherished here; the first encounter between Sky and Sarah yields real tension.

Julie Covington sings beautifully as Sarah, but could afford to be, literally, more-out-front; Ian Charleson delivers a gutsy 'Luck Be a Lady', but does not justify the awe in which Sky is held by his fellow high-rollers.

Bob Hoskins's Nathan is superbly vulnerable, notably when hoisted shoulder-high by a couple of dancing admirers. It is a shame he is starved of songs. (Actors who sing as badly as Sam Levene, the original Nathan, are hard to come by.) He is the evening's linchpin; its star is Julia McKenzie as Adelaide, 'the well-known fiancée,' a paragon of put-upon-poise; her delivery of the glorious Lament ('a person could develop a cold') sets the show unshakably on its feet. Hers are the funniest numbers, and the most touching.

Bill Paterson's Harry the Horse has the weirdest accent I have ever heard, but he also has a sinister jack-knifed walk like Eagle Eye Fleagle in 'Li'l Abner'. This brings me to David Toguri's choreography which, after an overly studied opening montage, gets steadily better, progressing through the Havana and crap-game ballets to a staging of 'Sit Down, You're Rockin' the Boat' that, to judge from the photographs, improves on the original, and in which David Healy's Nicely-Nicely justifies his encores.

John Gunter has designed a wonderful surround of shopfronts, neon ads, scrapered skyline and – my special delight – a real solid subway entrance. Two final thoughts. A crucial difference between Runyon's hoods and those of the show is that you always believe the former capable of real mayhem, but never the latter. This was only Loesser's second theatre score, but how strongly even a conventional ballad like 'I've Never Been in Love Before' takes the stage. There are 16 songs in the score and, dramatically at least, 16 hits.

Eric Bentley once wrote that as a piece of art 'Guys and Dolls' far surpasses Broadway's efforts to be artistic, and Lillian Hellman's 'The Little Foxes' is at the Victoria Palace to prove the point. It seems unfair, since Miss Hellman made a far better showing in front of the Un-American Activities Committee than Mr Burrows, but her melo-drama of Deep Southern greed is now very dead indeed, and this production – in the dying-fall manner deemed appropriate by Amer-icans to a native classic – embalms it.

But such criticisms are probably irrelevant. The audience come to see a star: not to see her act but just to see her. Elizabeth Taylor's performance hardly carries into the auditorium. The first night, for which many citizens in penguin suits shell out £25-notes each and which has the gendarmes out with barricades, is as grisly as an undertaker's picnic, and maybe grislier. *(14.3.82)*

A Twinkling Superstar
Sue Arnold

The delicate problem of overmanning in Fleet Street might well have been solved last week when Miss Elizabeth Taylor, the film actress, held a press conference.

A high percentage of the 300 hacks who converged on the London Palladium to witness the historic event fell in active service while attempting to storm the Cinderella Bar.

Miss Taylor, who was 50 yesterday, is over here to appear in her first West End play, 'The Little Foxes' by Lillian Hellman.

The conference was less theatrical than zoological. Bear garden, lion's den, snakepit and bunfight were phrases that sprang to mind as a herd of crazed cameramen shooting from the hip, the head, and in some desperate cases the heel, trampled through a jungle of rent-a-plant shouting 'Miss Taylor, over here!' from the quality press and 'Come on, Liz, give us a twinkle!' from the tabloids.

Miss Taylor twinkled. With all that hardware strapped to her neck, wrists, fingers and ears, she could hardly do anything else.

On the third finger of her left hand a diamond as big as a gob-stopper out-twinkled the rest of her tackle, but it was not, hissed an American female snapper clawing at my back, the famous Burton diamond. This remains in its Washington bank vault because it is too heavy to wear.

Those of the press who made it to the bar were rewarded by the sight of the actress in burgundy suede sitting behind a balustrade draped with royal purple and more hired foliage. Then, quite suddenly, after all the initial frenzy the hard-nosed news hounds became shy.

It was understandable. We were, after all, in the presence of a living legend. Here she was, at arm's length, Elizabeth Taylor – movie queen, megawoman, one-time child star, two Hollywood Oscars, three face-lifts, four decades in show business, five bodyguards, six husbands, seven marriages.

It all added up to a package as awe-inspiring as Cleopatra, Joan of Arc and the Dagenham Girl Pipers. And she is still ravishingly beautiful.

The ping-pong began. Was she nervous about her first London show? Of course. Would Mr Burton be coming to see the play? No comment. Why did she always wear purple? Why not. What advice would she give to other 50-year-olds? Enjoy. Would she do it all over again? Sure.

An Israeli reporter raised the intellectual tone. 'Miss Taylor,' he said. 'Would you agree with Raquel Welch, who once said that comparing films to theatre was like comparing industry to art?' Stunned silence both sides of the net. It was probably the first time any of us had realised that Raquel could speak, let alone compare.

It was over. The bodyguards moved in to hustle Miss Taylor through the media mob inside and the public mob outside to her waiting limo. Hacks with stamina and elbows to spare raced after her.

'This isn't theatre,' said an American reporter, unpinning himself from a wall. 'This is rock 'n' roll.' *(28.2.82)*

Reassessing Sutherland
William Feaver

Douglas Cooper's assertion that 'Graham Sutherland is the most distinguished and the most original English artist of the mid-twentieth century' raised hackles in 1961, and not just because the notoriously combative Douglas Cooper said so. Sutherland's fame was then at its height: the Churchill portrait was widely remembered, and the Coventry Cathedral tapestry, still being woven, was in the news. He had recently been awarded the OM. His reputation, though, was already over the hill.

The time has now come, two years after his death, to work out what happened – what went wrong – and to try and get Sutherland's distinction and originality into perspective.

Obviously the Sutherland memorial exhibition at the Tate is the ideal opportunity for reassessment.

It demonstrates throughout the graphic qualities of his art, the arresting colour-schemes, the heavy shadows lying like forelocks across remote places, the treatment of people and things as either basking or transfixed. Sutherland wasn't versatile. He relied on shock tactics to see him through. He played on universal fears: fear of the needle and the sting, fear of solitary confinement, fear of the dark. The technical draughtsman in him kept any tendency to go soft or wild or overtly passionate in check. Numbering off and squaring up, he turned *frissons* into set-pieces.

Sutherland was, if anything, over-anxious and therefore over-deliberate; at his best not in a crisis, when he responded with stock-horror (crowns of thorns for every occasion), but in circumstances where things seemed to conspire to stir his curiosity. He had a prowler's instincts. Hence the fascination with clefts and hollows, with screens and lairs, with the next bend in the lane. He kept exploring the same haunts, always reverting, when at a loss, to the same old themes.

'The Black Rabbit', for example, one of his first etchings, done in 1923, a few months before he discovered the joys of Samuel Palmer, shows a road near Arundel curving away to the right among bulky trees. Twelve years later, in South Wales, he repeated the composition: Arundel with a Shoreham accent transposed to Porthclais, Sutherland's Valley of Vision. And 40 years after that he went back to these, his origins, searching through the sketchbooks, making an imaginative leap back to the same spot overlooking the same bend.

Sutherland's portraits, his thorn heads and boulders, are interchangeable. That is, they all have a caged look. The sitters are shoved up against the lattice or stuck on their perches; they have hard, fissured faces and the twinkle in the eye is simply the reflection of the interrogator's spotlight. A toad raises one leg and its orange eye gleams.

In the portrait category some significant works are missing: the Churchill, of course, and, less well-known though it met the same fate, Sutherland's painting of Douglas Cooper, destroyed apparently in 1975 when the friendship came to an abrupt end. No Lord Beaverbrook either and no heads of industry. Two of his last, and previously unexhibited, portraits, however, have been included: Mrs Emery Reves, treated in a curiously bedraggled manner, and the 13th Earl of Airlie, sporting a kilt and looking as though he has been landed with a walk-on role in Harry Lauder Night at the Glasgow Empire. This spectacularly bad painting can be regarded as a sort of classic: the worst Graham Sutherland ever, crudely drawn, clumsily assembled and, above all, niggly.

So it's back to the early period for respite, particularly to the Welsh hills. Sutherland's lyricism, fitful though it was, found expression in scenes of sunset desolation. Before the war, in the period when, hard on the heels of Paul Nash, he cultivated 'the element of the accident and the accidental encounter', he achieved lightness of touch. Paintings like 'Gorse on Sea Wall' and 'Entrance to a Lane' have a genuine sense of drama. Colour is used to tinge, not to overstress; shadows define the forms instead of covering up for them.

Sutherland worked as an Official War Artist for long periods between 1940 and 1945. The Tate selection concentrates on his more finished works, among them views of bombed-out terrace-houses, charred rolls of newsprint and drawings of steel-workers tending vats and furnaces. A large collection of his war drawings, however, is being shown at the Imperial War Museum. These are Sutherland's intimacies, notes made of torn buildings, rafters laid bare like ribs, of tangled girders, mountainous spoil heaps. The war took him to places beyond everyday experience, down the Cornish tin mines, into deep recesses where men scrambled and delved like a lost species burrowing nowhere.

Re-emerging, free to travel, for the first time, to France, Sutherland drew wrecked railway engines and abandoned flying-bomb stores. The war ended and, back in fully civilian life, he found himself, along with Bacon and Moore, a leading artist in his generation. Hopes were pinned on him. He undertook increasingly difficult commissions.

The first of these, the 'Crucifixion' for St Matthew's, Northampton, was praised at the time for being strikingly contemporary and relevant to the age of Auschwitz. Removed from its church setting and hung on its own at the Tate, occupying a whole wall, it doesn't hold up too well. The influences of Grünewald and Bacon are so strong it's impossible to regard the painting as anything but a grim attempt at a grand manner.

Sutherland's next whopper, 'The Origins of the Land', painting as a symbolic adornment for the Festival of Britain, contains the seeds and pods of all his later developments. Incubation has reached an advanced stage. Flames spurt at the base of the yolky yellow canvas, forms are splitting open, beaks gape, hills erupt and a pterodactyl soars, mad-eyed, like a society hostess desperate to get her portrait painted.

Sutherland thrived in the Fifties. His derationed, delicatessen, sunshine and espadrille imagery, his Triffid-girt pergolas, his air of not-too-stark modernity, were just the job in a Britain where Picasso was still considered the last word in daring. On Jennie Lee's suggestion, an all-party committee of MPs commissioned the Churchill portrait.

If there was a single moment of truth in Sutherland's career it wasn't when that work was unveiled, in 1954, but 20 years ago exactly, in May 1962, when the new Coventry Cathedral was consecrated. Sutherland himself wasn't present to see his Christ in Majesty revealed to the public; every fault blown up out of all proportion in the world's largest tapestry.

The design looks much better in cartoon form, as shown at the Tate; less cramped and vapid and without the wrinkled green immensity. But then Sutherland always was better in miniature; or, to be precise, on a 5,000-times-smaller scale. His optimum size, this exhibition proves, was about 10 inches by nine, the size of his unused design for a George V 7d. postage stamp, the size of a sketchbook page. *(23.5.82)*

An American Comedy
D. M. Thomas

Saturday 16 January. Arriving in blizzard-numbed, disaster-prone Washington, I wait in the passport queue behind a boiler-suited delegation of Chinese. After 15 hours by train and plane, I'm exhausted and hungry. The head of the Literature Department at American University greets me warmly, and drives me to the apartment block where I'm to live. Once he's unlocked us, with three keys, into my apartment, he shows me the fridge they've kindly stocked with groceries; gives me directions on how to find the university on Monday morning; says, 'Well, I guess you're tired,' and leaves. Since I don't fancy trudging out through darkness and snow to search for a restaurant, I make tea, toast a crumpet, and crawl into bed.

Sunday. Jet-lagged, I wake at 4 a.m. I smoke a cigarette, and wonder what I'm doing here. Eight months ago, when I was invited to be a visiting professor for the spring semester, it seemed like a good idea. At home, in Hereford, I'd been made redundant as an English lecturer: the colleges I applied to, including Hereford's sister college at Worcester, didn't seem to think I could offer them anything: yet here was an American university – no, damn it, *the* American University – ringing me up all the way from Washington begging me to come! Injured pride, if nothing else, said accept. But now, in the middle of the night, I wonder why I'm here. I develop a fear that I'll fall suddenly ill; no one has given me their home telephone number, and I'm not sure if 999 summons an ambulance in the States.

With the morning, I unpack, gaze out at a frozen road and another apartment block. It's preternaturally silent. When they'd rung to offer me the apartment, they told me the block was postgraduate accommodation; I had Oxbridge dreams of noisy parties to which I'd been invited; of students popping their heads round my door at all hours, saying, 'Don, there's a cup of coffee brewing.' But no. You need three keys to get into any apartment. For signs of life, I am grateful to the cockroaches that dart about the sink.

The day is saved by Brigitte Weeks, book editor of the *Washington Post*. When she found out I was coming to the city, she offered to put on a reception. She collects me in the evening in her car, and drives me to her civilised, friendly house. I enjoy her food, her drink, her log fire, and meeting her thoughtfully chosen guests. Someone hands me a note from John Irving, welcoming me to America. That, too, is heartwarming, and I ask for his address, so I can thank him.

Monday I venture out, get lost, eventually find the University Literature Department, up a hill. I'm greeted by friendliness and a mass of phone messages, from people who would like me to do this or that. I see that my time is going to be fully employed, since – unwisely perhaps – I have accepted reading engagements all over America, at weekends. Thank God, though, that I've finished my new novel.

I waffle a good deal in my first meeting with the Modern British Literature class. I should have prepared it better. After a four-year lay-off, it's strange to be teaching again; nor am I quite a teacher, but in the students' curious eyes a visiting 'celebrity'. This makes me uncomfortable. My words assume a hollow, portentous air, as if someone else is speaking.

Back at the apartment-block, I find I've lost one of my precious keys. Panic. I knock on a neighbour's door. He opens the door an inch. I explain my predicament. He tells me where I can find the student-janitor. I knock up the janitor, a black American. In the elevator he says, 'If you need the exterminator, let me know.' I reply: 'I probably will.'

Tuesday. My hour with my postgraduate Writing class is the most enjoyable and rewarding yet. They are gracious, welcoming, good-humoured, bright. They seem to come from all over the world. I talk about 'The White Hotel' for a while, answering their questions, then read and discuss a poem about a suicide. Eagerly they accept my challenge to write something inspired by postcards of paintings that I give them. I have a drink in a bar with a few of them.

I return to the apartment, feeling much more cheerful. My colleagues, including the Head of Department (who is only anxious not to invade my time too much) have also been kind: offering me a radio, a portable TV, hospitality. I've accepted all their invitations, needing company, yet aware that my time for writing is further eroded. And now, late at night, pacing the apartment, I realise my novel isn't finished after all. It needs a lot more work. I haven't even brought the typescript with me.

Wednesday. Kurt Suplee of the *Washington Post* interviews me for three hours. He shows me the five covers Pocket Books have chosen for their paperback editions of 'The White Hotel', and I wince at four of them. But he is taken aback at the delight I show at their publicity key-rings! I take one, as a child grabs a toy, and he grins. Well, I need it so I don't lock myself out again. . . .

After the interview I go up to the Department, even though I haven't a class. I feel agitated; there are still more phone-memos, which in desperation I bury in a drawer. Walking around the snow-bound campus, I feel isolated and exposed – a sham, a shaman, a showman. I feel about 70, a visiting Frost. I've even developed a stoop. I'm a 'successful author', and it gives me the horrors. I shan't be able to write a word while I'm here.

Thursday. Yeats with my Modern British Literature class. Just about my favourite poet, and I think I teach him with a little passion, throwing myself into a performance of 'Purgatory'. I don't seem to break through, however. It's perhaps because I'm a museum specimen to them. 'You should see our museums,' they keep telling me. Why doesn't someone say, 'We know this great nightclub we'll take you to'? Because they think I'm a Man of Letters, beyond such trivia. . . . Still, I'm only here for four months, with a two-week break back home in the middle. I'll survive.

Friday. I awake, with the instant knowledge that I'm going to pack it in, do a bunk. Save myself. Become the unsuccessful author of my next book. I get up quickly and pace around, horrified and joyful at my nocturnal decision. *Out, out!* as a Frost poem has it. I'll go to New York to meet my editors and give a lecture I promised – then home to England. I spend the day writing remorseful letters of resignation. Guilt-ridden, I still roar with laughter as I mistype 'mindless' for 'kindness' – I have drunk a lot of bourbon. The publicity director of Pocket Books rings up with a suggested extra promotion. Wanting the university to hear first, I stall her: can I see her in New York on Monday? Sensing that she senses what I'm going to do and sees all their promotional plans coming to nothing, I tell her don't worry and she says OK, obviously worried.

Saturday. I post my letters, the die is cast. In the spacious tundra of Washington – how masculine it is in the snow, like Petersburg without Pushkin – I slither, frozen, from a car to my solitary piece of 'sight-seeing' of the whole 'semester': a glimpse of Lincoln, before the biting wind forces me back to the car.

Sunday. Having left my keys in the locked apartment, I go by train to New York. At Penn Station I bump into the novelist Susan Shreve, whom I'd met at Brigitte Weeks's party. She must have travelled by the same train. She is startled: I'm to have dinner with her and some friends on Tuesday. 'Are you coming back tomorrow?' she inquires; I say 'Yes,' and try to hide my two suitcases. I go to ground with an Armenian friend in the Bronx. From his apartment balcony I can just see Manhattan. The river and the graceful curves of skyscrapers seem wonderfully feminine.

Monday. Meet the Pocket Books director for lunch and break the news. She says, 'I'm not surprised.' I assure her I'll come back later for a short period, if she can re-schedule the promotions. She is relieved and understanding: offers the comfort of a hotel. Feeling like a secret agent – which is what writers are – I slink into the St Regis hotel.

Tuesday. I rest, waiting for the storm.

Wednesday. My birthday; and my present is the *Washington Post* profile and scoop together: 'The Flight of D. M. Thomas'. The book covers and key-rings are blamed. Suplee quotes my anecdote of a Cornish ancestor who brought his family to New York, took one look and sailed home on the same ship. Maybe it runs in the family, he suggests. I smile: it's well-deserved. It appears that in desperation I asked for John Irving's phone-number, in order to ask him how to cope with media attention . . . another distortion I hear about (not in the profile) is that my students, when I don't turn up for class, recall my poem about suicide, and rush to my apartment-block to break into my room.

Thursday. I attend the National Book Award at the New York Public Library. Of the winning novel, the adjudicator, through a blurred loudspeaker, proclaims: 'This is where we live. This is who we are.' 'They're awarding it to the telephone directory,' I say to Susan Ginsburg of Pocket Books. She chuckles, but I roar with laughter at my own joke. I realise, suddenly, it's the first joke I've cracked since arriving in Washington. It's a sign of recovered health. I know that my decision, though I've let down my students, was right. Others, too, offer me undeserved congratulations. In the night, I'm awakened by what seems like a Mafia war breaking out: explosions, gunfire. I lie dazed, untroubled, believing it to be a thunderstorm, stressed and made strange by the skyscrapers. But the war grows louder. I get up and look out. The skyscraper across the way is on fire. I almost expect falling bodies, but thank God it turns out to be empty.

Friday. A talk on Freud, to the Bronx Institute of Psychiatry – as a gypsy astrologer might lecture to the Royal Astronomical Association. But it goes down well.

Sunday, 31 January. I fly home. England, its snows gone, looks kindly and homely.

Friday, 2 April. I re-enter Washington. The weather is sunny, the promised cherry-blossom is out, and the city looks beautiful. I give the first of my re-scheduled readings at Glen Echo, a former Amusement Park, and feel an undeserved warmth in the audience. I fear keeling over after five minutes, but I complete the reading. Some of my former students are among those who shake my hand afterwards. I wince with embarrassment, but they speak generous, forgiving words. One of them gives me back a postcard. All say they learnt something from my brief appearance among them; but they don't say what. And I re-learn from their faces – though I never quite forgot it – the generosity of youth, and of America. *(2.5.82)*

The Making of a Composer
Gillian Widdicombe

With most composers one can only guess at the beginning of the creative process, but with William Walton one can actually see why and how a pale, blue-eyed choirboy became a composer. Both his parents were singers – his mother a mezzo-soprano, his father a baritone – and singing lessons filled the Victorian redbrick terrace house in Oldham.

William, the second of four children, was no young Mozart; for years the Waltons considered Noel, his elder brother, much brighter and more musical than William; Noel was sent to the grammar school, became a music teacher and spent the rest of his life in Oldham. William apparently suffered from a lack of muscular co-ordination and, no matter how hard he tried, he could never organise fingers, wrists, arms and brain so that the right notes went down at the right time.

Their father obliged Noel and William to sing as trebles in his local choir; musical discipline was rapped into William at a very early age. He was intimidated by his father, particularly when strong liquor and professional failure generated a bitter and violent temper. Charles Walton never believed that William had any musical talent and died before the extent of it was proved.

An advertisement in the local paper changed William's fate. 'Christ Church Cathedral, Oxford . . . Sons of clergy or professional men . . . Exceptional opportunity for good preparatory education at £25 per annum. No fees on becoming choristers in due course.' With two more children beginning to over-crowd the small terraced house, and William obviously doing badly at a rough local school, it seemed a golden opportunity – though neither of the Walton parents had any idea what going to Oxford would mean to William.

In September 1912 the 10-year-old boy arrived for his first term at Christ Church Cathedral Choir School. He had already been to Oxford, with his mother, for a hasty audition; but this time they were able to explore the noble college buildings in grey and golden stone, the unexpected lawns, the celebrated spires, cupolas and pinnacles. William was overwhelmed by the beauty of Oxford. The first term was hell until he had lost his Lancashire accent, but the choir school was a happy little family of some 30 boys, presided over by a benevolent clergyman.

He dreaded the day when his voice would break. There was no way William could be sent to public school. He would have to return to a local school in Oldham, then leave as soon as possible and assist the family income, probably by working in a cotton mill. His voice was late to break, so the cruel day was somewhat delayed, giving him time to wonder how best to circumvent his fate. The trouble was, he was still unable to play two notes together.

But he loved the choir work; and when he eventually became head chorister the cathedral and its music became the passion of his life. The letters he wrote to his mother every Sunday turned into proud lists of the services and anthems they had done and the solos he had sung. 'I had a solo in Stainer in E flat . . . the solo in Garrett in D . . . in "God of my Righteousness" by Greene. . . . We are having "Praise the Lord" by Wesley. I have got three out of the four solos! I had a solo in Arnold in F. . . . We are having "When Jesus was born", Mendelssohn . . .'

It was in this atmosphere that Walton began to compose, quickly finding that his highly developed musical ear could at last be expressed in an 'interesting' way. There was no provision, in the small choir school, for teaching composition.

William was encouraged, but not taught. He would sit at his desk, dash something off in pencil, tuck it out of sight, then return to it, again and again, and eventually make a fair copy in ink (usually a clumsy, splodgy business), which he would present to Henry Ley, the young, jolly organist and choirmaster of Christ Church Cathedral. Ley would play the piece through and make helpful comments; sometimes he would misread the ink splodges and remark, 'That doesn't sound very nice,' only to be admonished by the composer, 'But, Sir, that's not what I wrote.'

Most of these early pieces were obvious imitations of the cathedral music that formed his daily diet; and those that have survived have a sense of fluency even when they break all rules. By the time he began to be told what the rules were, he had already found a natural and original musical language of his own, using the added seventh, the distorted cadence or the irregular rhythm without fear. The fact that he could not hope to play the end-result himself saved him from inhibition. He relied on his ear and his cathedral experience, and then added a personal flourish of deliberate imagination.

The best of all these juvenile works (and the only one Walton preserved) was a setting of a religious poem by Phineas Fletcher, 'Drop, drop, slow tears', obviously composed after the choir had sung the famous setting by Orlando Gibbons during Lent in 1917. Christ Church lore maintained that the Dean, a distinguished amateur musician, had probably helped with it. But pencil parts, obviously made for the choristers while William was still at the choir school, prove beyond doubt that by the age of 15 he was capable of a mature and beautiful work, expertly written for voices.

Instrumental music came less easily. But there was a first attempt at opera, after his father had taken him to a performance of 'Tosca' given in Manchester by the Beecham Opera Company. Back at Oxford, Walton composed his own 20-minute 'Tosca', complete with rudimentary set and costumes.

The Dean was quick to realise that Walton was trying to do something interesting and had a good chance of succeeding. He arranged for Walton to stay on for an extra year at the choir school after his voice had broken and have harmony and counterpoint lessons free of charge with members of the music faculty. Dean Strong was interested in musical adventure and experiment, and it was he, rather than Henry Ley, the dons or Walton's family, who opened the teenage boy's ears to composers such as Debussy, Stravinsky, even Schoenberg.

There was a close link between Oxford and the Royal College of Music during those years. Sir Hubert Parry had been professor at the university and head of the RCM simultaneously; and so was his successor, Hugh Allen, who also took an interest in Walton's earliest compositions, though he did not think much of them. The Dean obviously hoped that Walton would be able to go directly from the choir school to the RCM; if only he could play a musical instrument, it would have been simple.

Alas, the only thing that Walton could do, or wanted to do, seemed to be composing, and he made remarkable progress through the early stages of a Mus. Bach. When war ended in 1918 the university was in a chaotic situation, so Dean Strong saved Walton from the return to Oldham by squeezing him into Christ Church as an undergraduate.

He must have known that Walton would never be able to muster the academic requirements and would inevitably be sent down – he had not made much of a showing in the Oxford Senior exams and subjects such as Greek and algebra were obviously beyond him. But the ploy worked. By the time he was sent down he had become an honorary member of the Sitwell family, in whose Chelsea attic he lived for some 14 years.

The Sitwells believed he was a genius in need of a patron: Walton spent the next 20 years doing his best to fulfil that expectation. He continued to absorb and make use of the music around him – from Debussy, Stravinsky and Sibelius to jazz and Gershwin; he continued to rewrite and abandon things that didn't sound right and tuck ideas away in his desk when they got stuck. Such habits had become an essential part of his creative technique. Without them, there would not, I think, be such a heartfelt and widespread celebration of his eightieth birthday. *(28.3.82)*

Last Laugh to Wodehouse
Auberon Waugh

P. G. Wodehouse was born the son of a Hong Kong magistrate and a clergyman's daughter on 15 October, 1881, the same year that Disraeli died and fuzzy-wuzzies rose in revolt under the Mahdi in Sudan. His childhood was spent entirely separated from his parents, being boarded out at various prep schools in Kent and Guernsey and passing the holidays with a terrible regiment of aunts. After Dulwich he had his first and only experience of Work, that terrible fate which all sensible men struggle to avoid, serving two years as bank clerk in the Hong Kong and Shanghai Bank in Lombard Street. Thereafter – he left the bank in 1902 – he lived the quiet, uneventful life of a professional writer.

As it was, he lived through the Russian Revolution and two World Wars, not to mention the uprooting of whole populations, genocide, the collapse of the British Empire and independence of the Third World with its attendant wars, massacres, brutal despotisms and scenes of mass starvation, but he does not seem to have noticed any of these things. One has to search the seventy-odd novels with a tooth comb to find the slightest reference to either World War – although the first one is anticipated in his little-read anti-war farce of 1909, 'The Swoop' – and so far as I can recall there are no references at all to Russia or the Third World.

On one occasion Jeeves is on loan to Lord Towcester, who asks him 'Were you in the First World War, Jeeves?'

'I dabbled in it to a certain extent, m'lord.'

'I missed that one because I wasn't born, but I was in the Commandos in this last one. This is rather like waiting for zero hour, isn't it?'

'The sensation is not dissimilar, m'lord.'

In fact, 'The Return of Jeeves' (published in 1953) is one of the few novels in which Wodehouse shows any awareness of political events or social change. The reason Jeeves is on loan to Lord Towcester is that Wooster has gone to attend a sort of school where gentlemen are prepared for the rigours of the impending social revolution:

> 'An institution designed to teach the aristocracy how to fend for itself, m'lord. Mr Wooster . . . I can hardly mention this without some display of emotion . . . is actually learning to darn his own socks. The course he is taking includes boot-cleaning, sock-darning, bed-making and primary-grade cooking.'

Jeeves never seems to be in any doubt about where he stands in the social revolution. This fish-fed mastermind, his eyes ever shining with the light of pure intelligence, who resembles 'the High Priest of some refined and dignified religion,' even makes a few astute political comments while explaining to an enraged White Hunter why his employer, Lord Towcester, who has been posing as a bookmaker in order to gain enough money to marry his beloved, is unable to pay up on a successful double accumulator at Epsom:

> 'Socialistic legislation has sadly depleted the resources of England's heredit-
> ary aristocracy. We are living now in what is known as the Welfare State,
> which means – broadly – that everybody is completely destitute.'

I have never seriously doubted that Jeeves was, like all the best servants, a left-winger, and probably a member of the Communist Party. And I could make out a very good case for suggesting that there was a homosexual element in the relationship.

Jeeves frequently attends upon his young master in the bath. Perhaps it was normal for valets to do this, but I do not think so. And I know what people would think who saw a bachelor and his valet arrive for the weekend sitting side by side in a two-seater.

Jeeves deliberately wrecks Bertie's chances of marriage – not just once but five or six times. Many of the women in these scenarios were not entirely suitable, it is true, but then how many women are? However, I feel sure that Bertie could have settled down and lived happily with Roberta Wickham, the red-headed practical joker whom Jeeves condemns as too volatile and frivolous, despite her undoubted *espièglerie*. Bobbie has the figure and general comportment of a boy, which might have helped, too. But Jeeves saw to it that when Wooster died – as he must have done, with his creator – he had never known the delights of feminine love.

Time and again Bertram is driven by the machinations of his valet into a sort of whimsical misogyny:

> '. . . the more a thoughtful man has to do with women, the more extraordin-
> ary it seems to him that such a sex should be allowed to clutter the earth.
> Women, the way I looked at it, simply couldn't do. . . . What a crew! What a
> crew! I mean to say, what a *crew*!'

So far as one can judge from his books, Wodehouse had no impure longings of any sort. To say that sex was a complete stranger to him might be thought insulting to a man and his wife married with every appearance of happiness for an enormous number of years; however there is something almost monotonous in the way that so many of his characters come around to the view – usually attributed to

Shakespeare – that a woman is only a woman, but a good cigar is a smoke. We must conclude that whatever part sex may have played in his life – and I hope we never learn – it was not allowed to intrude into his art.

Nor is there any mystery about his politics. There was a memorable passage in his television interview with Malcolm Muggeridge in May 1965 when it seemed that even Muggeridge for once was nonplussed. On religion, Wodehouse had simply said that he did not have any particular thoughts on that subject. Muggeridge mentioned politics. No, he had no time for that sort of thing. Where does the interviewer go from there?

Until a few years ago, I supposed that Wodehouse had successfully spent his life avoiding politicians. Then I was amazed to discover, when reading a history of The Other Club – the small Conservative dining club founded by Churchill for his special cronies – that Wodehouse had been a member of it in the 1930s. Another member was Duff Cooper, a penniless but ambitious Tory MP who shared with Churchill some rather dubious literary aspirations.

One cannot believe that Wodehouse attended many meetings of The Other Club, since he was living for the most part in America, and later in the north of France, throughout this time. But he must have attended a few, and he must have met the two men who were later to persecute him so bitterly. Lady Diana Cooper's biographer, Philip Ziegler, tells us that Cooper was a great admirer of Wodehouse, although I venture to doubt it. At any rate, we know what Wodehouse thought of politicians, and it would be interesting to know what these two men thought of him. Politicians do not, as a rule, take very kindly to anyone with an imperfect appreciation of their own importance. Both these men, as I have pointed out, had literary pretensions, and it was about this time (1934) that Belloc was hailing Wodehouse as 'the best writer of English now alive, the head of my profession.' Not Churchill, nor Cooper, but Wodehouse.

Retribution came in the summer of 1941. At the outbreak of war Wodehouse was living quietly with his wife Ethel at their home in Le Touquet. After the surrender of France he was interned in a camp in Silesia as an enemy alien, since he was still technically a British subject, although he had been an American resident pretty well since 1909. Released a few months before his sixtieth birthday after representations on his behalf from the United States – which was not at war with Germany at that time – he was allowed to stay in the Hotel Adlon, Berlin, where his wife (who had not been interned) was waiting for him.

There he was approached by the Berlin representative of the

American Broadcasting System and asked to make five broadcasts for the American public describing his prison camp experience. This Wodehouse did in all innocence. The broadcasts have been published, and are exactly what one would expect them to be – funny, mildly derisive of German authority and devoid of all political content. But the broadcasts had to go out over the German network, and Wodehouse was guilty of the technical offence of using enemy air waves – as were British prisoners of war who used the German facility for sending messages to their families.

The question of Wodehouse's culpability has been discussed at length by Malcolm Muggeridge who, by one of those freakish coincidences which might have persuaded even Wodehouse that there was Someone Up There looking after him, was the MI6 officer put in charge of his case in Paris at the end of the war. Muggeridge concluded, if I may paraphrase him, not only that Wodehouse was totally blameless of all charges levelled against him at the time, but that Wodehouse himself, by his very nature, added a whole new dimension to the concept of innocence.

However, this was not until the war was over. In the summer of 1941 Cooper, who was on a sticky wicket at the time as the Minister of Information who had sent his son to America, launched a ferocious onslaught against Wodehouse on the BBC, as if he had been broadcasting enemy propaganda. For this purpose he used Bill Connor, better known as Cassandra of the *Daily Mirror*. Many years afterwards, Bill (by then Sir William) Connor told me that he bore no malice towards the old boy, had not been shown the text of his broadcasts and had only Cooper's word for it that they were of a disreputable or treasonous nature. But he still thought Wodehouse was wrong to have made them.

My only authority for asserting that Churchill was behind these attacks is the late A. P. Ryan, who occupied a high position in the BBC at the time and tried to suppress Cassandra's blackguardly attacks. Cooper left him in no doubt that they were strongly supported, even if not originally inspired, by the old brute himself.

The post-war inquiry concluded that while there were no charges to be made against Wodehouse, except of an unimportant and technical nature, it would be better if he were kept out of the jurisdiction, to avoid any possibility of unpleasantness in the aftermath of the violent accusations. This amounted to an unofficial sentence of exile.

Whether Wodehouse observed it, and never set foot in his native land again, as most people seem to believe, or whether he discreetly – almost furtively – paid occasional visits to the family of his step-daughter, Leonora Cazalet, as I have been told, the result might seem a victory for the politicians.

Politicians, as I have frequently observed, can forgive almost anything in the way of abuse; they can forgive subversion, revolution, being contradicted, exposed as liars, even ridiculed, but they can never forgive being ignored. That was the true nature of Wodehouse's crime; only that explains why, even on his ninetieth birthday in 1971, Mr Heath's Government was not prepared to make the slightest friendly gesture towards the man who had delighted and inspired four generations of Englishmen. Our greatest anti-political thinker had to wait until a few weeks before his death when Harold Wilson, to his eternal credit, made good Mr Heath's disgusting lapse.

So it might seem, as I say, to have been a victory for the politicians. But I would argue that Wodehouse has had the last laugh. He has influenced the political thinking of the nation more than any of them – always subliminally, nearly always at one or two removes – until he now colours our entire perception of the subject. The English attitude to work is one of the wonders of the world. Its literary inspiration can be traced unfailingly to P. G. Wodehouse, and I would maintain that our attitude to politics and politicians is similarly derived.

Mr Ken Livingstone, the revolutionary new GLC Chairman, might have inspired terror among Londoners – until they learned that he keeps newts in his bedroom. No longer a figure of terror, he is now a figure of harmless fun. This is not just because Gussie Fink-Nottle also kept newts in his bedroom (and in his bath). More significantly, Mr Livingstone is now identified as a Wodehouse type – the enthusiast – along with Uncle Tom Travers, who collects silver cow creamers, and Madeline Basset, who thinks the stars are God's Daisy Chain. In the same way, one can unhesitatingly identify Mrs Thatcher as an Aunt, Lord Carrington as a member of the Drones. And so it goes on, as Bertie says, so it goes on. *(11.10.81)*

Breaking the Mould at Hillhead
Clive James

Terry Wogan, currently hosting the best radio show on the air, hosted the worst television show just to stay in practice. 'A Song for Europe 1982' (BBC1) plumbed new troughs.

Most ghastly development is the tendency for every other singing group to field a sub-Hot Gossip group of leather fetishist dancers. The song 'Dancing in Heaven', featuring a lot of space talk about radar and countdowns, was delivered by a squad of people in American uniforms and pressuresuits who gyrated to what they hopefully described as orbital be-bop. In all songs there were frequent mentions of U and R, as in 'U and R have just begun'. U might have been able to put up with this, but R couldn't stand it.

A series deservedly honoured, 'Arena' (BBC1) profiled author Salman Rushdie with a subtle thoroughness which incidentally told you a lot about his strange homeland. 'You literally aren't alone, ever,' was his most telling comment. Trains are a very big deal in India. During one train journey Rushdie looked out of the window and counted the amounts of time between people. Even in the most desolate stretches of countryside there was never more than a 15-second interval. Here was the governing factor of subcontinental politics laid bare.

If you subjugate India to the extent that the Indian ruling class will want to educate its young in your public schools, eventually you will get the occasional Salman Rushdie ready to take on the job of explaining his own country to you in terms you will understand. But who will do the same job for Britain? It is a country far weirder than India. From the window of a British Rail Intercity train the gap is often more than 15 seconds between people, especially if the train is stuck a mile outside Macclesfield 'owing to the engineering.' But in every other respect Britain is a teeming, jostling daydream of sacred cows, holy men, thugs, curry-merchants and people who will write letters for you in return for money. How, for example, do you begin to explain the mere existence of someone like Tony Benn?

In India the Tony Benns sit semi-naked under gnarled trees and pull greased cords through their nostrils while inhaling water through the penis. But in Britain they are prominent in what was, until last Friday, the leading political party of the opposition. 'Newsnight' (BBC2) was already predicting victory for Jenkins just after 11 p.m., basing its estimate on a poll taken of voters leaving the booth – the only kind of poll, experience suggests, on which you can ever begin to rely. Vincent Hanna was 'Newsnight's' man on the spot in Hillhead, with John Tusa anchoring in the studio. In charge of discussions: Sir Robin Day. Biffen, Hattersley and Shirley Williams represented the big three. 'If Roy Jenkins does win,' asked Robin, 'is the mould of British politics really broken?'

'No,' said Hatters, adding that even if the SDP did win it would in fact be a disappointment for them, because they would have won by much more had they not been morally defeated by a 'much underrated candidate', meaning the mysteriously taciturn Labour candidate with the beard. Robin's incredulity at this was beautiful to see, but far stranger things were happening on the commercial channel, where Tony Benn was now out of his tracksuit and warming up.

Alastair Burnett was in charge of the ITN studio, with Peter Sissons out in the field. Sissons convincingly argued that Jenkins had peaked at the right time and not by accident: he was a 'very, very astute campaigner' who had personally met twice as many constituents as any other candidate. Back in the studio, however, Benn knew that Jenkins was really just Reg Prentice in disguise and that the people had been fooled. Benn's propensity for going on television and telling the people that they are easy to fool could well bring about, in the course of time, the utter destruction of the Labour Party, but tonight he wasn't going to let a consideration like that slow him down.

'I'm absolutely amazed by Tony Benn,' said Jim Prior, representing the Tories. Dr Owen of the Alliance contented himself with a few rational statements while Benn mimed incomprehension and stoked his pipe, another of his delusions about television being that it is a medium which favours histrionics. Actually it exposes them ruthlessly, but some people are hams to the core.

'CND is four times as big as the SDP,' Benn announced, forgetting to add that the RSPCA is four times as big as CND. 'It may be that the SDP is past its peak.' On BBC2 they were interviewing local Scots politicians. Back at ITN, where Benn was saying, 'I believe the SDP is now past its peak.' He had gone from 'it may be' to 'I believe' in half a minute. 'I think what we're witnessing,' he went on, 'is Jeremy Thorpe reappearing in the guise of Roy Jenkins.' Back to the Beeb, before Benn could suggest that what we were witnessing was Flash Gordon reappearing as Ming the Merciless of Mongo, Emperor of the Universe.

Hatters was telling Robin that if Jenkins won it would really be a victory for Labour, because in the general election an SDP led by Jenkins would take votes from the Tories, whereas an SDP led by Shirley Williams would have taken them from Labour. 'I genuinely believe that this is an encouraging vote for Labour.' This was a pretty mad moment for Hatters, but he still sounded as judicious as Thucydides compared with what was going on back at ITN. 'I personally,' Benn was saying, 'think that the SDP has passed its peak.'

He could say that again and was plainly determined on doing so, but there was a big blur as both channels switched to Hillhead for the announcement. A total of 282 people had voted for the other Roy Jenkins, but in the end it was the real Roy Jenkins who stood up. Back in the BBC studio, Shirley Williams threw away her walking stick. 'We've got back into Parliament the man who will lead that Alliance.' On ITN, Owen said 'Fantastic'.

If this wasn't real generosity in both cases, it certainly sounded like it. If they were fooling the people about their own disappointed hopes, at least they had paid the people the compliment of employing a fairly high level of acting. Benn, on the other hand, the man who goes on endlessly about how the media manipulates the people, went on manipulating to the end. 'I think this means we'll have a Labour government . . . the SDP is on the way down . . . the SDP will disappear.'

Which is my cue. Last year in Las Vegas I met a blackjack dealer who told me there are only two kinds of gamblers, the dumb ones and those who know how to quit while they're ahead. After 10 years of writing this column I still face the gleaming tube with undiminished enthusiasm, but with increasing frequency I find my own face looking back at me. It is time to quit my chair, before I find myself reviewing my own programmes. Creativity and criticism, in my view, are more continuous than opposed, but there is such a thing as a conflict of interest. There is also such a thing as making way for fresh talent. By standing up and moving aside for my gifted successor, Julian Barnes, I avoid the possibility of finding him suddenly sitting in my lap. *(28.3.82)*

This was Clive James's last TV column for 'The Observer' after ten years. He was named Critic of the Year in the British Press Awards.

Confessions of a Dilettante Englishman
Maureen Cleave

New York had been hot in the early afternoon and at 3.30 there was a cloudburst; sheets of rain swept the street and the famous person scanning it from beneath the awning of the restaurant had no hope of a taxi. Almost at once, however, a huge motor caravan drew up and the driver, recognising the famous person as Mick Jagger, shouted, 'Where to?'

We clambered in. There were cameras and clothes and a table and seats. The driver, eyes front peering through the rain, waved an arm at a crate of beer on the floor behind him.

'Have a drink, man,' he said.

'Thanks, man,' said Mick Jagger, settling himself at the table with a can.

'OK,' said the driver.

'Cool, man,' said Mick Jagger, not meaning the beer. The encounter was cool. His home address and another 'Thanks, man' when we got there 20 minutes later completed the exchange, entirely satisfactory to both.

He spends half the year in New York and he always talks to Americans in a very pronounced, slightly phony pan-American accent. It is not the usual compromise of dropping a few consonants or flattening the odd vowel, but a completely different voice and vocabulary. 'After all,' he said, reverting to an English accent for me, 'I've been singing in it for 20 years, so why shouldn't I speak in it? In cabs and bars you needn't go through the "You're-from-England-I-was-in-England-during-the-war" bit. They just accept you as another person.'

This might not suit many famous people, but it suits him because he doesn't like fuss. He is 38 now, a 60s idol. Sixties idols were built to last; a 70s idol is a shoddy, throwaway thing by comparison.

He is interesting for two reasons: one is that he has stayed the course doing exactly what he always did, which is singing rock'n'roll music in an athletic and sexual manner. American singers like Jerry Lee Lewis kept on rocking into middle age, but the English rock singer of that era tended to become the dreaded all-round entertainer, doing Christmas TV spectaculars at home and appearing in white suits and costume jewellery in Las Vegas.

Mick Jagger wears a precious jewel in his head – in his tooth to be precise. He has a small but costly diamond set in the upper right lateral incisor. (It used to be an emerald until friends complained it looked like a bit of spinach.) Black singers favour jewels in the teeth, often set in gold, and he got the idea from a singer called Buddy Guy. 'He has a huge enormous diamond but I, being a discreet white person, have a small discreet diamond.'

Manhattan sped by in the rain as he talked. He is a nice likeable person and agreeable company; not that he bothers with charm or winning ways – doing things for effect is confined to his stage work – but he is honest, direct and intelligent. Because there is no side to him, he makes a good friend. He went on that famous pilgrimage to North Wales with the Beatles to see the Maharishi, but this seems to have been his only brush with fancy religions. His approach to life is essentially brisk.

Here is his analysis of American musical taste and why he caters for it:

'The Americans are a conservative society; they have three kinds of pop music and always have had. One: country music. Two: rhythm and blues or black or soul music. Three: white rock'n'roll, which is a mixture of the first two. This last is a huge industry. Eighty per cent of people like this music and it is what they will buy.

'Rock'n'roll is a spent force in that we can't expect any more from it, either as music or an instrument for social change. It is merely re-cycling itself and everything is a re-hash of something else. I'm not that good a musician to break out of it; it's all I can do. If I were a jazz musician with a brilliant technique, then to go on doing it would be galling; but as I'm not, it isn't galling. I can't go on leaping around for ever – it would be unseemly and perhaps I shouldn't be doing it even now – but it would be stupid not to do it while I still can.

'If you're a footballer and physically fit, you go on because there's going to be a time when you can't. If we were unsuccessful we'd certainly give it up.

'I suppose I could change my act and do more than just titillate little girls, but not the voice. I realise now you've got to take care of your voice: you go to bed, you don't take drugs, you gargle three times a day. I used to use very hot water and salt, but Stevie Wonder put me on to glycerine.

'In any case, if I can't hit middle C I'm not going to cancel; nobody's going to notice.'

At this point the driver indicated some biscuits in a tin. 'Cookies,' he said, speaking for the third and last time. We stuck to beer.

The second remarkable thing about Mick Jagger is that he stayed the course at all. In his line of business, mere survival is highly prized. There was an unpromising start at the Station Hotel, Richmond, Surrey, in 1963 when two prospective managers came to view a new group called the Rolling Stones. 'OK,' said one to the other, 'but the BBC will never take the vocalist. That vocalist will have to go.'

The Rolling Stones' early success was fostered by the rumour that they didn't wash, but fairly soon real life disasters took care of the publicity. They began in a small way: *ROLLING STONES AT LONGLEAT – 200 FAINT . . . STONES CONCERT AT BELLE-VUE – TWO POLICEWOMEN FAINT . . . FANS SLEEP ON PAVEMENT . . . GIRLS' CLOTHES RIPPED OFF . . . TEAR GAS USED . . . STAMPEDING FANS BREAK WINDOWS . . . SECURITY GUARDS HOSE FANS . . . POLICE WITH BATONS KNOCK DOWN RIOTING FANS,* the crescendo reaching triple sforzando at Altamont in California when a spectator was stabbed to death in front of the film cameras.

Nearer home there was worse trouble. Apart from the usual run-of-the-mill paternity cases, drug swoops and legal wrangles with managers, Brian Jones was found drowned at the bottom of his own swimming pool. Marianne Faithful, Mick Jagger's girlfriend, attempted suicide, attracting even more attention than her predecessor Chrissie Shrimpton, who had tried the same thing.

Mick Jagger, hitherto presented as a straightforward Viking figure, boozing and wenching, now became slightly sinister. It was rumoured that he had leukaemia, that he dabbled in the black arts; he was the demon king, the demon lover.

There was even a rumour, half credited by those who should have known better, that he had roasted Chrissie Shrimpton's poodle in the oven. This reputation left the real person so far behind as to be out of sight.

Through it all, he obeyed to the letter Colonel Tom Parker's instructions to Elvis Presley, which were to say nothing and keep it dignified.

But it was too late. Having worn a frock to a concert in Hyde Park, it was to be expected that his photograph would appear in the newspapers if he wore a collar and tie. He grew smarter and smarter, a *salonier* as welcome as Chopin not only in London and New York, but also in Paris. When he married the raven-haired Nicaraguan Bianca, his glamour enveloped her to such an extent that her public image was enhanced by their divorce.

He himself has survived barely rumpled in either body or spirit, a moderate man in a world of excess, a man who knew where to draw the line when others went over the top. Everyone in the pop world marvels at this ability.

He has it, he says, because he was well brought up in a middle-class home in Dartford, Kent. He got to the London School of Economics, leaving in mid-career to follow his calling. 'It only takes a conventional upbringing and education in the English style of life to produce a normal human being. It gives you equilibrium, the balanced view.'

He was wearing the jacket of a black silk suit, an odd pair of trousers in puffy black seersucker and bright blue socks. He is wiry and exceedingly healthy for a rock singer. Rock'n'roll is an after-dark activity, and rock singers never look good in daylight, let alone out of doors, but Jagger is rather reverting to type, for his father Jo was a lecturer in physical education and even used the young Mick to illustrate a television series entitled 'Seeing Sport'. Mick was depicted canoeing, rock-climbing and camping in a tent. His movements, animal and menacing on stage, are deft and nimble off it.

His father had been in America recently, lecturing in Georgetown, Washington. 'On the history of physical education from the Renaissance to the present day – something like that. He's terribly nice to me now but he was a very strict father, very severe – being a schoolteacher, I suppose. He loves Jade [Mick's daughter] very much, lets her do anything she likes. My mother was always lenient but they both hated it when I became a pop singer; they thought it meant I was gay, that pop singing and homosexuality went hand in hand.

'But there was a big difference when things began to go wrong: they became protective. "He's a nice boy really," they said to themselves, "we brought him up, so he must be." It was a stable upbringing to which I attribute my stability.'

What did worry him as a young man was that his father was completely bald, an anxiety that has so far proved groundless. He once looked up the curious name Jagger and found that it came from Northumberland; a jagger was a man who carried ore on packhorses. It also meant a vagabond or a knifer.

Celebrities of the top rank sometimes have a vulnerable childlike air because they cannot do things for themselves, like finding numbers in a telephone directory or waking up in the morning. They have people on the payroll, called aides, to do these things for them. Mick Jagger has as few people on the payroll as possible and he likes to organise his own life. He carries his own suitcase and cooks his own lunch. He doesn't have a bodyguard or a driver or a living-in maid.

'None of that,' he said. 'It's anathema to me. I'm on my own and apart from anything else, it's much cheaper. I get up at 11 and I make myself a cup of tea. Jerry [his girlfriend] has usually gone to work by eight. Then I go cycling in the park – everyone in New York does that.

'John Lennon lived next door to me but he never went out; he shut himself up in all those apartments for four years. I suppose it's easy to get into that interior sort of life. I used to leave little notes saying: "Mick was here." It's sad to talk about it now because we were good friends. I used to send him postcards from abroad saying, "Having a great time in Indonesia." He was terrified to leave the country in case they wouldn't let him back, but really our situations were very similar: we'd both been busted for drugs in 1969. I wasn't going to let them stop me getting back in, so I just whittled away at the establishment.

'I have to get out and see things for myself. That album "Some Girls" was about New York, the streets and the people. It was full of observations, and you can only make those by getting out there and looking and being ordinary.'

He loves travelling, particularly to where the music and dancing are good and where he can join in: Africa, the Caribbean, South America, especially Brazil. His French and Spanish are quite workable. He has a small house on Mustique and has just bought a small French château near Amboise; he'd been on to the mayor on the telephone that morning. The mayor was helping him to find a gardener.

In the past, he had rather avoided acquiring houses. 'If you do,' he said, 'you've got to spend time there and be part of the local community.'

He also organises – to the extent that they are organised at all – the Rolling Stones. They have had no manager since Andrew Oldham sold them behind their backs to Allen Klein in 1969 for three-quarters-of-a-million dollars.

By the time they were free of Klein they had, in a relative sense, no money. Mick Jagger bumped into the immensely grand Rupert Lowenstein (prince and banker) at a party. 'I said to him: "Look, you're a banker; you must have some sort of brain. We've been dropped in the hole by this American. Can you bring your intellect to bear on this rock'n'roll world?" He's a good bloke. I've known him for 10 years and he tells you exactly what he's doing, doesn't just give you the bottom line.'

Few details of the Rolling Stones' financial arrangements are available; they are said to own a fish factory in Japan. Their record albums, one a year, sell on average three million copies. 'Some Girls' sold seven million, 'Emotional Rescue' sold eight. An album may take up to six months to record: they do this at night in Paris. Recordings made in England are liable to a tax of 60 per cent on profits.

What he had to organise that afternoon was a governess for his 10-year-old daughter Jade. Jade and her mother Bianca were coming from Chelsea to live in New York in the autumn.

'We think she'll get a better education here and I can spend more time with Jade if she's here. I do think a neglected child is a terrible thing, and if the parents are separated and live in different towns, it's hard to give the child enough attention. I love children very much. I really do like them and not just my own.'

He has married only once and wouldn't do it again. 'I'm almost a Catholic in the way I feel about it. If you aren't successful at it, it isn't a case of try, try again. In our society, there's no reason to get married again; even illegitimate children aren't thought of badly.'

How did he think of women? Crudely, it seemed from his songs. On 'Rolling Stones Tattoo You', their new album, he is singing:

> My eyes dilate, my lips go green,
> My hands are greasy, she's a mean, mean machine.

A car/woman metaphor that is not at all romantic.

He laughed and said this was just a pose. 'Rock'n'roll is not a tender medium; it's raunchy and macho. There's no such thing as a secure family-orientated rock'n'roll song. I suppose I'm a bit hidebound by the tradition, but I don't really think like that. In actual fact I love women; I'm absorbed by them and if you ask any of my women friends, not just the ones I've had affairs with, they'll tell you that I'm very nice. I have a lot of sympathy with women.'

The meaningful companion in his life is the Texan model Miss Jerry Hall, towards whom, in a rented apartment on the West Side overlooking Central Park, we were now speeding in the rain. Jerry, he said, was a nice simple Texan girl and good fun. One thing he particularly likes about her is that she earns her own living.

'Women should have jobs,' he said. 'Jerry owns a ranch and she runs that ranch and she breeds quarter horses. If a quarter horse comes first in a race, it can win $4 million.'

Jerry wore a very short sailor dress revealing yards of golden satin leg; she is as dainty as is consistent with being six feet tall. She is much prettier than in her photographs and looks slightly unreal in the way the 'Dallas' women do.

She was trying to be helpful, to get Mick out of the house for a video recording. She came in with two shirts on a hanger, one for Mick and the other for Charlie Watts, the Rolling Stones' drummer who, it was discovered, had been sitting silent and motionless as a statue in a corner behind the door all this time.

'Aren't you going to wear this shirt?' said Jerry, holding it out invitingly. Charlie did not permit himself to speak; he shook his head. He was dressed as a middle-aged American tourist in a horizontally striped shirt worn loose outside his trousers. He put on a long, rather depressing mackintosh and we set off for the studios.

Charlie Watts lives in Gloucestershire with his original wife and daughter; Bill Wyman lives in the South of France and has photography as a hobby; Ronnie Wood lives in California and Keith Richards lives in New York. They like each other but not, Jagger says, all of the time. 'We're only musicians, we don't have to *love* each other, but we get on pretty well.' His special friends are Watts and Richards.

Keith Richards looks marvellous with wild grey hair and sunken, burning eyes; he was dressed like a Principal Boy in black trousers that fitted him like tights, a grubby lilac satin jacket and Robin Hood boots. He and Ronnie do the fooling around, like stage drunks, showing off. They don't converse with outsiders but put on a dumb show. Richards had poured beer over Wood's hair to make it stick up in spokes; they looked frightening but were quite affable, sliding the litre bottle of Jack Daniels across the floor to whoever wanted a swig. Bill and Charlie behaved just as they do on stage, spectators at the sport, occasionally smiling in a small way. Richards pretended to treat Charlie like an invalid.

'All right, Charlie, up we get – do you need your wheelchair then?'

None of it very subtle, but it's how groups behave, man and boy.

Many have dropped out of the race altogether thinking they can keep up with Keith. 'Sure he goes to bed,' said their secretary Jane Rose, who thinks they're all wonderful, 'but not every night.' He can stay up all night three nights running. He had lost something. He moaned distractedly, rummaging through piles of kit.

'What is it, Keith?' she said soothingly, and she went to help him.

They all argue about cricket. Videos of the day's Test play are flown out each evening from Heathrow.

The studio staff were quite excited because the Rolling Stones hadn't played together before any sort of public for two years. There were huge blow-ups suspended above the stage of Mick and Keith and another of the devil's cloven hoof in a high-heeled shoe.

The Stones struck up. 'My eyes dilate, my lips go green,' sang Mick, cavorting about. Keith and Ronnie leapt and danced like flames on either side of him, a moving frame to a moving picture: Charlie and Bill looked as involved as passers-by brought in off the street to witness a wedding.

At the end of Take One Mick kissed the cheek of his own portrait and at the end of Take Two, he picked its nose. Everyone was delighted by these touches. One wondered which the producer would choose.

There was a break; Prince Rupert arrived and positioned his pince nez for a business meeting.

Success, Mick Jagger said, was good for you. 'When you are successful you have money and I think money's really good for you because it enables you to do what you want in life – no more being pushed around by dregs of managers saying: "You get up on that stage and you earn me my 25 per cent." I don't have to work every day, not because I'm so rich but because I don't want to.

'I'm a dilettante Englishman. It's our great forte. We know we're the best – we may not choose to do it everyday, but when we do, we know we're the greatest.' *(30.8.81)*

8.
Sporting Prints

Shanks for the Memory
Hugh McIlvanney

Opponents of Liverpool Football Club would be rash to assume that they have done with Bill Shankly. Once Bill's ashes have been scattered on the pitch at Anfield, any visiting forward who is setting himself to score an important goal is liable to find suddenly that he has something in his eye.

Certainly Shanks would want us to believe in the possibility. Even after the results were in the paper, showing a scoreline against his men, he always refused to give defeat houseroom. Maybe we should follow his example and regard his death as just an ugly rumour.

To those who knew him well his loss is about as sore as any could be. But there is some easing of the grief in the knowledge that few men ever had such a capacity for warming and delighting their fellows without being physically in their company. For many of us he really will always be there.

Most of the thousand and one Shankly anecdotes, the tales of his doings and his utterances, are distorted and diminished in the telling, but he communicated such a strong sense of himself that enough of what was unique and marvellous about him is bound to survive. Nearly everyone connected with British football has tried at one time or another to impersonate the accent and the mannerisms he brought out of the south Ayrshire coalfield as a teenager and guarded against even the tiniest erosion through half a century in England.

Few of the impersonators get within touching distance of the reality, but nobody minds. The Shankly legend is the living, genuine article and the smallest fragment of it can spread laughter in any group of football people.

Clearly, however, he needed far more than earthy, utterly original wit to make the impact he did. His unshakable attachment to the ordinary supporters of football ('I'm a people's man – only the people matter') was a big help, but his real strength was perhaps drawn from something even more unusual.

With his drill-sergeant's hairstyle, his boxer's stance and his staccato, hard-man's delivery, he did not fit everybody's idea of a romantic. But that's what he was, an out-and-out, 22-carat example of the species. His secret was that he sensed deep down that the only practical approach to sport is the romantic one. How else could a manager persuade grown men that they could find glory in a boy's game. Shankly did that and more.

Looking into the faces of some of his outstanding former players in the last few days, men like Ian St John and Ronnie Yeats and Kevin Keegan, we could see how much they felt they owed to the Boss. He gave them more than a share in trophies, nothing less than a wonderful dream.

He fed it into their spirits by many means; by humour, dedicated example and that romanticism that insisted on talking defeats away as if they were fleeting embarrassments that a malevolent and dishonest fate had inflicted on his teams without regard to their true worth. His performances in that line were like those of a witch doctor, full of blind faith and incantations. They worked so well that his players never allowed defeat to become a habit.

Of course, he had learned plenty about the nuts and bolts of the game in his long career as a player with Carlisle, Preston (where he developed a bottomless admiration for Tommy – never Tom – Finney) and Scotland, and his management years at Carlisle, Grimsby, Workington, Huddersfield (where he had a brief memorable alliance with the young Denis Law) and from 1959 at Liverpool.

His Liverpool won the Second Division championship in 1962 by eight points and by the time he retired prematurely in 1974 they had taken the League title three times, the FA Cup twice and the UEFA Cup once. It is no diminution of the splendid manager who succeeded him, Bob Paisley, to say that Shankly left behind a foundation that contributed hugely to the subsequent domination of Europe by the club.

He also left behind a great deal of himself, and the pathos of his self-precipitated conversion into a peripheral, haunting and sometimes embittered figure at Anfield was painful to his friends. But he was never reduced in the eyes of those who knew him best. No manager ever gave more to the spirit of a city or the folklore of a game than he did.

'Me havin' no education,' I once heard him say, 'I had to use my brains.' He used his heart, too. It was as big as a town. *(4.10.81)*

Hugh McIlvanney was named Journalist of the Year in the British Press Awards, the first sports writer to win that title.

A Simple Superman
Michael Davie

With his Henry VIII appearance of porcine eyes, massive bulk and animal good looks, Ian Botham, the cricketer, has in the past year become a symbol of the resurgent energy that this country evidently yearns to feel.

Unlike Henry VIII, however, Botham has not allowed his early promise to turn sour. Instead, a year ago, he recognised his limits by taking the unprecedented step of resigning the England captaincy. He had been a failure against Australia, especially as a batsman, and was wondering whether he would be picked for the next Test.

This week marks the anniversary of a born-again cricketer. At Headingley last year, hitting as he had never hit before in a Test (indeed, as few batsman have ever hit), Botham made 149 not out, and his fame and reputation have been growing ever since. Last week, after he had made 208 against India, his celebrity reached some sort of peak of popular esteem when the *Sun* newspaper announced that he was the best player of the century, and 'as good as W. G. Grace.'

He was a success from the beginning. He was born on 24 November 1955 in Heswall, Cheshire, where his father, a chief petty officer in the Fleet Air Arm, and mother, who trained as a nurse, lived while the father was stationed in Northern Ireland.

Both parents played cricket. When the family moved to Yeovil in Somerset, after Botham senior retired and took a job with Westland Helicopters, Ian was sent first to Milford Junior School. By the age of nine he was already prodigious, both at cricket and football. Aged 10, he hit a six out of the ground and out of sight. He went next to Butler's

Mead Secondary School nearby, where his feats continued. His father used to tell him that it was the next success, not the last one, that mattered. His hero was the great West Indian all-rounder, Gary Sobers.

By the time he was 15, he could have chosen a career in either football or cricket. Crystal Palace offered him a contract (and he has since played for Scunthorpe reserves.) Instead, he joined the Lord's ground staff, where he was reckoned to be a promising batsman but no sort of bowler. He is remembered for flinging down bad bouncers in the nets at elderly members of MCC.

He played his first full season for Somerset in 1974, was selected for England in 1977, aged 21, and two years later achieved the Test double of 1,000 runs and 100 wickets in record time. He was married in 1976, to Kathryn Waller, a Yorkshire girl, and they have a son, Liam, five next month, and a daughter, Sarah, who is three.

His physique has certainly helped his success, even though first-class cricketers come in all shapes and sizes. When Botham was 17, Brian Close, the former England captain who was then captaining Somerset, pointed him out to a friend and said: 'Take a good look at that bloke. He's going to be a great player, and he's built like a shithouse door.' Botham may have picked up his competitive aggression from Close.

He is 6 ft 2 in., and weighs nearly 15 st. One winter, after an accident, he went up to 17 st. His shoulders, despite all the sixes, are not particularly broad, but he has a colossal torso and thighs.

He hits the ball exceptionally hard – something he may have picked up from his Somerset team-mate, Viv Richards, and uses a fearfully heavy bat. Sir Leonard Hutton once picked it up after Botham had been batting in the nets: 'It was like a railway sleeper', he says.

He likes to appear indestructible. After he had smashed up two sports cars on a motor-racing circuit near Andover earlier this season, although badly shaken in private, he surfaced like Superman for the public and the photographers. In Sydney in 1979, when it was so hot that Willis, the England fast bowler, left the field dehydrated, Botham bowled 18 overs as England's only surviving pace bowler and that night, while everyone else flopped early to bed, went to see 'Midnight Express' for the second time to watch the gruesome bits. Yet he is prone to occasional migraines, and is partially colour blind.

Because of his raw energy, his blatant desire to be a winner, and his occasional spectacular rudeness, some people in the outside world regard him, not to put too fine a point on it, as a lout, though a lout, to be sure, of exceptional sporting talents. This is not how he is viewed by his team-mates. They see him as basically a shy character who would much prefer to be one of the lads, and who likes to submerge himself in the camaraderie and protection of whatever cricketing company he happens to be in.

He is loyal. If he hears a stranger criticising one of his colleagues, he is liable to barge over and ask for the evidence. If a member of the Somerset team is in financial trouble, it is usually Botham who helps him out. He is a close friend of Richards, a West Indian, who is godfather to his son. It was partly for this reason that he refused to play in South Africa.

Botham is not a thinker, though he has common sense. However, he was forced into a period of self-doubt when, after being made at the age of 24 the youngest England captain of the century, his world slowly began to crack last year. He stopped making runs – a matter of luck, according to him, not the burden of captaincy. His bowling lost effectiveness, owing to trouble with a vertebra in his back. He was up on a charge of 'occasioning actual bodily harm.' He felt the Press was out to get him.

But he was found not guilty of the charge, and he fought back as a cricketer. He had averaged 13 as captain; since giving the job up, he has averaged 64.26.

No doubt he was made captain too young. One of his best friends in the Somerset side says he is 'really a simple country lad at heart.' He likes shooting and fishing, and goes salmon-fishing in Scotland every autumn, though he has yet to catch a salmon. He stays in the best hotels, but drinks lager in the pubs round the corner. He has built a snooker room onto his house and keeps his sporting and animal trophies there.

In the West Indies, when he was captain of England, he lacked the capacity to make small talk to local officials, but was superb at fostering good relations between the two teams. At the end of two Test matches, he arrived back at his hotel at dawn after a night's carousing with his West Indian cricketing mates. In his drinking he is in a long West Country cricketing tradition: Sammy Woods of Somerset used to drink champagne (and eat lobsters) for breakfast.

Botham could afford the same breakfasts, if he liked. These days he is said to earn, with sponsorships and endorsements, £60,000 to £70,000 a year. South Africa offered him over £50,000 last winter for the four 'rebel' Tests which he declined. But not long ago he was nearly broke, and as recently as the spring of last year did not find it easy to raise the money for his court case.

His current cash flow means that he can afford to take flying lessons regularly, and he has done so for a year. He sees it as another challenge. In his Saab turbo car he has reached his limits of speed on earth (while he was England captain he was fined for speeding) so he has now conceived the ambition of flying to Australia and, eventually, round the world. (W. G. Grace went ballooning over the Avon Gorge.)

As his father long ago advised, Botham is always looking to the next milestone. At Kanpur at the beginning of February, he accepted a bet of 20–1 with an English reporter that he would make 1,000 Test runs during this calendar year: not a unique feat, but at the time of the bet he had made only 2,000-odd Test runs since 1977. Already this year he has made 699, with three Tests against Pakistan still to come and four in Australia. Challenges keep Botham going.

He has set himself another statistical goal, connected with Boycott. The relationship between the two might be described as one of mutual disrespect. It was Botham who ran out Boycott in New Zealand, when Boycott, who was captain, appeared to be absorbed in remaining not out and to have forgotten the good of the side. Botham is now determined to overtake Boycott's record aggregate of Test runs. If it were Hutton or Compton or Hammond who held the record, he might be much less interested. Boycott made over 8,000, but if Botham, whose total is now 2,833, keeps going at his current rate, he should dethrone Boycott before he hangs up his pads.

He has one more ambition. One of the few cricket skills he still has to master is that of bowling off-breaks. Again there is a spur. The two current players he regards as his equals, Viv Richards and Mike Procter, can also bowl them. Botham reckons he can bowl off-breaks better than either of the two specialists in the Somerset side, and on the last day's play at the Oval last week all four of his overs were off-breaks. He knows that his pace bowling will get fewer wickets as he gets older and stiffens up – already, as his batting improves, his average haul of wickets per Test match has gone down from five to three – so he will need his off-break if he is going to break Fred Trueman's England record of 307 Test dismissals. So far, in 51 Tests, he has taken 231. It is conceivable that he could end up with more runs *and* more wickets than any cricketer in England's history. He would probably then chase the score for catches.

But is he really, as the *Sun* thinks, 'as good as W. G. Grace'? Comparisons with Grace are futile, except in the matter of vitality. Botham has had no part in shaping the game's evolution or techniques. Richie Benaud, the former Australian captain, ranks him with Sobers and Keith Miller, two of the outstanding all-rounders in cricket history. T. E. Bailey says he is the best cricketer England has produced this century.

These judgments sound extravagant, but they are partially endorsed by Len Hutton, an exacting judge. 'Botham is not as good a bowler as

Miller, who could bowl slow as well as fast: at least, he has some way to go before he is as good an off-spinner as Miller. He is very close to being as good as Sobers, but not quite, either with bat or ball. The variety that Sobers had with his bowling was unique.' It may safely be concluded, in sum, that Botham is as exceptional in his era as any cricketer has been in any former era, apart from Grace himself and Bradman.

He says he will retire at 30. So long as he does not seriously injure himself flying or driving, what will Sir Ian do then? Governor of the Falklands? *(18.7.82)*

Best of the Breed
Clem Thomas

William Blackledge Beaumont is a splendid name, but then he is a splendid man. The premature passing of his career will be mourned as much by the Welsh, Irish and Scots as by his own Englishmen, for whom he is the archetypal example of the very best characteristics of his breed.

The injury which finally snuffed out Bill's delightful career was a culmination of three hard blows on the head in a year. The worst of these by far was sustained at Beziers at the start of the current season and the final one came while playing for his beloved Lancashire two weeks ago.

A computerised brain scan revealed that there were grave risks of permanent injury if he continued to play. Wisely he read the medical evidence correctly and ended one of the most distinguished careers in the history of the Rugby Football Union.

I am not surprised that he acquired so many head injuries, for he was never an instinctive footballer. His greatest attributes were honesty, integrity and courage. He will not be remembered for jumping like a stag in the line-out: instead he was a compressor at the front of the line, where his concentration and determination invariably saw him snatch his fair share of the ball.

His principal strength was that, in the idiom of the game over the past decade, he was a marvellous ground player. He would drive fiercely into rucks and mauls, using his head like a battering ram, propelled by what Steve Smith called his outboard motor, which is perhaps the most famous and prominent posterior in the game. His courage in driving into a maelstrom of flying boots and bodies was his danger and eventually his downfall. He contested everything.

Bill will never be forgotten for the charm of his captaincy. He led England a record 21 times, winning 11 times and drawing twice. In 1980 he took England to the Grand Slam for the first time since 1957, when they were led by another Lancastrian, Eric Evans.

If it is a cliché to say that he led by personal example, it is nevertheless entirely true. He had an immense charisma both on and off the field, and perhaps a reflection of his strength of character was that he was always at his best when things were going badly. In adversity in South Africa in 1980 he could shrug his shoulders and say 'Come on, lads,' and then take 10 minutes to get to the coach as he politely signed autographs.

The first major impression he made on me was in 1977, when he arrived in New Zealand as a replacement for Nigel Horton on that difficult, ill-fated tour. I will never forget when the Lions met him at the airport. Willie Duggan stepped forward to shake his hand and said, 'If I were you, Bill, I would flick off home again on the next plane.' Bill smiled and replied: 'Not Pygmalion likely.' Immediately he established himself alongside Gordon Brown as an automatic choice for the Tests.

I used to look at Bill Beaumont and wonder what he reminded me of, and finally decided that he was like a St Bernard, a loveable, bulky, gentle old thing possessing great strength underneath the gracefully floppy exterior, someone who would always come to your rescue.

Yes, Beaumont was everybody's favourite. You see, he always had an advantage over the kind of man who recently broke Geoff Wheel's nose in two places with two punches at the last line-out of the game. It would never have occurred to Bill to act like that. The very idea would be abhorrent because he loved the game, its ethics and its people and the little man who feels that punching or kicking is part of the game would never morally or physically survive against Beaumont, who was a big man in every sense. He may have finished as a player but not as a rugby man and we will, I know, hear and see a lot more of him yet.
(14.2.82)

The Cup that Cheers
Julian Barnes

The Two Brians, ITV's occasional sit-com, is back on our screens for a four-week run. Originally conceived as a reply to 'The Two Ronnies', it is perhaps closer to 'The Odd Couple'. A pair of men in early middle-age live in a television studio; they sit discussing reruns of soccer games. Sometimes they agree; more often they disagree; occasionally there are tears before bedtime. It doesn't sound much of a formula, but it works.

Brian One introduces the football clips. He is affable and balding. As a boy, we learn, he used to sing out imaginary football commentaries while bicycling to school. He believes in everybody having a good time; he is life-affirming; some call him softie, others idealist.

Brian Two, by contrast, looks saturnine and squash-fit; he doesn't believe in anybody having a good time unless they have thoroughly earned it; he is vinegary, with a philosophy of advanced scepticism which makes everyday sceptics seem like realists. Brian One is a doe-eyed masochist, shocked by his partner's harshness; Brian Two is a belligerent sadist, shocked by his partner's squishy liberalism.

The couple also have a lodger, Greavesie, a genial fellow with an unconvincing haircut, who sits between them not noticing that anything is wrong. He spends most of his time thinking up funny remarks about the old soccer-clips. If a player takes a dive in the penalty area, Greavesie dubs this 'a Jacques Cousteau effort.' Neither of the Two Brians take much notice of Greavesie, as he sits between them like a dormouse. Soon one of them (Brian Two, no doubt) will probably stuff him in the teapot.

The Two Brians are surely winning the ratings scrap. The BBC panels are worthy, responsible and patriotic, but lack ITV's contrasts of character. Brian Moore offers cloudless enthusiasm, Jimmy Greaves local colour, Ian St John scholarly expertise; while Brian Clough adds that valuable rogue element, not least in the vigour with which he gores his own club players.

John Robertson in particular provokes him to go recklessly over the top. Ian St John, worrying about this forward's physical condition, commented with a sideways nod, 'I've been speaking to Brian Clough about his fitness and he says it's all in his head.' Clough broke in with a joyous confirmatory snort: 'There's not much else there.'

The Cup's opening ceremony contained even more *opéra bouffe* than usual: flags, streamers, fireworks and that much-abused creature, the dove, as symbolic centrepiece (given some of the play, the dingo would be a better emblem). The richest moment came when girl usherettes bearing trays of carnations went to the touchline and 'threw flowers to the crowd.'

The inverted commas are required because Spanish grounds wisely have moats between the pitch and the terraces. Most of the flowers were therefore scattered over a puzzled band of kneeling photographers; while a brave, hard-flung few just made it into the moat. A couple of days later a ball disappeared down one of these anti-fan trenches. Commentator Gerry Harrison gave a private chuckle: 'There's all sorts of things in there – I just couldn't talk about them at this time of the evening.' I don't think he meant dead carnations either.

*   *   *

Last week the nation cheered the birth of a child, a timely symbol of hope in the difficult weeks ahead. I refer, of course, to Charlotte, second daughter of Bryan Robson, England's midfield lion, main scorer, schemer, prince and philosopher-king.

Soccer-haters facilely assume that for the fan the World Cup is largely a matter of quantity: that the ping-pong game in the head between ecstasy and despair is simply being played out more often. Not so. This quadrennial event ensnares not by its quantity – or even necessarily by its quality – but because it unleashes the full spectrum of fandom's emotions. That bored scold who rails at the slumped figure watching eleven lethargic Slavs doggedly scything their way to a goalless draw with eleven thespian Latins little appreciates the vivid inner life unreeling within the apparently dozing viewer.

Beyond the normal wary love for one's own team, and the neurotic fear and hatred of the immediate enemy, there lies an unguessed-at range of response to the other 22 teams. These four weeks have room – like some Club Meditérranée holiday – for everything from a brief flirtation with the gaudy Hondurans up to a grand passion for the quite unsuitable Argentines; elsewhere, there is a batch of emotions available for teams such as Austria (civil respect), Kuwait (humorous approval) and Italy (keen, unshadowed contempt).

The second week brought a straightening out of two basic World Cup rules. Rule One: Spain are allowed one penalty per game. Rule Two: No team can be awarded a penalty against Spain. It also brought the slow but traditional rising curve of onfield violence. This always extracts certain key euphemisms from the commentator, which need to be memorised. 'They're not interested' = they're more or less playing according to the rules and not fouling anyone. 'They're showing a lot of enthusiasm' = they're being fairly violent. 'Some of these tackles are very borderline' = an indictable offence has probably been committed. 'Well, they've got a few devious tricks, the Italians' = elbow in the face off the ball, spitting, and that incredibly painful Latin ploy of chivalrously helping a player up with one hand while tweaking his nipple violently with the other (this usually provokes a 'very borderline' response from the victim, followed by his sending-off). 'Things are getting a bit out of hand' = the players have bazookas on the pitch and are setting up their Rapier missile-systems.

*   *   *

Just in case my distinguished predecessor nurses any bubbling nostalgia for his old job, I'd like to declare that 'Clive James Live in Las Vegas' (LWT) was a delightful, entertaining and searingly compassionate piece of film-making, and that Mr James has definitely found his true métier. I always thought his artful play of wit and good sense was rather wasted when set in narrow columns of drab newsprint: how much more satisfying to flesh it out, to see the lips that speak the words, to view the body that holds the lips that speak the words . . .

A fizzing script won through, even against the competition of some crassly chosen music: 'Clive James in Las Vegas' was at least as good as 'Ian Wooldridge in Las Vegas,' and much better than 'Whicker in Las Vegas,' 'Fyfe Robertson in Las Vegas,' 'Liberace in Las Vegas' and 'Sooty in Las Vegas.' I formally wish Mr James a very long and successful (but especially long) career in the field of TV-documentary. *(1.8.82)*

9.
A Backward Glance

Back to Vietnam
William Shawcross

On modern maps of Vietnam there is a town called Ho Chi Minh Ville. Don't be deceived. No such place exists.

But Saigon does.

Saigon – tawdry, brash, sad, resilient and touching – Saigon is still Saigon. Six years after it was conquered or liberated by the North (depending on your politics) the Saigonese are still *méfiant* of their new rulers; indeed, in some ways the men from Hanoi are having as much trouble as the French and Americans before them.

One night in Saigon I took a cyclo to a café in the suburbs. It was a dark little house on the banks of the river. Vietnamese of all ages sat around drinking *café filtre* or orange juice or crême de menthe *frappé*, talking softly. The furniture was rattan, the lampshades were dark green cognac bottles with the bottoms knocked out and with scenes of Vietnamese villages scratched on their sides.

An old man played the piano, another warbled on the sax, and a few customers sang quiet Vietnamese songs about freedom. These songs had been banned under the anti-Communist regime before 1975 and they were still banned today. Neither ban had been terribly effective.

The café and its clients could have been there since the early Fifties, long before the Americans or the Communists came, so little seemed to have changed. On my second night people began to talk to me – about their fears, about their relatives in California, about their relatives in re-education camps, about their sons fighting in Cambodia, about the difficulties of making a living, and about their hopes, very fragile hopes, of a better future. One beautiful girl, who wanted to leave Vietnam, gave me her photograph.

It was my first visit to Saigon since 1975, my first visit ever to Hanoi. Officially Vietnam has been reunified since 1976. In fact, to fly from North to South, from Hanoi to Saigon, is still to fly between two different worlds.

All of Vietnam is terribly poor – most people earn only about £60 a year and many, particularly children, are now starving – but the North is far poorer than the South. The poverty is tangible from the moment you land at Hanoi. The Customs area at the airport is an old shed. The road into town is crowded with ancient carts filled with wood or bricks and pulled by thin horses or even people. The bridges over the river, bombed by the Americans, have not been repaired; traffic crawls over flimsy, temporary structures.

Clothing in Hanoi is drab and hard to come by. The State shops are gloomy as morgues. Markets hardly exist and contain no luxuries. A rich man owns a bicycle. A chicken costs almost one month's wages. The mood is one of resignation.

But fly, in a plane full of Russians, Poles and Czechs, to 'Ho Chi Minh Ville' and it is another land. The girls wear bonnets, some still ride Hondas, the markets are filled. Not only with rice and fruit and meat and fish, but also with beer, cassette players, lipstick, cognac and music. The mood is not of resignation but disappointment, mingled with anger, a determination either to leave or not to give in. And, in some people, there are glimmers of hope that life is going to improve.

In the streets of Saigon there is music. The fronts of the old downtown bars, which turned them into perpetually darkened caves for wretched GIs to fumble with wretched bar girls, have been torn down. The bars were completely closed for a time as the government tried in vain to abolish all private enterprise. But now private business is being encouraged again and when I was there the bars were thriving. Then, in a new drive against 'corrupt influence', many were closed again.

Most of the bar girls (not all) have vanished, but the music of the Sixties and early Seventies lingers. No, it does more than linger, it blares defiantly across a decade and more.

Some of the tunes played are deliberately nostalgic and ironic: 'I gotta get outta this place, if it's the last thing I ever do,' 'Spaceship to the Moon', 'Yesterday'. Perhaps most poignant of all in the city of the boat people, a song by the black American group, Boney M:

> 'I see a boat on the river
> It's sailing away.
> Down to the ocean.
> Where to, I can't say.'

The boat people are no longer a story in the Western Press – our disasters are very fleeting – but last year 76,000 Vietnamese fled by boat to other countries of Southeast Asia. So far this year over 41,000 more have arrived. That's 117,000 people who managed to run the strict gauntlets the Government has set up and also survived the horrors of storms and Thai pirates who rape, rob and often even kill helpless boatloads.

I met one boy who had tried four times to leave and each time was stopped by the police, imprisoned, then managed to bribe his way out. (The corruption of poor officials sometimes humanises the State.) His exquisite sister had tried once and was about to try again. She shrugged off the danger of pirates. 'I must go,' she said.

Everywhere I went in Saigon, children and grown-ups jeered: 'Lien So, Lien So,' meaning 'Soviet, Soviet.' The one phrase a Westerner needs is 'Khong Phai Lien So' – 'I am not a Soviet.' Russians are not popular in the South; they are less visible than Americans were, but also much less rich. They are known as 'Americans without dollars', and many people blame them for the poverty which has followed the end of the war.

I met, driving a cyclo, an old man I had known in American days. Then, he drove one of the ancient little blue and white taxis which puttered around Saigon tied together with string. After liberation, the government dispatched him, along with several hundred thousand other Saigonese, to 'New Economic Zones' in an attempt to reduce the war-swollen population of the city and to increase food production.

It was a sensible policy, but in too many cases the land chosen was infertile, and the people were given hardly any tools to work it. 'I stayed there a year,' said my driver, 'but I couldn't make a living. So my family came back to Saigon illegally. Now we sleep in the streets.' He said he was far poorer than before 1975, so what was Communism all about?

I asked to see a collective farm in the Mekong Delta, that miraculous leaf of land through which the water flows like a million tendrils and which is fertile enough to feed the whole country; it produces a surplus which the government fails to distribute. In 1976 the government started to collectivise land in the South. But peasants were not pleased and today less than a third of the land in the area is collectivised; the rest is still farmed under the system devised by the Americans and incentives for private production and sale have recently been introduced in both North and South. All is irony.

We travelled by boat up a stream to the fine concrete home of what was clearly a rich old man. He had a visitors' book filled with the names of all those 'foreign friends' from East and West who had been brought to admire his estate. One explanation of his comfort lay in four portraits hanging along the wall; they were his children and they had all been killed while fighting for the Viet Cong. The revolution rewards its own.

We visited a small handicraft factory which had just been set up to export baskets to Poland. The director, a beautiful woman in her fifties, was 14 years in the Viet Cong. She was a naval officer charged with meeting and unloading boats which came from the north to the Delta. 'The Americans always tried to intercept our ships, but did not often succeed,' she said.

Then I went to the Children's Hospital in Can Tho. The director, Dr Kien Tung Khan, was trained in Moscow and sent down the Ho Chi Minh Trail to the South in 1971. She worked in the jungle about 40 miles from Saigon. 'We were well supplied with drugs in those days,' she said. Today there is a terrible shortage.

Finally that day I met the Party Secretary for the whole region, Comrade Thiep Bin. He had been sent from Saigon to Can Tho in 1979 after Hanoi acceded to Western pressure to limit the flow of boat people. His predecessor had been profiting rather too obviously from the traffic. In Saigon people spoke of Thiep Bin as a decent and humane man.

He received me in the Party guesthouse, a large suburban villa which boasted red pelmets over every door, wearing sports slacks and Ho Chi Minh sandals. He did not tell me anything vastly new, but he had a modest, pleasant demeanour. He was born in the North in 1918 'but I took up my revolutionary work in the South in 1949,' he said. 'Many Northerners would not now think I was one of them. During the Thieu regime I was a political commissar. I lived in a resistance area, but I travelled quite often into the Thieu areas, even to Can Tho city. That was quite normal for an activist.'

So, in just one day I had met in just one town four people, all of whom had held responsible positions in the Communist maquis in South Vietnam. When I was last here these people were invisible workers in another Vietnam, one which few foreigners ever saw and at whose extent we could only guess. To see them now was to glimpse only a tiny corner of the revolution, but it helped underline the futility of the American effort.

It is fashionable in Reagan's America, and in magazines like the

Economist, to say that America could have won the war in Vietnam 'if its hands were not tied' and 'if the war had not been lost on television.' It is dangerous nonsense. It serves only to feed the illusion that 'next time' might go better. Half a million American troops failed to 'pacify' South Vietnam. The enemy was everywhere and his cause, which was seen as nationalism before Communism, was popular.

That popularity has gone now. There was no bloodbath in Vietnam, as American officials had constantly warned. (There was in Cambodia.) But the government in Hanoi has disappointed even its own allies in the South. 'They promised to liberate us, but they tried to conquer us,' says one disillusioned former Minister.

This same person, a Communist, compares Vietnam unfavourably with Hungary. The Hungarian Government embarked on a policy of national reconciliation after 1956. Its slogan was 'Who is not against us is with us,' and it succeeded brilliantly. In Vietnam there has been no such reconciliation; the Northern leadership still seems to regard the South as an untrustworthy enemy.

Central to this attitude is the continued system of re-education, known as 'the Vietnamese Gulag'. No one knows how many Southerners have been 're-educated' since 1975. Some refugees claim that the camp population is over 200,000. Hanoi has told Amnesty International that it was never higher than 40,000 and that now fewer than 20,000 people are still inside.

The task of the victors in 1975 could never have been easy. It has been made much harder by growing antagonisms and then wars with Kampuchea and China, by the continued mutually destructive rupture with the United States, and by the end of all aid except from the Soviet bloc. Underlying all these has been the Hanoi leadership's Stalinist siege mentality and its inability to compromise with its foes, real or imagined.

There is no end of these problems in sight. As a result Vietnam will get poorer and poorer, more and more dependent upon the Soviet Union. More and more children will die, more and more people will seek to flee by boat. The tragedy of Vietnam, with us since World War Two, will not yet go away.

As always, I found Vietnam passionate and moving. Just before I flew out on board an Air France jumbo, with an ease and in a comfort which seemed shocking, I had coffee in a bar with friends. The bar was filled again with the lyrics of Boney M: 'I see a boat on the river. It's sailing away. Down to the ocean. Where to I can't say.'

My friends were planning to sail away for Thailand in the next few days. They promised to write if they survived the police, the storms, the Thai pirates. There has been no letter. *(12.7.81)*

The Divisive Society
Richard Hoggart

I have been re-reading 'The Uses of Literacy' for the first time since it was published 25 years ago. After I had finished I certainly didn't feel like Swift, re-reading 'A Tale of a Tub' in old age: 'Good God! What a genius I had when I wrote that book.' I did feel: 'Good God! What a lot of *time* I had when I wrote that book.' A more important impression, obvious enough but it had to wait on a re-reading, is that looking back from 1982 the book seems to record a now vanished period of almost pastoral simplicity.

This book marked a period when I was between two worlds, still able to look back at my upbringing with some nearness but inevitably moving farther and farther away. I was 33 when I began it. Not many years later the picture had begun to fade. The book also seemed to body out something of the sense of change then at last clearly getting under way in British society after the post-war restraints.

People sometimes say now: Why don't you write a 'Uses of Literacy' for the Eighties? That would be impossible. There's no going back on that track. I am too old to be able to respond, except in a removed way, to the major social pressures on working-class people these days, to the stresses of inner city life, to the situation of the new immigrants, to one-parent families and feminism and all the rest.

What I might try to write would be a more analytic book that would include a discussion of the slow nature of change, for good and ill, in societies such as this. I did discuss this in 'The Uses of Literacy' so far as it seemed relevant to working-class attitudes then. I would now want to broaden it to all social groups and particularly to those who handle the main levers of power and influence. For it is not possible any longer to ignore, unless one is totally set on protecting one's own corner, the force of institutionalised privilege in Britain which, all the evidence suggests, has strengthened since the war. A democratic society which takes this high correlation between class of birth, a few schools and colleges, and access to some of the most important sectors of society as just, a true reflection of talent and merit, is a democracy only in name. To say this is not 'envy' or 'class rancour'; anger, maybe, or even outrage; and sadness at too easily tolerated injustice.

One analytical strand would be about the fact that societies have sets of attitudes, partly specific to particular classes but also more widely shared, which usually work in contrasting clusters. So on the one hand there is that habitual unexpectancy in the English spirit, that process by which the belief in gradualness and tolerance and lack of showiness is always threatening to change into a damp, dog-in-the-manger, slightly bloody-minded, going-on-going-on; as in the current quite healthy rejection of the high gloss of some aspects of prosperous Europe which can degenerate into a commitment to squalor, to grime in the grain.

Contrast that with the devotion to unselfseeking voluntarism, or the enormous preoccupation with gentle spare-time activities, that poetry of amateurism which occupies millions in their spare time; or with the neighbourliness which is still habitually practised whenever one is out of semi-anonymous, mass, public situations. Or the sudden creative, generous, public gestures by which we surprise ourselves, such as the founding of the National Health Service or the Open University.

Then one would have to talk about the movements of the pendulum of a society's attitudes. Just now we are in a watchful, self-protective phase; one in which BUPA speaks more for the dominant mood than the NHS, in which an Open University would never have got off the ground and this for more than financial reasons; in which it is becoming more apposite to adopt for the police the French phrase 'forces of order' rather than 'copper'. But that other side of the English character – charitable, chance-taking, idealistic, concerned – could come to the front once the climate begins to change; and in all classes.

Or one might talk about wave-breaking, that process by which a major change in an important group of attitudes builds up and then breaks irreversibly. Overwhelmingly the major example in the past 20 years is the changed attitudes of men and women towards one another, towards marriage and towards sexual life itself. I would be surprised if a full analysis did not decide that on balance this set of changes was for the good.

A more polemical and hardhitting book (which is just as much needed) would have a bolder shape. For me, it would be about the *polarisation* of British society, a polarisation encouraged by those very social reforms which were meant to make us more equal in humane provisions and in opportunity.

Polarisation is not the same as that privilege mentioned earlier. It is a direct result of the great provision made over the past 20 years for certain kinds of ability; it gives rise to the emergence of what are variously called the 'meritocracy' or the 'service group', people who have moved upwards from their class of origin (anywhere from the mid-middles to the working class) usually as a result of application and talent. The process of privilege operates on top of that movement, as still as a film of heavy oil on water.

Take one major example: the greater provision of funds for higher education from the early Sixties. That process enlisted the best instincts of many of us and it has many solid achievements. We now know, though, that because insufficient thought was given by all concerned, including those actually working in higher education, to the links between social class and the chances of arriving at a point where access to such an education might even seem possible, those billions did virtually nothing to improve opportunities for the main underprivileged groups. It ensured that virtually any middle or lower middle-class child whose parents so wished could go to university or polytechnic; not the *working*-class child.

The effects of such a huge, one-sided investment in higher education are now spreading into all parts of the general culture. The Arts Council has been caught in a similar trap.

Thirty years ago it was just possible to define 'access' to the arts merely geographically. Having found gaps in, say, theatre provision in various parts of the country, the Council helped create a national network so that hardly anyone need travel for more than an hour to find a professional theatre of high standard. But when, after 20 years or so, it looked at the social composition of the audiences for that impressive network, it had to recognise that what keeps theatre-going predominantly the preserve of a relatively small proportion of the population – the middle classes and the meritocrats – is a set of socio-cultural assumptions which are as deterring in their own way to those outside as a hundred miles of physical distance.

Under pressures from competition, broadcasting went the same way. Within the BBC, the dream of a national audience gave way to a division of the network by height-of-brow; however, following the age's capacity to find emollient evasives for unpleasant realities, it was called 'generic' broadcasting. In newspapers, the 'weightier' ones have gained ground overall, but the gap between their audiences and those of the populars is wider than ever (stylistically, though, they often seem to be overlapping more and more. But that is part of an even more subterranean trend). Add the enormous rise in specialist journals for the meritocracies, each with its own filtered and angled approach to the treatment of more general issues, and the whole process is seen to have a comprehensive logic of its own.

I do not automatically blame the middle classes or the meritocrats for taking advantage or, to use a more neutral term, making full use of the new opportunities. Our own three children all went to university. Nor should we forget that children may be made deeply unhappy if parents too rigidly follow the logic of our own ideological positions and, for instance, insist that they attend clearly unsuitable schools. This is different from recognising what *is* a parental responsibility: to let our children see what values we respect and try to live by, and why.

But we should insist that in all social improvements special provisions are incorporated to encourage their use by people who don't at first see their value. Otherwise, well-intentioned reforms will further distort the inequalities and divisions within society.

So to the other side of the chasm. The gap between the two sides is now, in styles, expectations, attitudes, arguably greater than it was at the time of Butler's 1944 Education Act.

Conditions in the remaining working-class area of the inner cities, whether they are unreconstructed remnants or redeveloped, are in many cases appalling; the comprehensive schools struggle with these awful odds against a Press coverage which is almost uniformly hostile and distorted. No wonder that more than 50 per cent of those who leave school at the minimum age never think it relevant for the rest of their lives to set foot in any educational institution.

Again, in our society there are illiterates and near-illiterates in far larger numbers than most of us would like to recognise. Some of them seek help. But an underfunded provision does little more than scratch at the problem. Amazingly, some local authorities charge for attendance at basic education classes for illiterate adults.

But, the cry will go up, why shouldn't we be a divided society? What do you want: a grey uniformity? That is to confuse dividedness with diversity. We should be diverse; we are diverse anyway. It is this real diversity which divisiveness obscures. The 'quarrel of a society with itself' is one of the healthier occupations of a democracy; and it's quite different from a nagging, at-odds, fratching.

We are also in some ways a coherent society. But again, coherence is not the same as the consensus invoked in the speeches of some politicians, or in the sentimentalities of populist journalists or disc-jockeys. The Queen on Christmas Day, the Commonwealth goodwill hook-ups, the Boat Race, all those moments so loved by broadcasters, are curious and interesting but tell us more about the backgrounds and assumptions of the broadcasters themselves than about the possible real coherences in British life. To understand them I would go first to those things which touch the collective national funny bone . . . some cartoons, some broadcast comedies . . . as well as to the more demotic current affairs programmes.

About all that we have thought hardly at all and this at the very period – and it will be a short period – which will see the end of the regulated years in broadcasting and the start of the free-for-all. As we go into all the multiple possibilities of the new technology, to the accompaniment of loud hurrahs from both tycoons and the more thoughtless 'progressives', we ought to be asking ourselves instead about how the best in the public service idea in broadcasting may be carried over.

Certainly our material standard of living has undeniably improved over the past few decades. Whether the inward quality of most people's lives has improved, remained stable or deteriorated, is quite another question. *(21.2.82)*

A Botticelli Out of Budapest
Lajos Lederer

Half a century ago Hungarians wanted to make Harold Sidney Harmsworth, first Viscount Rothermere, their king. Thereby hangs a hitherto untold tale of the spiriting out of Hungary, just after the last war, of art treasures now worth tens of millions of pounds. The strange sequence of events that involved me in all this had begun nearly 20 years earlier.

Before the war I was London correspondent of *Pesti Hirlap*, the country's leading liberal newspaper. In 1927 an article appeared in Rothermere's *Daily Mail* headlined 'Hungary's Place in the Sun'. In it he supported Hungarian claims to the lands wrested from Hungary after the First World War – territories like the one I was born in, which became Czechoslovakia.

Overnight Rothermere became a hero in Hungary, but this was nothing compared to what followed the publication in my paper in Hungary, two months later, of an interview I had with him in which he said that Hungary's frontier would again be the Carpathian Mountains.

One result was that I went to work for Rothermere as a private secretary, to handle his Hungarian affairs. Hungarians wanted publicity for the restoring of the lost lands – the most they got in British newspapers normally was an occasional two-inch story in *The Times* and the *Manchester Guardian*, as it then was. Now, out of the blue, here was the mass-circulation *Daily Mail* devoting whole pages to Hungary's cause.

The reaction of the Hungarian people was astonishing. Telegrams by the hundred and tens of thousands of letters flooded into Rothermere's office, expressing the affection and gratitude for which he had been longing all his life. However, he had the reputation of taking up causes and dropping them equally suddenly, and I soon saw that this was so. How were we to keep up his interest in Hungary?

Then I had an idea. Hungary was a kingdom without a king. A throne was something even a multi-millionaire could not buy. Why not offer him the crown? I suggested this diffidently (I was only 24 at the time) to the editor of *Pesti Hirlap*, Dr Otto Legrady. He responded enthusiastically and floated the idea among his political friends. They, too, were enthusiastic; so were some of the country's most eminent aristocrats. Over the next three years delegation after delegation came to London begging Rothermere to become King of Hungary.

It was all rather bizarre, but although it did not come off (Rothermere pulled out), it had the effect of keeping Rothermere interested in Hungary for the rest of his life. I believe that one reason why he supported fascism and cultivated the friendship of Hitler and Mussolini was that he thought Hungary could expect more from the dictators than from the democrats.

In 1938, after Munich, Hungary recovered territories from Czechoslovakia, and Rothermere was invited to Budapest for the celebrations. He was received like the king he never became. A few months before this, he made a regal gesture to the people of Hungary: he sent them, on a long loan, his entire collection of Old Masters.

Eight of the paintings were: Virgin and the Dead Christ (Bellini); Portrait of a Young Woman (Botticelli); Portrait of Charles IX (Clouet); Madonna (Piero di Cosimo); Portrait of the Artist (Rembrandt); Virgin with Child (Rubens); Portrait of a Woman (Holbein); Portrait of a Woman (Cranach). They were hung in the Budapest Gallery of Fine Arts.

During the war I was interned, released as a 'friendly enemy alien', and spent the rest of the war monitoring broadcasts from Nazi-occupied Europe for the Rothermere newspaper group. I had heard nothing of my family – my mother and my two elder brothers (my father, a newspaper editor and politician, had died in the 1930s). I last saw them in January 1940, at the end of my last visit to Budapest, before Hungary formally joined the Axis Powers.

Now, in 1945, Hungary was a defeated enemy country. Getting into it would not be easy. To do so I needed the permission of the four-Power Allied Commission. I got that by becoming an accredited correspondent of *The Observer*.

Then I heard from Rothermere's son Esmond, who had succeeded on his father's death in 1940. He asked me to contact the trustee department of Coutts Bank. They gave me the list of the art treasures lent to Hungary and asked if I would discover if they had survived the conflict. If so, 'perhaps you will then be so good as to ascertain what formalities it would be necessary for us to comply with in order to have these pictures and effects sent to this country.' They gave me a handsome amount of money for expenses, some thousands of pounds.

It was a somewhat naive request – Hungary was occupied and controlled by the Red Army – but I accepted the commission and flew off to Budapest.

I arrived on a bleak October day in 1945 and went to my brother's flat in the centre of the shattered city. Here I found my brother, Aladar, the eldest. My mother, he told me, had died in May, during the last days of the Russian siege. The second brother, Zoltan, was dead too. He had been serving in a labour battalion on the Russian front and had been shot, possibly for refusing to work; I never found out. I set about reporting for *The Observer* – and looking for the Rothermere treasures.

I went to the Gallery of Fine Arts along what had once been familiar streets, now torn by shellfire. Soviet tanks were everywhere. Red Army patrols at every corner – the occupation forces were 1,500,000-strong. The head of the Gallery, Dr Istvan Genthon, was an old acquaintance. When I told him of my mission he agreed at once that the Rothermere paintings should go back to Britain, but, alas – he threw up his hands in despair. 'Come and see the gallery, my dear Lajos,' he said, and I trembled lest I should find the treasures damaged, even destroyed.

It was, if anything, worse than that. The gallery had escaped intact; it was one of the few public buildings still undamaged. But it was bare. 'Everything, yes, everything has gone,' said Genthon. And then he told me how.

In April, a day or two before the Red Army reached the outskirts of Budapest, some Hungarian Young Nazis had entered the gallery. They had come to strip it of its treasures – paintings, sculptures, priceless antiques – and take them to what was known as the 'Gold Train'. Already on board were Hungary's gold reserves and the crown jewels from the palace, including the 1,000-year-old St Stephen's Crown. The train was waiting at Deli (i.e. South) Station with full steam up, ready to go west, away from the advancing Russians. The art treasures were loaded and off it went with the Young Nazis acting as guards.

Their instructions were to meet the American forces advancing on Vienna and await further orders. Once over the Austrian border, however, some of the guards left the train, taking treasures with them, and went into hiding with their loot, including, of course. the Rothermere paintings. They found sanctuary with local Nazis in villages scattered over the mountainous borderlands of Austria and Bavaria.

How to find these people was the first and most urgent problem. In a matter of months, perhaps weeks, they could be anywhere – Australia, Canada, South America.

From the Gallery I went first to the home of Zoltan Tildy, the new Prime Minister. Tildy, leader of the Smallholders Party, was an old friend who also wrote for *Pesti Hirlap*. He arranged for me to be appointed to the Hungarian Commission of National Property Abroad, with an official letter saying: 'You are hereby empowered on behalf of this government commission to negotiate with every responsible government authority both in Austria and elsewhere, and to conclude agreements.'

Armed with this warrant I travelled from Budapest to Vienna inquiring at all the Allied headquarters – except the Russian – about the Young Nazis who had been on the train with the treasures.

The British and French clearly knew nothing. The Americans knew about the 'Gold Train', but were not going to talk to a newspaperman, even one armed with authority from the Hungarian Prime Minister.

However, there were also Hungarian refugees in Vienna. Some of them knew my name – and my connections with Rothermere. From them I engaged two young men as agents to seek out and report to me the whereabouts of the vanished Nazis. I paid them with money I had from Coutts Bank.

Days went by before the discovery of any clue. Then one of the agents contacted me. He had found Denes Csanky, himself a painter who, it was believed, had directed the transfer of the treasures from the Fine Arts Gallery to the 'Gold Train', and, so other refugees said, would know where the dispersed paintings were. I also knew that Csanky had catalogued the Rothermere paintings in Budapest in 1938.

Now, my agent reported, he was living with his wife in a remote mountain village in Bavaria, 250 miles away. I hired a car and set off. Vienna was in the Russian zone of occupation and a permit was required to leave it. I went without one, not wishing to risk a refusal or, worse, an inquiry into the purpose of my journey.

We reached the village without mishap. With a few discreet inquiries, coupled with an odd bribe or two, I found a cottage on the outskirts and knocked on the door. It was opened by Csanky. He welcomed me in, as a fellow Hungarian, but as soon as I told him what I was looking for, he clammed up. He knew nothing about any hidden paintings.

I tried to assure him that he was in no danger from me. I said I would help him with money if he needed it, and left him to mull over the offer.

But when I called the next day, the cottage was empty. Csanky had fled.

Again I set out, and found him two days later in another village. Again I tried to convince him that he was in no danger from me and that I would help him – he and his wife were obviously desperately poor. Food was scarce, there was no fuel for heating except bits of wood that could be gathered on the mountainside. Winter was approaching. We talked all afternoon; then I went back, empty-handed, to Vienna.

As soon as I could, I returned in a Jeep laden with food, which I obtained from a British NAAFI store. I unloaded it at Csanky's door and promised him $3,000 to help stir his memory. He asked for time to think it over. I left the food with him.

Next day, when I came back, he handed me a list of 14 villages in the border regions. In these villages, he declared, I would find what I was looking for. I gave him $1,000 and promised him a further $2,000 if his list worked. Then I left for Munich and the headquarters of the American Third Army.

There I showed my list of villages and asked for help in my search. After much anxious consideration the Army commander, Lieut-General L. K. Truscott, assigned me two military policemen and an American secret service man. Together we drove in a staff car to the first village on the list, in the Bavarian Alps. Here I found more Hungarian refugees. When I had managed to convince them that I was only looking for art treasures and had no political motives, they gave me clues to the whereabouts of someone, also a Hungarian, who could help me.

He turned out to be as suspicious and hostile as Csanky had been. It took a long time to persuade him, in our native language, that I was not trying to hand him over to the authorities.

At last he pulled out from under a bed a number of paintings; others came from under the rafters. Some were still in their frames, more were rolled up. I stowed them in the car and drove back to Munich, handing them for safe keeping to the Americans, who now organised a wider search. I told them of my fears for the paintings, having seen the miserable conditions of Csanky and his wife, and the Americans agreed that if they were not found soon, they might be sold for food, and so lost to their owners for ever.

Csanky's list was indeed working. Two more paintings (not Rother-mere's), a Tintoretto and an El Greco, were found in an open cart covered with snow in a Hungarian border village. Neither was harmed.

A few days later I had wonderful news: the eight Rothermere paintings had been found. But to my dismay the Americans had unaccountably sent them back to Budapest, where they had been restored to the Fine Arts Gallery.

I went back to Budapest too. There I found some consolation. More and more paintings were turning up, and on 11 December the head of the Commission to which Zoltan Tildy had appointed me wrote to the Coutts trustee department: 'With Dr Lajos Lederer's energetic and valuable help we have located most of Hungary's precious treasures,' among them 10 more Rothermere paintings. These had been handed over to the American Third Army. The letter ended, 'We have no objection if you take possession of them as the rightful owner of the estate.' (These paintings were shortly returned to London.)

As far as I could see, there was nothing more I could do for the moment. I returned to London. But those eight paintings still in Budapest went on nagging at me. How was I to get them out of a country in the iron-grip of the Red Army.

I decided to go back to Budapest and seek help from the British representatives on the Allied Control Commission there.

Sir Alvery Gascoigne, head of the Political Mission, and Lieut-General H. Edgcumbe, head of the Military Mission, both agreed that to consult their Allied Control Commission colleagues might put paid to getting the paintings back to London. Courageously they were prepared to take the risk of allowing a British military plane into Hungary, to land after dark in a field on the outskirts of Budapest.

In great secrecy I began to make my preparations. I hired carpenters to make wooden crates and deliver them, at night, to a spot in the public park, near the Fine Arts Gallery. Then, in a hired van with a Russian-speaking driver – and a member of the British Military Mission – I drove to the park. We collected the crates and took them to the gallery, where Istvan Genthon and a trusted assistant were waiting. We packed the paintings, reloaded the crates in the van and drove out to the field where the plane was due to land.

We took a roundabout route, but we still had to go through four roadblocks. Luckily the guards were either drunk, or asleep, or just not expecting traffic on the sideroads; anyway, there were no challenges, and no shots.

When we reached the field we sat there in the dark for two hours before we saw the twinkling lights in the sky signalling the plane's approach. It landed, we loaded the paintings, and it took off again. In Vienna, the paintings were handed over to Lieut-Colonel T. Humphrey Brooke, who was in charge of the Monuments, Fine Arts and Archives branch of the British element in the Allied Commission for Austria.

Brooke, who later became Secretary of the Royal Academy, wrote to me on 1 April 1946: 'Having seen the pictures which have been recovered by your initiative, I would like to congratulate you on the amazing feat of saving these valuable British treasures. When one considers the condition of Hungary today, it is nothing short of a miracle that these works of art should have been brought back intact.'

The remaining Hungarian paintings were sent back to Budapest by the American forces. So was the gold reserve. The regalia, including St Stephen's Crown, were returned by the United States to Hungary in 1978.

And Denes Csanky, the man who gave me that first, vital clue that enabled me to track down the treasures? We last met in Vienna, in the autumn of 1946. He had some sort of job, restoring paintings, I think, and I was able to hand over the $2,000 I had promised him if his list worked. It had. *(9.8.81)*

Pearl Harbour: The View from Cape Cod
Mary McCarthy

7 December 1941: We heard the news that afternoon, on the radio. We were living – my husband, Edmund Wilson, and I – in Wellfleet, on Cape Cod, with our child, Reuel, who was going to be three on Christmas Day. The Cape, because of its position, jutting out into the Atlantic, was prone to spy and submarine alarms. Once we did have a real submarine surface in Provincetown Harbour, and Dr Herbert, the local MD, who seldom got to diagnose anything more interesting than a case of measles, had the adventure of being sped aboard the vessel by the Coast Guard to look at a sick crew member.

We also had at least one rubber boat, with a complement of saboteurs (one guessed), land on the back shore near Truro, though in my memory that is mixed up with an invasion of rubbery black dogfish that came to grief on the same stretch of sand. As for local spy scares, the surrealist painter, Max Ernst, of German origin, was held for questioning right in Wellfleet and left the Cape, vowing never to return; it was a disgruntled real estate agent, we heard, who had turned him in because he and his then wife, Peggy Guggenheim, had backed out on an agreement to rent a house near the beach.

Now that I think of it, my own behaviour could have appeared questionable: I was a Trotskyite sympathiser, and I steadfastly refused to instal blackout shades. That was because they would uglify our pale yellow living room; eventually I got hold of some expensive thick white roller shades through which the light didn't show. Though not regulation, they passed inspection, fortunately, by the Wellfleet Air Defence authorities. I felt quite a heroine in this episode, and Edmund, who opposed the war, didn't know (I think) whether to be proud of me for my obstinacy or annoyed with me for my extravagance.

It is hard to explain to younger people how we could be anti-Hitler and yet opposed to the war, and without even being pacifists. Our positions were not quite identical. He took an old-fashioned Isolationist stand – he never had any use for the British and during the lend-lease period was convinced that they were trying to trick us into intervention. I had nothing against the British but as a Trotskyite (somewhat platonic) I accepted the line that this was just another imperialist war and would change nothing. Had we known of Auschwitz then, I could not have stuck to that line. But it was easy for me to maintain it in the prevailing state of ignorance and also because nobody I was close to was fighting; my youngest brother was a Navy pilot in the Aleutians but, having been separated in 1923, we scarcely knew each other.

The young critics of the *Partisan Review* circle – *my* circle – were 4F to a man, having been turned down by their draft boards mainly for 'psychiatric disabilities'; Edmund's friends were past the draft age; a few youngish, married men I had known were working for propaganda agencies like the OWI (Office of War Information), which I scorned. One poet I knew – Robert Lowell – was soon in jail for refusing the draft, not for pacifist reasons but as a protest against the Dresden and Hamburg fire bombings; another, who was also a teacher at Harvard, had actually tried to get into the Navy as an officer but had been turned down because of his height – 6ft 5 in. – which meant he could not fit into a bunk. My actor-brother Kevin had got transferred from the MPs to the Air Corps and was performing in an air force play called 'Winged Victory'; he was never sent overseas.

In fact, though I followed the news, especially of North Africa and the European theatre, I felt far more remote from that war than I ever did from the one in Vietnam.

Thus Pearl Harbour did not affect my life except in such things as food and petrol rationing, all of which I enjoyed, for it made you plan ahead and be resourceful. Practically the only meat obtainable on the Cape was Portuguese sausage – linguiça and chorizos – but we got chickens from Mrs Higgins up the road and we could go m100mselling off the old pier on the Pamet River road, not to mention clamming. I made many a paella.

The oil shortage was a good reason to dress warmly and keep the thermostat down in the Wellfleet house and to burn anthracite in Victorian coal grates during the winter we spent in a tall house in Hendersons Place in New York. Petrol rationing was not a problem: you could pool, and occasionally I hitch-hiked.

All the things I cared about – mutual aid, self-help, rejection of temptation to self-pity – were handed to us civilians on a platter. Needless to say, hoarding was anathema to me. The only adversity I suffered on account of Pearl Harbour was to have Clifton Fadiman review my first book, 'The Company She Keeps' (June 1942), in the *New Yorker* magazine and declare that, since Pearl Harbour, there was no place in our literature for 'high grade backfence gossip,' if I recall his words right. No doubt that unsold a few copies.

Yet Hitler, if not Pearl Harbour, did change my life, and for the better. He made us a present of the refugees: the psychoanalysts on Ballston Beach with their radio sets; the surrealists – Breton and Matta – in the Thoreau country by Slough Pond playing in the dark with phosphorescent wood and describing the scenery as 'very Ludwig of Bavaria'; most importantly, my friends-to-be Nicola Chiaromonte and Niccolo Tucci and Hannah Arendt, though she, like Nicola, brought to us by the fall of France, appeared in New York and not on the Cape.

Meanwhile, my position on the war was eroding. I don't know what happened. But I came to realise that, whatever I *said*, I was cheering the Allies on. This was clear to me, finally, during the British film, 'Desert Victory', which showed Rommel's Afrika Korps and Mont-gomery and bagpipers. I came out crying with happiness that those pipers had won, which let me know that I was a hypocrite, politically.

In Truro that summer I told my friend Chiaromonte about this troubling gap between thought and feeling, or maybe between theory and practice. Although he did not believe for his own part, having fought in Spain, in war as a solution for politics, he did not seem at all shocked. This encouraged me to become a blood donor – a sin, as I felt, against Trotsky which I had been longing with passion to commit. I gave the blood, once; then Hiroshima came, and the war ended, while we were all still on the Cape – the Chiaromontes, Dwight Macdonald, Tucci, James Agree, the psychoanalysts, probably the surrealists in the woods.

It was the most wondrous summer in my life; on the beach I translated Simone Weil's 'The Iliad, or The Poem of Force', getting sand in my typewriter; in the fall with Reuel I went off to teach at Bard College – chiefly the Russian novel. *(6.12.81)*

Two Men in a Boat
Eric Newby

I joined the Special Boat Section in September 1941, having arrived in the Middle East by a circuitous route. There, in Cairo, at the bar in Shepheard's Hotel which, like White's Club, was a good place to seek extra-regimental employment, I met two officers of my regiment who had already joined SBS. They thought that, having been a sailor before the war, I might be accepted.

What is now the Royal Marines Special Boat Section was not originally a force run by the Royal Navy. Over drinks at Shepheard's, my Black Watch colleagues put me in the picture. . . . The origins of the unit went back to the summer of 1940, after Dunkirk, when Bob Laycock, an officer in the Royal Horse Guards later to be immortalised by Evelyn Waugh as Tommy Blackhouse in 'Officers and Gentlemen', had been ordered to form 8 Commando, one of nine commandos that came into being that summer. This he did with men from the Household Cavalry, the Foot Guards, the Somerset Light Infantry and the Royal Marines.

What was later to become the Special Boat Section consisted of a handful of men with 10 folding canvas canoes called folboats which, although a German invention, never really commended themselves to the Germans for warlike purposes. Their task was to carry out beach reconnaissances for commando landings and engage in sabotage.

This minute force was commanded by 2nd Lt Roger Courtney, who before the war had been a big game hunter in Africa and had already paddled a canoe down the White Nile from Lake Victoria.

Having trained his men in the unpredictable waters of the Firth of Clyde off Arran, Courtney proceeded to prove their potential worth by putting a canoe alongside a Navy ship lying in the Clyde under cover of darkness, boarding it undetected and stealing a gun cover. The following day he presented it to the ship's captain at a conference.

On 22 June 1941 the first recorded successful SBS operation took place when Lt 'Tug' Wilson of the Royal Artillery and Marine Hughes ferried a large quantity of explosives ashore from a submarine on the west coast of Italy and blew up a train in the mouth of a tunnel. It must have been one of the first known landings on the Italian peninsula.

In November, SBS took part in the raid on Rommel's HQ, 500 miles west of Alexandria, from which Laycock and Sgt Terry of SBS walked for 41 days through the wilderness before reaching the Allied lines. 'Trust Bob to beat Jesus Christ by one day,' was the SBS reaction.

My interview took place aboard HMS *Medway*, the First Submarine Flotilla depot ship in Alexandria harbour. I was not optimistic. I had already been rejected by the Long Range Desert Group with which, as with David Stirling's SAS, SBS was closely connected. I was interviewed by Courtney, now a Major, who could drink anything on two legs under a table. Over his desk was a device which read 'ARE YOU TOUGH? IF SO, GET OUT! I NEED BUGGERS WITH BRAINS' which made me feel that I would not be accepted; but I was. By this time Courtney was feeling the strain of sending his men out without himself participating. Many of them failed to return (two SBS were shot by order of General Bellomo in an orchard in Sicily: one miraculously survived to spend the rest of the war in prison, after which he returned to confront the general, who was subsequently shot).

Courtney consigned me to the training camp, next to David Stirling's at Kabrit, on the shore of the Bitter Lakes on the Suez Canal. There, in company with other aspirants, rank meant nothing and discipline was of the self-imposed kind. In company with the soldier or marine who was to become your 'mucker' on future operations, you were taught to handle folboats and explosives, sent off to marshalling yards to learn to sabotage trains and to sink ships in the Bitter Lakes, which lived up to their name in winter.

Wearing long-johns and covered with grease you swam towards the ship off shore that had been chosen for you, pushing a magnetic limpet mine in front of you supported by a net inside a car inner-tube. This was Britain's primitive equivalent to the highly sophisticated Italian two-man submarines of Count Borghese's Decima Mas, his 10th light flotilla, which in December succeeded in exploding charges under the battleships *Queen Elizabeth* and *Valiant* – disabling both of them and affecting the balance of sea power in the Mediterranean – at about the same time as Wilson and Hughes were swimming in long-johns in Navarino Bay, trying to attack an Italian destroyer flotilla.

To set the limpet in its correct position on the ship's side meant diving deep and on my first training run, underwater alongside a Dutch ship, I found myself enveloped in the contents of a Dutch lavatory pan which someone had released. Coming to the surface in brilliant moonlight I found myself being addressed by a voice saying 'Better luck next time, Mynheer.'

By 1941 SBS was engaged in regular hazardous operations across the Channel. In 1943 a unit from Australia sank seven ships in Singapore. In 1944 SBS blew the Peudada river bridge in Sumatra, reconnoitred the Chindwin, operated in Arakan and in 1945 landed at Rangoon and operated in the Irrawaddy.

The year 1943 was a big one for SBS, as it was for SAS and the

LRDG in the Mediterranean, with attacks on Axis airfields in the desert, Crete and Sicily, from which last place my 'mucker' and I failed to return, as did a number of other officers and their 'muckers'.

SBS then went on to fight in the Aegean, in Greece, in Italy on Lake Comacchio, where Anders Lassen, a Danish member, got a VC, and in Albania where, it is said, fed up with the commissars, some of them took a drop of gold intended for the Albanians. We shall probably never know. The relative parts of the War Diary mysteriously went up in flames after the war.

After the war, SBS was taken over by the Royal Marines, who had already been engaged in similar work during the war. Today, those who survive among the unit's founder members will be thinking of their lineal descendants who, both reason and rumour lead one to suppose, are now operating in some of the nastiest canoeing waters in the world. *(23.5.82)*

Eric Newby was captured off Sicily in 1942 after landing from a submarine in a sabotage attack on a German airfield. He was later awarded the Military Cross for this operation.

Suez: The Inside Story
Anthony Sampson

A quarter of a century ago, when British forces invaded Egypt and seized the Suez Canal, *The Observer* faced the most testing time in its history, when it totally condemned the Government's action, incurring the fury of readers, advertisers and Trustees.

To anyone who was on the newspaper at the time, as I was, it was a heady experience to feel so intimately involved in contemporary history, when the Suez Canal seemed to be flowing through the old offices in Tudor Street. But the newspaper's position was more tense than most journalists realised at the time.

To many people in Fleet Street, *The Observer* seemed enviably independent from pressures. Its circulation had been growing spectacularly, and apparently effortlessly: a week before the Suez war it had, as it happened, just overtaken its rival, the *Sunday Times*. Its Editor, David Astor, had the advantage that his paper was owned by a

Trust set up by his father, which made him appear almost uniquely secure.

But that was not how it seemed to him, for the Trustees had ideas of their own. Only a few months earlier, Lord Portal, wartime Chief of Air Staff, had protested as a Trustee against the paper's attitude over the newly-formed Central African Federation, where he was in sympathy with the white Rhodesians. Astor had been taking the side of the Nyasa chiefs, who had not been consulted when the Federation was formed, and was supporting civil disobedience.

His attitude was shared by the Chairman of the Trustees, Dingle Foot (Michael's Liberal brother), who had been involved in Africa as a barrister. Portal had complained that Dingle Foot could not remain as Chairman; and he and another Trustee, Sir Keith Murray (now Lord Murray), had insisted on replacing him with a more conservative Chairman, Sir Ifor Evans.

David Astor was also taking a close interest in the growing Arab nationalism, advised by the Middle East correspondent, Robert Stephens; and when President Nasser nationalised the Suez Canal Company in August 1956, *The Observer* warned firmly of the dangers of using force. The paper knew that the Prime Minister, Sir Anthony Eden, was intent on taking some action. William Clark, who had recently been the paper's Diplomatic Correspondent, was now Eden's Press Secretary and he warned Astor and the current Diplomatic Correspondent, Alastair Buchan, that Eden was in an uncompromising mood – though the plans for an invasion were kept secret.

Meanwhile, the paper's Political Correspondent, Hugh Massingham, was receiving leaks from two Cabinet Ministers. Walter Monckton, the Minister of Defence, was very worried about Eden's attitude, while not actually resigning; and R. A. Butler, without going into details, let it be known that he thought that Eden and his immediate colleagues 'had all gone mad'. Astor knew that Eden was in a dangerous mood, but he did not believe that he could be foolish enough to order a military attack, and an editorial in late September said so.

When the attack came, then, the sense of shock was all the greater: *The Observer*, like many others in the country, felt betrayed and misled. It was Dingle Foot, outraged by the news, who first drafted an angry editorial attacking Eden, which he passed to Astor – who, instead of toning it down, added his own stronger phrases.

The finished editorial bore all the marks of a sense of personal outrage: 'We had not realised that our Government was capable of such folly and such crookedness . . . it can never live down the dishonest nature of its ultimatum . . . in the eyes of the whole world, the British and French Governments have acted, not as policemen, but as gangsters . . . Sir Anthony Eden must go. . . .'

No other newspaper was so consistently outspoken over the following weeks. The *Guardian* was at first uncompromising against the use of force, but more cautious after a British officer in Egypt was killed. The *Mirror* modified its attack after many working-class readers turned out to support the invasion, and *The Times*, which alone in Fleet Street had been forewarned about the planned invasion, published editorials which often appeared contradictory.

The Observer's sustained attack on the Government, at a time when British troops were engaged at Suez, provoked an immediate uproar. Among its own journalists, as I recall, there were only two dissidents: O. M. Green, the expert on China, and Haro Hodson, the cartoonist. But the two Trustees who were already worried about the paper's African policy were now both very upset.

Lord Portal promptly resigned, and wrote a letter to *The Times* insisting on the need to support the British forces. Keith Murray announced that he would resign at the end of the year. An elderly director, Arthur Mann, the former editor of the *Yorkshire Post*, also said he would resign. But the new Chairman of the Trust, Sir Ifor Evans – to Astor's intense relief – sustained him as Editor and recruited new Trustees.

As for the readers, many of them were astonished by *The Observer*'s attack on Eden, even though it was in keeping with its earlier line. The week after the first editorial, 1,227 readers had written to the paper, of whom 866 were against the editorial; by the next week, the numbers had doubled and 428 readers had written to say they had given up the paper. ('It is not the Conservative Party which is finished for a generation,' wrote Neil Hughes-Onslow from SW3, 'it is *The Observer*.')

Certainly, many Conservative readers did give up *The Observer*, though new and younger readers replaced them, and the total orders went up. The management were more worried by the signs of discontent among advertisers, who regarded *The Observer* as being pro-Arab, anti-Israeli, or simply unpatriotic. In the war fever of the time, with the whole country divided, *The Observer* was depicted by Right-wing Conservatives as subverting the national effort, as 'the Traitors' Paper.' When an *Observer* representative turned up at one City company meeting, the chairman asked him to leave.

The Suez crisis, as it happened, came at a critical time for the commercial future of newspapers, for by the end of the year newsprint rationing was lifted for the first time since the Second World War. Competition for advertisers, as well as readers, was immediately intensified. The *Sunday Times*, which was much more commercially prepared, rapidly fattened with advertising, and put on extra readers with a succession of serialisations of war memoirs, which were in keeping with the mood of the time. The wounds and humiliations of Suez soon encouraged a retreat into the glories of the past. *The Observer* undoubtedly suffered commercially from its stand over Suez.

In the following months, however, many of *The Observer*'s worst fears and warnings were borne out. The legitimacy of Eden's 'police action' to stop the fighting between Egypt and Israel was never believed by the rest of the world. President Eisenhower refused to come to Britain's support, as Eden had hoped: he too had tried hard privately to persuade Eden that Nasser was not a threat comparable to Hitler. The evidence of secret collusion with the French and Israelis increased over the next 25 years. The idea that Eden was effectively defending British trading interests was never believed by the oil companies, the biggest interests of all, who were appalled by the consequences for their relations with Arab states.

A month after the first attack on Eden, *The Observer* had written: 'The legend that we were really forestalling a Russian military coup in the Middle East (yet did not inform America of our plan) is too difficult to believe. The fact that our military action has actually stimulated Russian activity in that area, while losing us the goodwill of Arab states, is all too apparent.' The Suez adventure was, in fact, followed by a long period of Russian military support for Egypt. And the British militarism at Suez helped the Russians erase the memory of their own military ruthlessness in Hungary, just before.

In the light of history, there is no doubt that Suez was the critical turning-point in Britain's retreat from Empire. At that time there was a real danger that a Conservative backlash would lead to a major political crisis, as in France, but the dishonesty and incompetence of the Suez affair served to discredit any subsequent attempts to turn back the post-imperial tide.

But in domestic political terms, *The Observer*'s predictions were followed by some ironic twists. It was true that Eden *did* go, and that his Government never lived down 'the dishonest nature of its ultimatum.' It was true that there was something very close to a Parliamentary rebellion. But Harold Macmillan, by his skilful ambiguities, was able to disguise the Conservative retreat, while Hugh Gaitskell, as Opposition Leader, was inhibited by the jingo reactions in his own party.

The Observer continued to maintain that the Conservatives could not be trusted, all the more after their continuing indifference to the rights of Africans in Nyasaland; and it advised its readers not to vote for the Conservatives in the 1959 election. But the Labour Party was never able to get much electoral advantage out of the Tories' mistakes in Africa.

Over the years, many Conservatives came to recognise the importance of coming to terms with African and Arab nationalism, and to understand the danger that military force would encourage Communist activity, rather than suppress it. Many years after the Suez and Nyasaland conflicts, Iain Macleod came to lunch at *The Observer* and began talking eloquently about the crucial importance of recognising national aspirations in Africa and the Middle East. I noticed David Astor listening somewhat restlessly, until he finally burst out, 'But that's just what *The Observer* has been saying for *years*!' 'Ah, yes, David,' Macleod replied with a disarming smile, 'but you can be wrong by being right *too soon*.' *(1.11.81)*

10.
Hail and Farewell

The Self-Appointed Scapegoat
Neal Ascherson

The night of Albert Speer's second birth was warm, and the darkness
outside Spandau prison had that scent of water-weed and stagnant
lake-water which is the smell of Berlin. It was September 1966, the end
of the 20-year sentence which he and Baldur von Schirach received at
Nuremberg and which they served to its last evening.

We waited outside as night fell; a large crowd stood on the grassy
bank opposite the prison gate, behind the television lights trained on
the closed door. And when the door did open, it was all over very
quickly. Headlights, a car accelerating towards us, a glimpse of two
faces bleached with astonishment, and then there was only the red
tail-lamps vanishing and the soft, persisting applause from thousands
of unseen hands.

It took time to understand that applause. It was certainly not
anything to do with sympathy for Hitlerism, or with any notion that
Speer and von Schirach would take some active political part in West
German life. Neither was it, on the contrary, sympathy for Speer's
personal repentance as the only prominent defendant at Nuremberg to
accept guilt for the crimes of the Third Reich.

It was something much simpler. Speer and von Schirach were the
personification of all those millions of Germans who had come home
from all the captivities which followed on the fall of Nazi Germany,
limping back years later from camps scattered between Caithness and

the Arctic regions of Siberia. These two men were welcomed not as released criminals but as the last of the *Heimkehrer* – those who had been 'away'.

In the 15 years of his second life, which ended last week in London, Albert Speer found his own way to show gratitude for that welcome. He spent the rest of his time reflecting on the Third Reich and his part in it, and inviting others to share his reflections. He made himself, through the countless press and television interviews he gave, infinitely available; it was on another such project that he died.

In all that he wrote and said, there was not one word which could be construed as an attempt to rehabilitate or excuse Hitler's regime. Neither did he try to excuse himself. And yet it was just in this taking of personal blame, which he first accepted at his trial in 1946, that Speer – consciously or unconsciously – contributed to an alternative myth about Nazi Germany which is almost as misleading as the myth that Hitler did not order the physical extermination of the Jews.

Speer always insisted that the great mass of the German people were ignorant of the worst crimes of the regime, and were in any case in no position to do anything to stop them. Moral responsibility lay exclusively on the members of the small Nazi elite, of which Speer willingly admitted his own membership. The German population, unenthusiastic about the war and sceptical about their leaders, were passive objects of a terrorist government.

There can therefore – so the Speer thesis implies – be no question of a 'collective guilt' in which every German must share. The guilt is clearly defined and closely limited. The Germans were victims of the evil orders issued by Hitler or Himmler – or Albert Speer – in the same way, though with less final results, as other races confided to the care of the SS.

Speer, in short, appointed himself Germany's scapegoat. There were decent, driving motives for this which were private; his need to seek out and confront his own guilt was genuine enough. But he also knew that he was doing his country one last service of atonement – and doing history some violence in the process. The Germans were, after all, agents as well as victims of their regime. Most served it and many, perhaps most, continued doggedly to support it in its last and worst years, if only for fear of what might follow its collapse.

In their smaller ways, they acted rather as Speer did on the grand scale. They and he wanted to believe that Hitler's genius somehow remained intact, especially as they became aware of the vice and incompetence of those who were his political henchmen. They and he reserved their most desperate efforts and ingenuities for the period when the war was lost beyond retrieving. The more one learns of

Speer's wartime attitudes, the more he comes to resemble his fellow countrymen – not to be isolated from them in some dark tower of command.

Nor was the fence between a few who knew the full horrors and the many who did not know as high and impenetrable as Speer wanted to make out. Walter Laqueur's recent book 'The Terrible Secret' demonstrates how many fragments of this awful knowledge lay around in wartime Germany. Had they been pieced together, a pretty full picture of the worst crime in European history would have emerged. It was because Speer's fellow-citizens sensed this that they let the fragments lie where they were.

Albert Speer himself always used to say about his own awareness of the gas chambers: 'I did not know, but I *could* have known if I had wanted to. . . .' He would make this point in order to demonstrate his own guilt, as opposed to the relative innocence of ordinary people who did not share his access to secrets. But the point does not spare the German population either. They too could have known much; they preferred not to.

Speer also assented, almost with enthusiasm, to being cast as a cautionary tale for technocrats. He had been, in his own version, a young and unpolitical architect for the gigantic neo-classical Berlin and Linz (of which only the new Chancellery in Berlin was built, and only a few lamp standards remain), then chief designer of the stupendous scenario of towers, hordes and searchlights for the Nuremberg Rallies, and finally as wartime Minister of Munitions, challenged to maintain and increase armaments production under the growing onslaught of the Allied air offensive.

In all this, Speer invited the world to believe, he paid no attention to Nazi ideology or to the political and human consequences of his own efficiency. Only at the end did he witness the reality of slave labour in his own factories. Shortly afterwards, he lost his faith in the Führer and toyed – he never pretended to have done more – with plans to murder him.

In the post-war world of nuclear weapons and military-industrial complexes, this was a priceless lesson to teach. Albert Speer followed Einstein and Oppenheimer in his proclamation that the scientist without social responsibility, the planner absorbed in his own virtuosity, the technocrat without a political sense, are a threat to the human race. It was the fads of the Sixties which Speer especially helped to puncture. He too was 'unstuffy', he too did his own thing, he too was a 'thrusting young technocrat' impatient with taboos. His war economy came to run on slave labour, his State collapsed and was partitioned, he and his colleagues ended in the dock.

But was Speer really so unpolitical? Certainly his bond to Hitler was emotional rather than political, a bond to the mesmeric leader who walked up to this unknown young architect, flung his own coat with its golden Party badge about Speer's shoulders and told him to follow.

Fascism is a bundle of disparate beliefs, and no Fascist believes each and every one. Speer was no anti-Semite, neither did he lust to settle Germans all over Russia. But in the way of the German middle-class at that time, he regarded democracy as a failure and the left parties as traitorous. To have 'no views' in such circles then was to have those views.

It was such assumptions which removed any defences Speer might have had to the man with pale blue eyes who summoned him, or to the principle that one man can have the destined right to command millions. Speer would have been drawn to the Nazis even if Hitler had never heard his name. *(6.9.81)*

The Hero They Loved to Hate
Colin Legum

Jews, especially Israelis, appear to be incapable of abiding their heroes for too long. In their history they have worshipped very few among their number (apart from the great religious teachers), and almost without exception – perhaps because every *Yankele* feels himself the equal of any man – they have torn down their heroes from their pedestals, leaving it to history to re-evaluate their contributions. So it was with Herzl, Chaim Weizmann, David Ben-Gurion – and now with Moshe Dayan.

Ben-Gurion and Dayan were probably the two most important figures in the making of modern Israel; yet, in their lifetimes, both were cast aside and, for a time, even openly reviled. While there is something healthy about this refusal to be beguiled by great men, there is also something unattractive in the extreme lengths to which Israelis will go in attacking those whom they once extolled.

Ben-Gurion, a true king among Jews, never completely recovered from the treatment he received. In his last years he seldom ventured forth from his desert kibbutz retreat. It was Dayan's special achievement that he doggedly chose to remain at the centre of political affairs, even enduring being spat at in the streets by the families of soldiers who had died in the Yom Kippur war.

This was hard to bear for one of the heroes of the Israeli war of independence, the Sinai campaign and the Six Day War in 1967, but he defiantly refused to accept the role of scapegoat into which he was cast for the early defeats of the 1973 war and proved himself in adversity to be as fine a soldier as he was in victory.

Moshe Dayan, with the famous black patch over the sightless eye he had lost in fighting with the British in Syria in 1941 – an injury that troubled him painfully ever since – became a legend in his own lifetime. His military contributions were of two kinds.

First, he brought to a new pitch of perfection the art of mobile warfare by selecting the right kind of weapons, daringly exploiting the element of surprise which called for bold, even reckless, initiatives and, above all, for highly trained men of exceptional morale. He was harsh on everybody, regardless of rank, who he felt had let him down.

His second contribution was to put into practice the teaching of Ben-Gurion that the Israeli Defence Force should remain 'a voluntary association of citizens profoundly oriented towards civilian life' – the spirit which has kept the Israeli army democratic, young and open to new ideas.

Like Ben-Gurion, Dayan abhorred war and military instruments as ends in themselves. Ruthless as an enemy, he saw wars as having a value only if they brought peace closer to Israel. When he entered the Old City after its capture from the Jordanians in 1967, the prayer he scribbled on a piece of paper lodged into a crack in the Wailing Wall read: 'Let peace reign in Israel.'

But he always understood that there could be no peace in Zion unless it found ways of dwelling in peace with its Arab neighbours. He was as persistent in his search for that kind of peace as he was in minding Israel's own security interests.

As early as 1949–50 he acted as Ben-Gurion's go-between in secret negotiations with King Abdullah of Jordan to find an accommodation between the Arab kingdom and the new Jewish republic. His close personal links with King Hassan of Morocco resulted in the decision of President Sadat to make his historic peace pilgrimage to Jerusalem.

Because Dayan did not trust the politicians and diplomats to exploit the fruits of war in the interests of peace, he pursued a relentless ambition to win a key role in government, even if it meant abandoning his close political allies – as he did when he made his controversial decision to join the Cabinet of his lifelong enemy, Menachem Begin. He did so because he was convinced that, whatever Begin's faults, it would be possible for himself as Foreign Minister to make peace with Egypt and, he hoped, also with Jordan and eventually with the Palestinians.

Although Dayan was right on the first score, he failed on the second. When he realised that Begin was not prepared to listen to his advice on how to carry forward the Camp David peace process by involving the Palestinians, he resigned rather than cling to office.

A crucial issue in his resignation was the Begin Cabinet's refusal to accept his advice that the Israeli military government should be withdrawn from the West Bank and Gaza, and that the Palestinians should be allowed to resume responsibility for their own affairs.

Like all his successful military operations, his proposal to demilitarise the West Bank required an act of imagination and great confidence. Sadly, his Cabinet colleagues lacked both his vision and his confidence.

The history of Dayan, of Israel and of the Middle East would probably have been very different if the ageing idol had not been made the scapegoat for what had gone wrong in the Yom Kippur war.

The details of that tragic episode are still matters of dispute, much of it still wrapped in secrecy. But the main facts are now fairly well established. Israel's unpreparedness for the surprise Egyptian attack was due mainly to the bitter in-fighting which had broken out between Israel's famed political intelligence service, Mossad, and the military intelligence service.

The former was convinced that Egypt was ready to strike; the latter clung to what has come to be known as 'The Concept', which was that the Arabs were unprepared for war and there was nothing to fear from Sadat's sabre-rattling. Dayan chose to support his military intelligence; hence the state of Israel's unpreparedness.

That Dayan should have recovered from that bad period in his life is a tribute to his resilience – a quality deriving from his enormous self-confidence, or what his critics preferred to call his arrogance. There was an unpleasant side to his public image: downright rudeness in his dealings with people, other than soldiers under his command or his very small coterie of intimate friends.

On a kibbutz one day a helicopter was seen to make a forced landing. Out of the crippled machine stepped three of Israel's top military leaders followed by Dayan. He emerged with a book and proceeded to read it under the slight shade provided by the helicopter while the mechanics set about repairing it. When some kibbutzniks approached Dayan with an offer that he might wish to rest in a bungalow and have some tea, he answered brusquely:

'Look here, when your tractor breaks down you don't expect people to come along and say have some tea, have a rest in the shade. Please go away and let us get on with our job.'

It was certainly the reply of a professional, but the tone was hurtful. And Dayan hurt many people in his time. He was essentially a private person who liked to be left alone. Even in the Knesset, he did not socialise with other members; he was usually to be seen sitting alone in the cafeteria engrossed in a book – usually one on archaeology, which was his private passion. But as an archaeologist he upset the professionals because of his insistence on carrying out digs on his own.

Dayan always lived by his own rules, and remained to the end of his days something of a maverick in Israeli politics. In a community which demands exceptional standards of morality from its leaders, Dayan scorned the conventional by his private behaviour. He enjoyed the (no doubt apocryphal) story told about him and Ben-Gurion who, when asked what he would do if he found that one of his ministers was a philanderer, replied: 'I would blacken his other eye.'

He was a man who, if his luck had held a little longer, would most likely have emerged as the country's Prime Minister and, because of his charisma, could have brought Israel further along the road to peace. *(18.10.81)*

The First of the Wets
Anthony Howard

R. A. Butler, who has died at the age of 79, ceased to be an active force in British politics 17 years ago. But there could be no more eloquent tribute to the surviving power of his reputation than the fact that his name always remained the brand-image for a certain type of progressive Conservatism.

More than any other individual, Lord Butler shaped and moulded the post-war Conservative Party. Even within today's Tory Party there are those who would say that, in rejecting his legacy, Mrs Thatcher has already ensured that she will leave no similar inheritance.

In Conservative circles it was always customary to refer to 'Rab' – the soubriquet his father gave him – as 'an enigma'. Indeed, in his heyday one much-quoted Tory gibe went: 'Anyone who understands

Rab Butler must be gravely misinformed.' But it could be argued that the British public understood him, even if his own colleagues did not.

Throughout his political career he always enjoyed far greater support among the electorate than he did within the ranks of the Conservative Party. To the ordinary voter, particularly perhaps the independent, uncommitted one, his presence in any Conservative government was, in effect, a guarantee that there would be no return to the more fundamentalist, tribal aspects of traditional Toryism.

In a sense, indeed, he was the first of the 'wets' – the term was used in White's Club and elsewhere to refer to him long before the present Prime Minister floated it into circulation as a characterisation of some of the less favoured of her current Cabinet colleagues. And, although intended opprobriously, the description had a certain appositeness: for Rab was always an unrepentant believer in consensus politics, of a government, whatever its majority, not pushing its electoral luck too far. The title he gave his autobiography was no accident: it was called 'The Art of the Possible' – and for Rab what was possible meant what public opinion, not mere party opinion, would be willing to accept.

When he arrived at the Home Office in 1957 (he was to stay there five years), he would have liked to abolish both capital punishment and the provisions of the criminal law that then oppressed adult homosexuals. He did neither – and the reason he gave in each case was a revealing one: that the British public was not yet ready to see such changes made. When they *were* made, as a result of Private Members' Bills, in the succeeding decade, no one rejoiced more than Rab. He had witnessed the vindication of his other great maxim – 'the patience of politics.'

Few politicians can ever have needed, or had to display, more 'patience' than Rab. He was a Member of the House of Commons for 35 years, more than 26 of them as a Minister. And yet, though he twice seemed within grabbing distance of it, he never attained the top prize.

He bore both his major public disappointments (in 1957 and 1963) with great fortitude – even, characteristically, remarking after the second occasion, 'If you're not made Pope in the Roman Catholic Church, you can still be a perfectly good Cardinal Archbishop of Milan.' That the wounds went deep, however, there was never any reason to doubt. I got to know him only after his retirement both from politics and his highly successful 13 years as Master of Trinity College, Cambridge. One remark recurred more often than any other in our conversations together. It was: 'I may never have known much about ferrets or flower-arranging – but one thing I did know was how to govern the people of this country.'

The first part of that sentence was, of course, a typical Butlerian shaft aimed at Lord Home, who snatched the Prime Ministership from Rab in October 1963. And in his later years Rab would always draw a distinction between the separate party rivals who had denied him the tenancy of Number 10. Harold Macmillan, he would say, 'whatever you thought of him, was a considerable figure'; Alec Home, despite his having written him the most chivalrous possible letter the day he kissed hands as Prime Minister, he would describe, by contrast, as 'an amiable enough creature – I'm afraid, you know, I grew rather bored with him.'

Alas, it was Rab's capacity for boredom, and his total inability to conceal it, that ultimately proved part of his undoing. He did not so much suffer fools badly as refuse to tolerate them at any price. Necessarily, down the years, this had the effect of limiting his range of acquaintanceship in the House of Commons – especially among the backbench Knightage of the 1922 Committee who effectively wielded the veto against his succession both in 1957 and 1963.

In the more formal sense, however, he was a House of Commons man through and through – probably the best defuser of storms and rows that the House has ever had. As Leader of the Commons from 1955–61, he surpassed even Herbert Morrison as a mollifier of the Opposition. But then, as he himself once said: 'It takes a very funny temperament to be Leader of the House.' Rab had that temperament in abundance – up to, and including, the capacity to announce 'We are a united party and a united government' and then promptly burst into a fit of giggles, overcome by the all-too-apparent absurdity of his own statement.

It was that kind of performance at the despatch box that led his critics, particularly on the Right of the Conservative Party, to charge him with an essentially flippant attitude to politics. 'Flippant' was almost certainly the wrong word – though throughout his career he never quite succeeded in subduing the vein of irreverence that caused him, as a young man, to change the opening verse of 'Land of Hope and Glory' into his own version of

> Land of Hope and Glory,
> Mother of the Free,
> Keep on voting Tory
> Until eternity.

He was well aware of the price he paid for such iconoclasm – but, try as he might, he could never quite rid himself of it.

Yet it was his irreverence that did a good deal to explain the British public's affection for him. His various indiscretions may have horrified the party stalwart but they endeared him to the British voter: far from an enthusiast for the party battle himself, the ordinary citizen welcomed a leading politician who was clearly not a partisan fanatic. It was for that reason that, in denying itself the services of Rab as leader in 1963, the Conservative Party made a monumental error. He was a ready-made 'national candidate' – and had he, instead of Sir Alec Douglas-Home, led the Conservative Party into the 1964 election, its result would almost certainly have been reversed.

It was typical, though, of the modesty that lay below the superficial vanity that Rab himself ultimately took the view that by then it was already too late. With the realism that he brought to examining any question, he *knew* when he should have been Prime Minister, even if no one else ever spotted it.

In the summer of 1953, when both Churchill and Eden were ill, he, as Chancellor of the Exchequer, carried for a number of months the whole burden of running the Government. He was told later that, had he insisted on having the job as well as doing the work, the office could not have been denied to him. He was then just 50 years old and at the height of his powers – not just the renowned framer of the Education Act but the architect of Britain's all-too-brief post-war economic recovery. For the second time in less than two decades the man and the hour could have met. That, unlike in 1940, they failed to do so was not just the first of Rab's many disappointments: it was also, in retrospect, a tragedy for Britain. *(14.3.82)*

Reporter of Style and Compassion
Michael Davie

Patrick O'Donovan was perhaps the most original reporter of his time. He was 62 and had been a member of the staff of *The Observer* for 35 years. No one, among English-speaking journalists, was his superior at conveying the look and smell and drama of great events.

His father was a Harley Street specialist and Conservative MP, though Patrick would boast of his humble ancestors in Clonakilty, County Cork. He was educated at Ampleforth and Christ Church, Oxford. During World War Two, he served in the Brigade of Guards. Some might say he never got over it. As a tank commander, he used to read poetry to his men and insist that every bolt on the tank was polished until it shone. (His one full-length book, 'For Fear of Weeping', about the Far East, was dedicated to his tank crew, 'who will never read it.')

After he joined *The Observer* he was sent briefly to the *Manchester Evening News* to learn the rudiments of the business. Then he was dispatched to Greece and Israel, where civil wars were in progress, and then to Africa, with general instructions to investigate the territories for which Britain was responsible. This he did. News scarcely came into it. He travelled about and described what was going on as if he were an explorer, in the process making large numbers of readers aware of the convulsions that were taking place as the imperial powers withdrew or were forced out. This was pioneering journalism, achieved – probably unconsciously – by adopting the methods of nineteenth-century reporters who sent home descriptive dispatches rather than 'stories'.

Africa established his reputation. Next, he went to the Far East; and again (before instant television) told the readers what a region in turmoil looked and felt like; this time the revolutionary war that turned China into a Communist state. He may have been the first to grasp what was going on. He wrote from Shanghai in 1949 as Chiang Kai Shek's regime tottered: 'China has collapsed like an old tent.'

Once you started to read an O'Donovan piece, it was hard to stop. He used short sentences and more adjectives than manuals of good writing recommend. He liked to begin a series of sentences with the insignificant word 'it', a device fatal to other writers but one that he somehow made to work.

At taking the reader there, and telling him what the place was like, whether it was Korea or the interior of a Suffolk church, O'Donovan had few rivals. He rarely came up with an idea for a story. But he never turned down an idea of anyone else's either. Even in his later years, after he had tired of wars, earthquakes and assassinations, and his health was starting to go, he could produce something memorable from unexceptional events: the disappearance of watercress beds near his home at Alresford in Hampshire, or the closing of an unimportant railway station.

He was conscious, though, of the irony of a former foreign correspondent, his briefcase still covered with labels, earning his salary by making day-trips from his country home. But he did not repine, and never boasted of his past. He was the least sour of men.

For a reporter who was involved in seismic political events, O'Donovan was curiously uninterested by politics in the conventional sense. He was much more stimulated by the underlying moods and emotions that produced the politics. In the Middle East, he described the attitudes of the men and women who were making Israel, and thereby prefigured the development of the state. In Africa, he concentrated on the relations between particular blacks and whites, and again foreshadowed the future. When election-reporting in Britain, he used to ignore the candidates and report the electorate.

He did not look, sound or behave like the popular notion of a journalist. As a young man, he was handsome with an Irish potato face, tall with black hair, dressed often in a black-and-white houndstooth suit, white shirt, Brigade tie, and perhaps yellow socks. Sometimes he affected a silver-topped cane. He might have been a junior guards officer off duty; perhaps in those days that was how he (for he had a powerful romantic and even flamboyant streak) thought of himself, though the pride was always tempered with self-mockery.

He was highly professional as a reporter, in the sense that he got his copy in on time, wrote to length, never complained about the way his stuff was handled, and knew when to bribe Telex operators; but he insisted that he was an amateur.

By current standards, he was indeed amateurish. He knew no shorthand. He spoke no language except English. He scarcely bothered with notes. When Gavin Young, a new colleague, was sent to take over from him during the Congo crisis, Young, knowing nothing about the country, anxiously asked Patrick if he could turn over any notes or cuttings or background material. Patrick pointed to a corner of the hotel room and a few crumpled scraps of paper. 'You're welcome to those,' he said. Once he interviewed the King of Greece. At the end of the interview, the King requested Patrick to read back what he had said. All Patrick had in his notebook was a doodle of a black cat.

His drinking was legendary. You could not say he was a desperate drinker, though desperation must have been part of it, but he was certainly reckless, and he seemed disdainful of the damage that he was presumably inflicting on himself. When the doctors told him that he must stop drinking, he took up sherry, on the grounds that sherry did not count.

Yet he never, so far as I have heard, missed a deadline. In Washington, where his patrician air was much admired by the harried American press corps, I remember him going to bed at 10 o'clock after a day's drinking. He was not sober. At six the next morning I was aroused by the rattle of his typewriter, and he had filed by the time I got up.

On one occasion he appeared in a popular TV talk show called 'Open End', a late-night programme based on the dangerous principle that it went on until the participants ran out of things to say. The subject was the Third World. Liquor was available. O'Donovan, after a brilliantly articulate start, began to slow down after an hour or two, finally becoming wholly silent. After a commercial break, he failed to reappear, and the chairman implausibly announced (the time now being one o'clock in the morning) that Mr O'Donovan had been called away to another appointment. The episode became famous. As a celebrated Washington columnist observed, 'O'Donovan slid off the screen and into the hearts of the American people.'

The paper often used him to report English set-pieces – the Boat Race, Trooping the Colour, State funerals – which sound easier than they are. O'Donovan had an almost foreign relish for English absurdities. He took risks with his prose and rarely played it safe by 'sticking to the facts'. What news editors call facts did not much concern him. But he was far more than a 'colour writer'. Behind the surprise adjectives there was usually an original idea that gave the piece a point and an unexpected bite.

He was brought up a Catholic, and his wife, formerly Hermione Fitzherbert-Brockholes, who survives him, came from an old Catholic family. Outwardly at least, his belief never wavered. His attitude to his religion was more like that of Evelyn Waugh than the probing, uneasy sinner described by Graham Greene. Like Waugh, O'Donovan accepted without demur the dogmas of his Church, which did not prevent him from being critical of, and funny about, particular members of the hierarchy.

He was well-versed in ecclesiastical history, and recently published a study of St Benedict and a monograph about Dr Richard Challenor, an eighteenth-century prelate whose importance for Catholicism in Britain had been, O'Donovan thought, underestimated. He was commissioned to write a biography of Cardinal Heenan, but abandoned it from boredom.

Whether his unconventional way of being a reporter will have any lasting effects on the trade is hard to say. Probably it will not. He had a certain style and presence, in his daily life as in his prose, that enabled him to bring off something exceptional. But there must be a lot of readers who will not forget his unmistakable writing. At its best, it possessed and conveyed qualities of love and generosity that are, in newspapers, quite unusual. *(3.1.82)*

Index of Authors